Contents

The 2nd Law
Make It Attractive

The 3rd Law
Make It Easy

The 4th Law
Make It Satisfying

Advanced Tactics
How to Go from Being Merely
Good to Being Truly Great

Appendix

ATOMIC HABITS
An Easy & Proven Way
to Build Good Habits &
Break Bad Ones

Introduction

My Story

ON THE FINAL day of my sophomore year of high school, I was hit in the face with a baseball bat. As my classmate took a full swing, the bat slipped out of his hands and came flying toward me before striking me directly between the eyes. I have no memory of the moment of impact.

The bat smashed into my face with such force that it crushed my nose into a distorted U-shape. The collision sent the soft tissue of my brain slamming into the inside of my skull. Immediately, a wave of swelling surged throughout my head. In a fraction of a second, I had a broken nose, multiple skull fractures, and two shattered eye sockets.

When I opened my eyes, I saw people staring at me and running over to help. I looked down and noticed spots of red on my clothes. One of my classmates took the shirt off his back and handed it to me. I used it to plug the stream of blood rushing from my broken nose. Shocked and confused, I was unaware of how seriously I had been injured.

My teacher looped his arm around my shoulder and we began the long walk to the nurse's office: across the field, down the hill, and back

into school. Random hands touched my sides, holding me upright. We took our time and walked slowly. Nobody realized that every minute mattered.

When we arrived at the nurse's office, she asked me a series of questions.

"What year is it?"

"1998," I answered. It was actually 2002.

"Who is the president of the United States?"

"Bill Clinton," I said. The correct answer was George W. Bush.

"What is your mom's name?"

"Uh. Um." I stalled. Ten seconds passed.

"Patti," I said casually, ignoring the fact that it had taken me ten seconds to remember my own mother's name.

That is the last question I remember. My body was unable to handle the rapid swelling in my brain and I lost consciousness before the ambulance arrived. Minutes later, I was carried out of school and taken to the local hospital.

Shortly after arriving, my body began shutting down. I struggled with basic functions like swallowing and breathing. I had my first seizure of the day. Then I stopped breathing entirely. As the doctors hurried to supply me with oxygen, they also decided the local hospital was unequipped to handle the situation and ordered a helicopter to fly me to a larger hospital in Cincinnati.

I was rolled out of the emergency room doors and toward the helipad across the street. The stretcher rattled on a bumpy sidewalk as one nurse pushed me along while another pumped each breath into me by hand. My mother, who had arrived at the hospital a few moments before, climbed into the helicopter beside me. I remained unconscious and unable to breathe on my own as she held my hand during the flight.

While my mother rode with me in the helicopter, my father went home to check on my brother and sister and break the news to them. He choked back tears as he explained to my sister that he would miss her eighth-grade graduation ceremony that night. After passing my siblings off to family and friends, he drove to Cincinnati to meet my mother.

When my mom and I landed on the roof of the hospital, a team of nearly twenty doctors and nurses sprinted onto the helipad and wheeled me into the trauma unit. By this time, the swelling in my brain had become so severe that I was having repeated post-traumatic seizures. My broken bones needed to be fixed, but I was in no condition to undergo surgery. After yet another seizure—my third of the day—I was put into a medically induced coma and placed on a ventilator.

My parents were no strangers to this hospital. Ten years earlier, they had entered the same building on the ground floor after my sister was diagnosed with leukemia at age three. I was five at the time. My brother was just six months old. After two and a half years of chemotherapy treatments, spinal taps, and bone marrow biopsies, my little sister finally walked out of the hospital happy, healthy, and cancer free. And now, after ten years of normal life, my parents found themselves back in the same place with a different child.

While I slipped into a coma, the hospital sent a priest and a social worker to comfort my parents. It was the same priest who had met with them a decade earlier on the evening they found out my sister had cancer.

As day faded into night, a series of machines kept me alive. My parents slept restlessly on a hospital mattress—one moment they would collapse from fatigue, the next they would be wide awake with worry. My mother would tell me later, "It was one of the worst nights I've ever had."

MY RECOVERY

Mercifully, by the next morning my breathing had rebounded to the point where the doctors felt comfortable releasing me from the coma. When I finally regained consciousness, I discovered that I had lost my ability to smell. As a test, a nurse asked me to blow my nose and sniff an apple juice box. My sense of smell returned, but—to everyone's surprise—the act of blowing my nose forced air through the fractures in my eye socket and pushed my left eye outward. My eyeball bulged out of the socket, held precariously in place by my eyelid and the optic nerve attaching my eye to my brain.

The ophthalmologist said my eye would gradually slide back into place as the air seeped out, but it was hard to tell how long this would take. I was scheduled for surgery one week later, which would allow me some additional time to heal. I looked like I had been on the wrong end of a boxing match, but I was cleared to leave the hospital. I returned home with a broken nose, half a dozen facial fractures, and a bulging left eye.

The following months were hard. It felt like everything in my life was on pause. I had double vision for weeks; I literally couldn't see straight. It took more than a month, but my eyeball did eventually return to its normal location. Between the seizures and my vision problems, it was eight months before I could drive a car again. At physical therapy, I practiced basic motor patterns like walking in a straight line. I was determined not to let my injury get me down, but there were more than a few moments when I felt depressed and overwhelmed.

I became painfully aware of how far I had to go when I returned to the baseball field one year later. Baseball had always been a major part of my life. My dad had played minor league baseball for the St. Louis Cardinals, and I had a dream of playing professionally, too. After

months of rehabilitation, what I wanted more than anything was to get back on the field.

But my return to baseball was not smooth. When the season rolled around, I was the only junior to be cut from the varsity baseball team. I was sent down to play with the sophomores on junior varsity. I had been playing since age four, and for someone who had spent so much time and effort on the sport, getting cut was humiliating. I vividly remember the day it happened. I sat in my car and cried as I flipped through the radio, desperately searching for a song that would make me feel better.

After a year of self-doubt, I managed to make the varsity team as a senior, but I rarely made it on the field. In total, I played eleven innings of high school varsity baseball, barely more than a single game.

Despite my lackluster high school career, I still believed I could become a great player. And I knew that if things were going to improve, I was the one responsible for making it happen. The turning point came two years after my injury, when I began college at Denison University. It was a new beginning, and it was the place where I would discover the surprising power of small habits for the first time.

HOW I LEARNED ABOUT HABITS

Attending Denison was one of the best decisions of my life. I earned a spot on the baseball team and, although I was at the bottom of the roster as a freshman, I was thrilled. Despite the chaos of my high school years, I had managed to become a college athlete.

I wasn't going to be starting on the baseball team anytime soon, so I focused on getting my life in order. While my peers stayed up late and played video games, I built good sleep habits and went to bed early each night. In the messy world of a college dorm, I made a point to

keep my room neat and tidy. These improvements were minor, but they gave me a sense of control over my life. I started to feel confident again. And this growing belief in myself rippled into the classroom as I improved my study habits and managed to earn straight A's during my first year.

A habit is a routine or behavior that is performed regularly—and, in many cases, automatically. As each semester passed, I accumulated small but consistent habits that ultimately led to results that were unimaginable to me when I started. For example, for the first time in my life, I made it a habit to lift weights multiple times per week, and in the years that followed, my six-foot-four-inch frame bulked up from a featherweight 170 to a lean 200 pounds.

When my sophomore season arrived, I earned a starting role on the pitching staff. By my junior year, I was voted team captain and at the end of the season, I was selected for the all-conference team. But it was not until my senior season that my sleep habits, study habits, and strength-training habits really began to pay off.

Six years after I had been hit in the face with a baseball bat, flown to the hospital, and placed into a coma, I was selected as the top male athlete at Denison University and named to the ESPN Academic All-America Team—an honor given to just thirty-three players across the country. By the time I graduated, I was listed in the school record books in eight different categories. That same year, I was awarded the university's highest academic honor, the President's Medal.

I hope you'll forgive me if this sounds boastful. To be honest, there was nothing legendary or historic about my athletic career. I never ended up playing professionally. However, looking back on those years, I believe I accomplished something just as rare: I fulfilled my potential. And I believe the concepts in this book can help you fulfill your potential as well.

We all face challenges in life. This injury was one of mine, and the

experience taught me a critical lesson: changes that seem small and unimportant at first will compound into remarkable results if you're willing to stick with them for years. We all deal with setbacks but in the long run, the quality of our lives often depends on the quality of our habits. With the same habits, you'll end up with the same results. But with better habits, anything is possible.

Maybe there are people who can achieve incredible success overnight. I don't know any of them, and I'm certainly not one of them. There wasn't one defining moment on my journey from medically induced coma to Academic All-American; there were many. It was a gradual evolution, a long series of small wins and tiny breakthroughs. The only way I made progress—the only choice I had—was to start small. And I employed this same strategy a few years later when I started my own business and began working on this book.

HOW AND WHY I WROTE THIS BOOK

In November 2012, I began publishing articles at jamesclear.com. For years, I had been keeping notes about my personal experiments with habits and I was finally ready to share some of them publicly. I began by publishing a new article every Monday and Thursday. Within a few months, this simple writing habit led to my first one thousand email subscribers, and by the end of 2013 that number had grown to more than thirty thousand people.

In 2014, my email list expanded to over one hundred thousand subscribers, which made it one of the fastest-growing newsletters on the internet. I had felt like an impostor when I began writing two years earlier, but now I was becoming known as an expert on habits—a new label that excited me but also felt uncomfortable. I had never considered myself a master of the topic, but rather someone who was experimenting alongside my readers.

In 2015, I reached two hundred thousand email subscribers and signed a book deal with Penguin Random House to begin writing the book you are reading now. As my audience grew, so did my business opportunities. I was increasingly asked to speak at top companies about the science of habit formation, behavior change, and continuous improvement. I found myself delivering keynote speeches at conferences in the United States and Europe.

In 2016, my articles began to appear regularly in major publications like *Time*, *Entrepreneur*, and *Forbes*. Incredibly, my writing was read by over eight million people that year. Coaches in the NFL, NBA, and MLB began reading my work and sharing it with their teams.

At the start of 2017, I launched the Habits Academy, which became the premier training platform for organizations and individuals interested in building better habits in life and work.* Fortune 500 companies and growing start-ups began to enroll their leaders and train their staff. In total, over ten thousand leaders, managers, coaches, and teachers have graduated from the Habits Academy, and my work with them has taught me an incredible amount about what it takes to make habits work in the real world.

As I put the finishing touches on this book in 2018, jamesclear.com is receiving millions of visitors per month and nearly five hundred thousand people subscribe to my weekly email newsletter—a number that is so far beyond my expectations when I began that I'm not even sure what to think of it.

HOW THIS BOOK WILL BENEFIT YOU

The entrepreneur and investor Naval Ravikant has said, "To write a great book, you must first become the book." I originally learned about

---

* Interested readers can learn more at habitsacademy.com.

the ideas mentioned here because I had to live them. I had to rely on small habits to rebound from my injury, to get stronger in the gym, to perform at a high level on the field, to become a writer, to build a successful business, and simply to develop into a responsible adult. Small habits helped me fulfill my potential, and since you picked up this book, I'm guessing you'd like to fulfill yours as well.

In the pages that follow, I will share a step-by-step plan for building better habits—not for days or weeks, but for a lifetime. While science supports everything I've written, this book is not an academic research paper; it's an operating manual. You'll find wisdom and practical advice front and center as I explain the science of how to create and change your habits in a way that is easy to understand and apply.

The fields I draw on—biology, neuroscience, philosophy, psychology, and more—have been around for many years. What I offer you is a synthesis of the best ideas smart people figured out a long time ago as well as the most compelling discoveries scientists have made recently. My contribution, I hope, is to find the ideas that matter most and connect them in a way that is highly actionable. Anything wise in these pages you should credit to the many experts who preceded me. Anything foolish, assume it is my error.

The backbone of this book is my four-step model of habits—cue, craving, response, and reward—and the four laws of behavior change that evolve out of these steps. Readers with a psychology background may recognize some of these terms from operant conditioning, which was first proposed as "stimulus, response, reward" by B. F. Skinner in the 1930s and has been popularized more recently as "cue, routine, reward" in *The Power of Habit* by Charles Duhigg.

Behavioral scientists like Skinner realized that if you offered the right reward or punishment, you could get people to act in a certain way. But while Skinner's model did an excellent job of explaining how external stimuli influenced our habits, it lacked a good explanation

for how our thoughts, feelings, and beliefs impact our behavior. Internal states—our moods and emotions—matter, too. In recent decades, scientists have begun to determine the connection between our thoughts, feelings, and behavior. This research will also be covered in these pages.

In total, the framework I offer is an integrated model of the cognitive and behavioral sciences. I believe it is one of the first models of human behavior to accurately account for both the influence of external stimuli and internal emotions on our habits. While some of the language may be familiar, I am confident that the details—and the applications of the Four Laws of Behavior Change—will offer a new way to think about your habits.

Human behavior is always changing: situation to situation, moment to moment, second to second. But this book is about what *doesn't* change. It's about the fundamentals of human behavior. The lasting principles you can rely on year after year. The ideas you can build a business around, build a family around, build a life around.

There is no one right way to create better habits, but this book describes the best way I know—an approach that will be effective regardless of where you start or what you're trying to change. The strategies I cover will be relevant to anyone looking for a step-by-step system for improvement, whether your goals center on health, money, productivity, relationships, or all of the above. As long as human behavior is involved, this book will be your guide.

THE FUNDAMENTALS

Why
Tiny Changes
Make a Big Difference

1

The Surprising Power
of Atomic Habits

THE FATE OF British Cycling changed one day in 2003. The organization, which was the governing body for professional cycling in Great Britain, had recently hired Dave Brailsford as its new performance director. At the time, professional cyclists in Great Britain had endured nearly one hundred years of mediocrity. Since 1908, British riders had won just a single gold medal at the Olympic Games, and they had fared even worse in cycling's biggest race, the Tour de France. In 110 years, no British cyclist had ever won the event.

In fact, the performance of British riders had been so underwhelming that one of the top bike manufacturers in Europe refused to sell bikes to the team because they were afraid that it would hurt sales if other professionals saw the Brits using their gear.

Brailsford had been hired to put British Cycling on a new trajectory. What made him different from previous coaches was his relentless commitment to a strategy that he referred to as "the aggregation of marginal gains," which was the philosophy of searching for a tiny margin of improvement in everything you do. Brailsford said, "The whole principle came from the idea that if you broke down everything you

could think of that goes into riding a bike, and then improve it by 1 percent, you will get a significant increase when you put them all together."

Brailsford and his coaches began by making small adjustments you might expect from a professional cycling team. They redesigned the bike seats to make them more comfortable and rubbed alcohol on the tires for a better grip. They asked riders to wear electrically heated overshorts to maintain ideal muscle temperature while riding and used biofeedback sensors to monitor how each athlete responded to a particular workout. The team tested various fabrics in a wind tunnel and had their outdoor riders switch to indoor racing suits, which proved to be lighter and more aerodynamic.

But they didn't stop there. Brailsford and his team continued to find 1 percent improvements in overlooked and unexpected areas. They tested different types of massage gels to see which one led to the fastest muscle recovery. They hired a surgeon to teach each rider the best way to wash their hands to reduce the chances of catching a cold. They determined the type of pillow and mattress that led to the best night's sleep for each rider. They even painted the inside of the team truck white, which helped them spot little bits of dust that would normally slip by unnoticed but could degrade the performance of the finely tuned bikes.

As these and hundreds of other small improvements accumulated, the results came faster than anyone could have imagined.

Just five years after Brailsford took over, the British Cycling team dominated the road and track cycling events at the 2008 Olympic Games in Beijing, where they won an astounding 60 percent of the gold medals available. Four years later, when the Olympic Games came to London, the Brits raised the bar as they set nine Olympic records and seven world records.

That same year, Bradley Wiggins became the first British cyclist to win the Tour de France. The next year, his teammate Chris Froome won the race, and he would go on to win again in 2015, 2016, and 2017, giving the British team five Tour de France victories in six years.

During the ten-year span from 2007 to 2017, British cyclists won 178 world championships and sixty-six Olympic or Paralympic gold medals and captured five Tour de France victories in what is widely regarded as the most successful run in cycling history.*

How does this happen? How does a team of previously ordinary athletes transform into world champions with tiny changes that, at first glance, would seem to make a modest difference at best? Why do small improvements accumulate into such remarkable results, and how can you replicate this approach in your own life?

WHY SMALL HABITS MAKE A BIG DIFFERENCE

It is so easy to overestimate the importance of one defining moment and underestimate the value of making small improvements on a daily basis. Too often, we convince ourselves that massive success requires massive action. Whether it is losing weight, building a business, writing a book, winning a championship, or achieving any other goal, we put pressure on ourselves to make some earth-shattering improvement that everyone will talk about.

Meanwhile, improving by 1 percent isn't particularly notable—sometimes it isn't even *noticeable*—but it can be far more meaningful, especially in the long run. The difference a tiny improvement can make over time is astounding. Here's how the math works out: if you can get 1 percent better each day for one year, you'll end up thirty-seven times better by the time you're done. Conversely, if you get 1 percent worse each day for one year, you'll decline nearly down to zero. What starts as a small win or a minor setback accumulates into something much more.

---

* As this book was going to print, new information about the British Cycling team has come out. You can see my thoughts at atomichabits.com/cycling.

1% BETTER EVERY DAY

1% worse every day for one year. $0.99^{365} = 00.03$

1% better every day for one year. $1.01^{365} = 37.78$

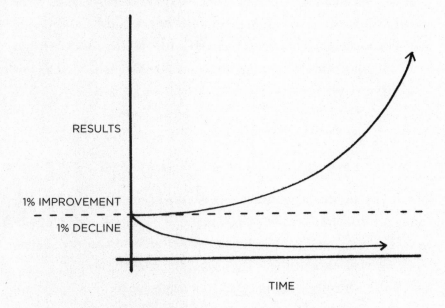

FIGURE 1: The effects of small habits compound over time. For example, if you can get just 1 percent better each day, you'll end up with results that are nearly 37 times better after one year.

Habits are the compound interest of self-improvement. The same way that money multiplies through compound interest, the effects of your habits multiply as you repeat them. They seem to make little difference on any given day and yet the impact they deliver over the months and years can be enormous. It is only when looking back two, five, or perhaps ten years later that the value of good habits and the cost of bad ones becomes strikingly apparent.

This can be a difficult concept to appreciate in daily life. We often

dismiss small changes because they don't seem to matter very much in the moment. If you save a little money now, you're still not a millionaire. If you go to the gym three days in a row, you're still out of shape. If you study Mandarin for an hour tonight, you still haven't learned the language. We make a few changes, but the results never seem to come quickly and so we slide back into our previous routines.

Unfortunately, the slow pace of transformation also makes it easy to let a bad habit slide. If you eat an unhealthy meal today, the scale doesn't move much. If you work late tonight and ignore your family, they will forgive you. If you procrastinate and put your project off until tomorrow, there will usually be time to finish it later. A single decision is easy to dismiss.

But when we repeat 1 percent errors, day after day, by replicating poor decisions, duplicating tiny mistakes, and rationalizing little excuses, our small choices compound into toxic results. It's the accumulation of many missteps—a 1 percent decline here and there—that eventually leads to a problem.

The impact created by a change in your habits is similar to the effect of shifting the route of an airplane by just a few degrees. Imagine you are flying from Los Angeles to New York City. If a pilot leaving from LAX adjusts the heading just 3.5 degrees south, you will land in Washington, D.C., instead of New York. Such a small change is barely noticeable at takeoff—the nose of the airplane moves just a few feet—but when magnified across the entire United States, you end up hundreds of miles apart.*

Similarly, a slight change in your daily habits can guide your life to a very different destination. Making a choice that is 1 percent better or 1 percent worse seems insignificant in the moment, but over the span

---

* I geeked out and actually calculated this. Washington, D.C., is about 225 miles from New York City. Assuming you are flying on a 747 or an Airbus A380, changing the heading by 3.5 degrees as you leave Los Angeles likely causes the nose of the airplane to shift between 7.2 to 7.6 feet, or about 86 to 92 inches. A very small shift in direction can lead to a very meaningful change in destination.

of moments that make up a lifetime these choices determine the difference between who you are and who you could be. Success is the product of daily habits—not once-in-a-lifetime transformations.

That said, it doesn't matter how successful or unsuccessful you are
right now. What matters is whether your habits are putting you on the
path toward success. You should be far more concerned with your current trajectory than with your current results. If you're a millionaire
but you spend more than you earn each month, then you're on a bad
trajectory. If your spending habits don't change, it's not going to end
well. Conversely, if you're broke, but you save a little bit every month,
then you're on the path toward financial freedom—even if you're moving slower than you'd like.

Your outcomes are a lagging measure of your habits. Your net worth
is a lagging measure of your financial habits. Your weight is a lagging
measure of your eating habits. Your knowledge is a lagging measure of
your learning habits. Your clutter is a lagging measure of your cleaning
habits. You get what you repeat.

If you want to predict where you'll end up in life, all you have to do is
follow the curve of tiny gains or tiny losses, and see how your daily choices
will compound ten or twenty years down the line. Are you spending less
than you earn each month? Are you making it into the gym each week?
Are you reading books and learning something new each day? Tiny battles like these are the ones that will define your future self.

Time magnifies the margin between success and failure. It will
multiply whatever you feed it. Good habits make time your ally. Bad
habits make time your enemy.

Habits are a double-edged sword. Bad habits can cut you down just
as easily as good habits can build you up, which is why understanding
the details is crucial. You need to know how habits work and how
to design them to your liking, so you can avoid the dangerous half of
the blade.

YOUR HABITS CAN COMPOUND FOR YOU OR AGAINST YOU

Positive Compounding	Negative Compounding
Productivity compounds. Accomplishing one extra task is a small feat on any given day, but it counts for a lot over an entire career. The effect of automating an old task or mastering a new skill can be even greater. The more tasks you can handle without thinking, the more your brain is free to focus on other areas.	**Stress compounds.** The frustration of a traffic jam. The weight of parenting responsibilities. The worry of making ends meet. The strain of slightly high blood pressure. By themselves, these common causes of stress are manageable. But when they persist for years, little stresses compound into serious health issues.
Knowledge compounds. Learning one new idea won't make you a genius, but a commitment to lifelong learning can be transformative. Furthermore, each book you read not only teaches you something new but also opens up different ways of thinking about old ideas. As Warren Buffett says, "That's how knowledge works. It builds up, like compound interest."	**Negative thoughts compound.** The more you think of yourself as worthless, stupid, or ugly, the more you condition yourself to interpret life that way. You get trapped in a thought loop. The same is true for how you think about others. Once you fall into the habit of seeing people as angry, unjust, or selfish, you see those kind of people everywhere.
Relationships compound. People reflect your behavior back to you. The more you help others, the more others want to help you. Being a little bit nicer in each interaction can result in a network of broad and strong connections over time.	**Outrage compounds.** Riots, protests, and mass movements are rarely the result of a single event. Instead, a long series of microaggressions and daily aggravations slowly multiply until one event tips the scales and outrage spreads like wildfire.

WHAT PROGRESS IS REALLY LIKE

Imagine that you have an ice cube sitting on the table in front of you. The room is cold and you can see your breath. It is currently twenty-five degrees. Ever so slowly, the room begins to heat up.

Twenty-six degrees.

Twenty-seven.

Twenty-eight.

The ice cube is still sitting on the table in front of you.

Twenty-nine degrees.

Thirty.

Thirty-one.

Still, nothing has happened.

Then, thirty-two degrees. The ice begins to melt. A one-degree shift, seemingly no different from the temperature increases before it, has unlocked a huge change.

Breakthrough moments are often the result of many previous actions, which build up the potential required to unleash a major change. This pattern shows up everywhere. Cancer spends 80 percent of its life undetectable, then takes over the body in months. Bamboo can barely be seen for the first five years as it builds extensive root systems underground before exploding ninety feet into the air within six weeks.

Similarly, habits often appear to make no difference until you cross a critical threshold and unlock a new level of performance. In the early and middle stages of any quest, there is often a Valley of Disappointment. You expect to make progress in a linear fashion and it's frustrating how ineffective changes can seem during the first days, weeks, and even months. It doesn't feel like you are going anywhere. It's a hallmark of any compounding process: the most powerful outcomes are delayed.

This is one of the core reasons why it is so hard to build habits that

last. People make a few small changes, fail to see a tangible result, and decide to stop. You think, "I've been running every day for a month, so why can't I see any change in my body?" Once this kind of thinking takes over, it's easy to let good habits fall by the wayside. But in order to make a meaningful difference, habits need to persist long enough to break through this plateau—what I call the *Plateau of Latent Potential*.

If you find yourself struggling to build a good habit or break a bad one, it is not because you have lost your ability to improve. It is often because you have not yet crossed the Plateau of Latent Potential. Complaining about not achieving success despite working hard is like complaining about an ice cube not melting when you heated it from twenty-five to thirty-one degrees. Your work was not wasted; it is just being stored. All the action happens at thirty-two degrees.

When you finally break through the Plateau of Latent Potential, people will call it an overnight success. The outside world only sees the most dramatic event rather than all that preceded it. But you know that it's the work you did long ago—when it seemed that you weren't making any progress—that makes the jump today possible.

It is the human equivalent of geological pressure. Two tectonic plates can grind against one another for millions of years, the tension slowly building all the while. Then, one day, they rub each other once again, in the same fashion they have for ages, but this time the tension is too great. An earthquake erupts. Change can take years—before it happens all at once.

Mastery requires patience. The San Antonio Spurs, one of the most successful teams in NBA history, have a quote from social reformer Jacob Riis hanging in their locker room: "When nothing seems to help, I go and look at a stonecutter hammering away at his rock, perhaps a hundred times without as much as a crack showing in it. Yet at the hundred and first blow it will split in two, and I know it was not that last blow that did it—but all that had gone before."

THE PLATEAU OF LATENT POTENTIAL

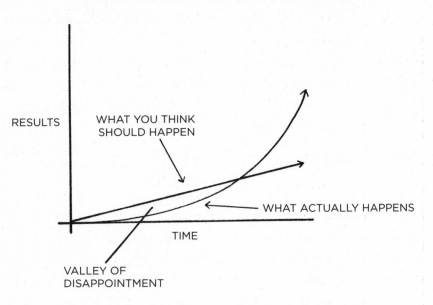

FIGURE 2: We often expect progress to be linear. At the very least, we hope it will come quickly. In reality, the results of our efforts are often delayed. It is not until months or years later that we realize the true value of the previous work we have done. This can result in a "valley of disappointment" where people feel discouraged after putting in weeks or months of hard work without experiencing any results. However, this work was not wasted. It was simply being stored. It is not until much later that the full value of previous efforts is revealed.

All big things come from small beginnings. The seed of every habit is a single, tiny decision. But as that decision is repeated, a habit sprouts and grows stronger. Roots entrench themselves and branches grow. The task of breaking a bad habit is like uprooting a powerful oak within

us. And the task of building a good habit is like cultivating a delicate flower one day at a time.

But what determines whether we stick with a habit long enough to survive the Plateau of Latent Potential and break through to the other side? What is it that causes some people to slide into unwanted habits and enables others to enjoy the compounding effects of good ones?

FORGET ABOUT GOALS, FOCUS ON SYSTEMS INSTEAD

Prevailing wisdom claims that the best way to achieve what we want in life—getting into better shape, building a successful business, relaxing more and worrying less, spending more time with friends and family—is to set specific, actionable goals.

For many years, this was how I approached my habits, too. Each one was a goal to be reached. I set goals for the grades I wanted to get in school, for the weights I wanted to lift in the gym, for the profits I wanted to earn in business. I succeeded at a few, but I failed at a lot of them. Eventually, I began to realize that my results had very little to do with the goals I set and nearly everything to do with the systems I followed.

What's the difference between systems and goals? It's a distinction I first learned from Scott Adams, the cartoonist behind the *Dilbert* comic. Goals are about the results you want to achieve. Systems are about the processes that lead to those results.

- If you're a coach, your goal might be to win a championship. Your system is the way you recruit players, manage your assistant coaches, and conduct practice.

- If you're an entrepreneur, your goal might be to build a million-dollar business. Your system is how you test product ideas, hire employees, and run marketing campaigns.
- If you're a musician, your goal might be to play a new piece. Your system is how often you practice, how you break down and tackle difficult measures, and your method for receiving feedback from your instructor.

Now for the interesting question: If you completely ignored your goals and focused only on your system, would you still succeed? For example, if you were a basketball coach and you ignored your goal to win a championship and focused only on what your team does at practice each day, would you still get results?

I think you would.

The goal in any sport is to finish with the best score, but it would be ridiculous to spend the whole game staring at the scoreboard. The only way to actually win is to get better each day. In the words of three-time Super Bowl winner Bill Walsh, "The score takes care of itself." The same is true for other areas of life. If you want better results, then forget about setting goals. Focus on your system instead.

What do I mean by this? Are goals completely useless? Of course not. Goals are good for setting a direction, but systems are best for making progress. A handful of problems arise when you spend too much time thinking about your goals and not enough time designing your systems.

Problem #1: Winners and losers have the same goals.

Goal setting suffers from a serious case of survivorship bias. We concentrate on the people who end up winning—the survivors—and

mistakenly assume that ambitious goals led to their success while overlooking all of the people who had the same objective but didn't succeed.

Every Olympian wants to win a gold medal. Every candidate wants to get the job. And if successful and unsuccessful people share the same goals, then the goal cannot be what differentiates the winners from the losers. It wasn't the *goal* of winning the Tour de France that propelled the British cyclists to the top of the sport. Presumably, they had wanted to win the race every year before—just like every other professional team. The goal had always been there. It was only when they implemented a *system* of continuous small improvements that they achieved a different outcome.

Problem #2: Achieving a goal is only a momentary change.

Imagine you have a messy room and you set a goal to clean it. If you summon the energy to tidy up, then you will have a clean room—for now. But if you maintain the same sloppy, pack-rat habits that led to a messy room in the first place, soon you'll be looking at a new pile of clutter and hoping for another burst of motivation. You're left chasing the same outcome because you never changed the system behind it. You treated a symptom without addressing the cause.

Achieving a goal only changes your life *for the moment.* That's the counterintuitive thing about improvement. We think we need to change our results, but the results are not the problem. What we really need to change are the systems that cause those results. When you solve problems at the results level, you only solve them temporarily. In order to improve for good, you need to solve problems at the systems level. Fix the inputs and the outputs will fix themselves.

Problem #3: Goals restrict your happiness.

The implicit assumption behind any goal is this: "Once I reach my goal, then I'll be happy." The problem with a goals-first mentality is that you're continually putting happiness off until the next milestone. I've slipped into this trap so many times I've lost count. For years, happiness was always something for my future self to enjoy. I promised myself that once I gained twenty pounds of muscle or after my business was featured in the *New York Times*, then I could finally relax.

Furthermore, goals create an "either-or" conflict: either you achieve your goal and are successful or you fail and you are a disappointment. You mentally box yourself into a narrow version of happiness. This is misguided. It is unlikely that your actual path through life will match the exact journey you had in mind when you set out. It makes no sense to restrict your satisfaction to one scenario when there are many paths to success.

A systems-first mentality provides the antidote. When you fall in love with the process rather than the product, you don't have to wait to give yourself permission to be happy. You can be satisfied anytime your system is running. And a system can be successful in many different forms, not just the one you first envision.

Problem #4: Goals are at odds with long-term progress.

Finally, a goal-oriented mind-set can create a "yo-yo" effect. Many runners work hard for months, but as soon as they cross the finish line, they stop training. The race is no longer there to motivate them. When all of your hard work is focused on a particular goal, what is left to push you forward after you achieve it? This is why many people find themselves reverting to their old habits after accomplishing a goal.

The purpose of setting goals is to win the game. The purpose of building systems is to continue playing the game. True long-term thinking is goal-less thinking. It's not about any single accomplishment. It is about the cycle of endless refinement and continuous improvement. Ultimately, it is your commitment to the *process* that will determine your *progress*.

A SYSTEM OF ATOMIC HABITS

If you're having trouble changing your habits, the problem isn't you. The problem is your system. Bad habits repeat themselves again and again not because you don't want to change, but because you have the wrong system for change.

You do not rise to the level of your goals. You fall to the level of your systems.

Focusing on the overall system, rather than a single goal, is one of the core themes of this book. It is also one of the deeper meanings behind the word *atomic*. By now, you've probably realized that an atomic habit refers to a tiny change, a marginal gain, a 1 percent improvement. But atomic habits are not just any old habits, however small. They are little habits that are part of a larger system. Just as atoms are the building blocks of molecules, atomic habits are the building blocks of remarkable results.

Habits are like the atoms of our lives. Each one is a fundamental unit that contributes to your overall improvement. At first, these tiny routines seem insignificant, but soon they build on each other and fuel bigger wins that multiply to a degree that far outweighs the cost of their initial investment. They are both small and mighty. This is the meaning of the phrase *atomic habits*—a regular practice or routine that is not only small and easy to do, but also the source of incredible power; a component of the system of compound growth.

———————————— Chapter Summary ————————————

- Habits are the compound interest of self-improvement. Getting 1 percent better every day counts for a lot in the long-run.
- Habits are a double-edged sword. They can work for you or against you, which is why understanding the details is essential.
- Small changes often appear to make no difference until you cross a critical threshold. The most powerful outcomes of any compounding process are delayed. You need to be patient.
- An atomic habit is a little habit that is part of a larger system. Just as atoms are the building blocks of molecules, atomic habits are the building blocks of remarkable results.
- If you want better results, then forget about setting goals. Focus on your system instead.
- You do not rise to the level of your goals. You fall to the level of your systems.

2

How Your Habits Shape Your Identity (and Vice Versa)

WHY IS IT so easy to repeat bad habits and so hard to form good ones? Few things can have a more powerful impact on your life than improving your daily habits. And yet it is likely that this time next year you'll be doing the same thing rather than something better.

It often feels difficult to keep good habits going for more than a few days, even with sincere effort and the occasional burst of motivation. Habits like exercise, meditation, journaling, and cooking are reasonable for a day or two and then become a hassle.

However, once your habits are established, they seem to stick around forever—especially the unwanted ones. Despite our best intentions, unhealthy habits like eating junk food, watching too much television, procrastinating, and smoking can feel impossible to break.

Changing our habits is challenging for two reasons: (1) we try to change the wrong thing and (2) we try to change our habits in the wrong way. In this chapter, I'll address the first point. In the chapters that follow, I'll answer the second.

Our first mistake is that we try to change the wrong thing. To

THREE LAYERS OF BEHAVIOR CHANGE

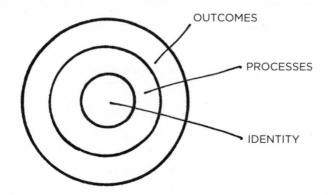

FIGURE 3: There are three layers of behavior change: a change in your outcomes, a change in your processes, or a change in your identity.

understand what I mean, consider that there are three levels at which change can occur. You can imagine them like the layers of an onion.

The first layer is changing your outcomes. This level is concerned with changing your results: losing weight, publishing a book, winning a championship. Most of the goals you set are associated with this level of change.

The second layer is changing your process. This level is concerned with changing your habits and systems: implementing a new routine at the gym, decluttering your desk for better workflow, developing a meditation practice. Most of the habits you build are associated with this level.

The third and deepest layer is changing your identity. This level is concerned with changing your beliefs: your worldview, your self-image, your judgments about yourself and others. Most of the beliefs, assumptions, and biases you hold are associated with this level.

Outcomes are about what you get. Processes are about what you do.

Identity is about what you believe. When it comes to building habits that last—when it comes to building a system of 1 percent improvements— the problem is not that one level is "better" or "worse" than another. All levels of change are useful in their own way. The problem is the *direction* of change.

Many people begin the process of changing their habits by focusing on *what* they want to achieve. This leads us to outcome-based habits. The alternative is to build identity-based habits. With this approach, we start by focusing on *who* we wish to become.

OUTCOME-BASED HABITS

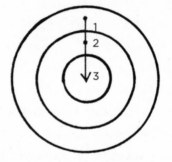

IDENTITY-BASED HABITS

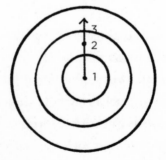

FIGURE 4: With outcome-based habits, the focus is on what you want to achieve. With identity-based habits, the focus is on who you wish to become.

...agine two people resisting a cigarette. When offered a smoke, the first person says, "No thanks. I'm trying to quit." It sounds like a reasonable response, but this person still believes they are a smoker who is trying to be something else. They are hoping their behavior will change while carrying around the same beliefs.

The second person declines by saying, "No thanks. I'm not a smoker." It's a small difference, but this statement signals a shift in identity. Smoking was part of their former life, not their current one. They no longer identify as someone who smokes.

Most people don't even consider identity change when they set out to improve. They just think, "I want to be skinny (outcome) and if I stick to this diet, then I'll be skinny (process)." They set goals and determine the actions they should take to achieve those goals without considering the beliefs that drive their actions. They never shift the way they look at themselves, and they don't realize that their old identity can sabotage their new plans for change.

Behind every system of actions are a system of beliefs. The system of a democracy is founded on beliefs like freedom, majority rule, and social equality. The system of a dictatorship has a very different set of beliefs like absolute authority and strict obedience. You can imagine many ways to try to get more people to vote in a democracy, but such behavior change would never get off the ground in a dictatorship. That's not the identity of the system. Voting is a behavior that is impossible under a certain set of beliefs.

A similar pattern exists whether we are discussing individuals, organizations, or societies. There are a set of beliefs and assumptions that shape the system, an identity behind the habits.

Behavior that is incongruent with the self will not last. You may want more money, but if your identity is someone who consumes rather than creates, then you'll continue to be pulled toward spending rather than earning. You may want better health, but if you continue to

prioritize comfort over accomplishment, you'll be drawn to relaxing rather than training. It's hard to change your habits if you never change the underlying beliefs that led to your past behavior. You have a new goal and a new plan, but you haven't changed *who* you are.

The story of Brian Clark, an entrepreneur from Boulder, Colorado, provides a good example. "For as long as I can remember, I've chewed my fingernails," Clark told me. "It started as a nervous habit when I was young, and then morphed into an undesirable grooming ritual. One day, I resolved to stop chewing my nails until they grew out a bit. Through mindful willpower alone, I managed to do it."

Then, Clark did something surprising.

"I asked my wife to schedule my first-ever manicure," he said. "My thought was that if I started paying to maintain my nails, I wouldn't chew them. And it worked, but not for the monetary reason. What happened was the manicure made my fingers look really nice for the first time. The manicurist even said that—other than the chewing—I had really healthy, attractive nails. Suddenly, I was proud of my fingernails. And even though that's something I had never aspired to, it made all the difference. I've never chewed my nails since; not even a single close call. And it's because I now take pride in properly caring for them."

The ultimate form of intrinsic motivation is when a habit becomes part of your identity. It's one thing to say I'm the type of person who *wants* this. It's something very different to say I'm the type of person who *is* this.

The more pride you have in a particular aspect of your identity, the more motivated you will be to maintain the habits associated with it. If you're proud of how your hair looks, you'll develop all sorts of habits to care for and maintain it. If you're proud of the size of your biceps, you'll make sure you never skip an upper-body workout. If you're proud of the scarves you knit, you'll be more likely to spend hours

knitting each week. Once your pride gets involved, you'll fight tooth and nail to maintain your habits.

True behavior change is identity change. You might start a habit because of motivation, but the only reason you'll stick with one is that it becomes part of your identity. Anyone can convince themselves to visit the gym or eat healthy once or twice, but if you don't shift the belief behind the behavior, then it is hard to stick with long-term changes. Improvements are only temporary until they become part of who you are.

- The goal is not to read a book, the goal is to *become* a reader.
- The goal is not to run a marathon, the goal is to *become* a runner.
- The goal is not to learn an instrument, the goal is to *become* a musician.

Your behaviors are usually a reflection of your identity. What you do is an indication of the type of person you believe that you are— either consciously or nonconsciously.* Research has shown that once a person believes in a particular aspect of their identity, they are more likely to act in alignment with that belief. For example, people who identified as "being a voter" were more likely to vote than those who simply claimed "voting" was an action they wanted to perform. Similarly, the person who incorporates exercise into their identity doesn't have to convince themselves to train. Doing the right thing is easy. After all, when your behavior and your identity are fully aligned, you

---

* The terms *unconscious*, *nonconscious*, and *subconscious* can all be used to describe the absence of awareness or thought. Even in academic circles, these words are often used interchangeably without much nitpicking (for once). *Nonconscious* is the term I'm going to use because it is broad enough to encompass both the processes of the mind we could never consciously access and the moments when we are simply not paying attention to what surrounds us. *Nonconscious* is a description of anything you are not consciously thinking about.

are no longer pursuing behavior change. You are simply acting like the type of person you already believe yourself to be.

Like all aspects of habit formation, this, too, is a double-edged sword. When working for you, identity change can be a powerful force for self-improvement. When working against you, though, identity change can be a curse. Once you have adopted an identity, it can be easy to let your allegiance to it impact your ability to change. Many people walk through life in a cognitive slumber, blindly following the norms attached to their identity.

- "I'm terrible with directions."
- "I'm not a morning person."
- "I'm bad at remembering people's names."
- "I'm always late."
- "I'm not good with technology."
- "I'm horrible at math."

. . . and a thousand other variations.

When you have repeated a story to yourself for years, it is easy to slide into these mental grooves and accept them as a fact. In time, you begin to resist certain actions because "that's not who I am." There is internal pressure to maintain your self-image and behave in a way that is consistent with your beliefs. You find whatever way you can to avoid contradicting yourself.

The more deeply a thought or action is tied to your identity, the more difficult it is to change it. It can feel comfortable to believe what your culture believes (group identity) or to do what upholds your self-image (personal identity), even if it's wrong. The biggest barrier to positive change at any level—individual, team, society—is identity conflict. Good habits can make rational sense, but if they conflict with your identity, you will fail to put them into action.

On any given day, you may struggle with your habits because you're too busy or too tired or too overwhelmed or hundreds of other reasons. Over the long run, however, the real reason you fail to stick with habits is that your self-image gets in the way. This is why you can't get too attached to one version of your identity. Progress requires unlearning. Becoming the best version of yourself requires you to continuously edit your beliefs, and to upgrade and expand your identity.

This brings us to an important question: If your beliefs and worldview play such an important role in your behavior, where do they come from in the first place? How, exactly, is your identity formed? And how can you emphasize new aspects of your identity that serve you and gradually erase the pieces that hinder you?

THE TWO-STEP PROCESS TO CHANGING YOUR IDENTITY

Your identity emerges out of your habits. You are not born with preset beliefs. Every belief, including those about yourself, is learned and conditioned through experience.*

More precisely, your habits are how you *embody* your identity. When you make your bed each day, you embody the identity of an organized person. When you write each day, you embody the identity of a creative person. When you train each day, you embody the identity of an athletic person.

The more you repeat a behavior, the more you reinforce the identity

---

* Certainly, there are some aspects of your identity that tend to remain unchanged over time—like identifying as someone who is tall or short. But even for more fixed qualities and characteristics, whether you view them in a positive or negative light is determined by your experiences throughout life.

associated with that behavior. In fact, the word *identity* was originally derived from the Latin words *essentitas*, which means *being*, and *identidem*, which means *repeatedly*. Your identity is literally your "repeated beingness."

Whatever your identity is right now, you only believe it because you have proof of it. If you go to church every Sunday for twenty years, you have evidence that you are religious. If you study biology for one hour every night, you have evidence that you are studious. If you go to the gym even when it's snowing, you have evidence that you are committed to fitness. The more evidence you have for a belief, the more strongly you will believe it.

For most of my early life, I didn't consider myself a writer. If you were to ask any of my high school teachers or college professors, they would tell you I was an average writer at best: certainly not a standout. When I began my writing career, I published a new article every Monday and Thursday for the first few years. As the evidence grew, so did my identity as a writer. I didn't start out as a writer. I *became* one through my habits.

Of course, your habits are not the *only* actions that influence your identity, but by virtue of their frequency they are usually the most important ones. Each experience in life modifies your self-image, but it's unlikely you would consider yourself a soccer player because you kicked a ball once or an artist because you scribbled a picture. As you repeat these actions, however, the evidence accumulates and your self-image begins to change. The effect of one-off experiences tends to fade away while the effect of habits gets reinforced with time, which means your habits contribute most of the evidence that shapes your identity. In this way, the process of building habits is actually the process of becoming yourself.

This is a gradual evolution. We do not change by snapping our

fingers and deciding to be someone entirely new. We change bit by bit, day by day, habit by habit. We are continually undergoing microevolutions of the self.

Each habit is like a suggestion: "Hey, maybe *this* is who I am." If you finish a book, then perhaps you are the type of person who likes reading. If you go to the gym, then perhaps you are the type of person who likes exercise. If you practice playing the guitar, perhaps you are the type of person who likes music.

Every action you take is a vote for the type of person you wish to become. No single instance will transform your beliefs, but as the votes build up, so does the evidence of your new identity. This is one reason why meaningful change does not require radical change. Small habits can make a meaningful difference by providing evidence of a new identity. And if a change is meaningful, it actually is big. That's the paradox of making small improvements.

Putting this all together, you can see that habits are the path to changing your identity. The most practical way to change *who* you are is to change *what* you do.

- Each time you write a page, you are a writer.
- Each time you practice the violin, you are a musician.
- Each time you start a workout, you are an athlete.
- Each time you encourage your employees, you are a leader.

Each habit not only gets results but also teaches you something far more important: to trust yourself. You start to believe you can actually accomplish these things. When the votes mount up and the evidence begins to change, the story you tell yourself begins to change as well.

Of course, it works the opposite way, too. Every time you choose to perform a bad habit, it's a vote for that identity. The good news is that

you don't need to be perfect. In any election, there are going to be votes for both sides. You don't need a unanimous vote to win an election; you just need a majority. It doesn't matter if you cast a few votes for a bad behavior or an unproductive habit. Your goal is simply to win the majority of the time.

New identities require new evidence. If you keep casting the same votes you've always cast, you're going to get the same results you've always had. If nothing changes, nothing is going to change.

It is a simple two-step process:

1. Decide the type of person you want to be.
2. Prove it to yourself with small wins.

First, decide who you want to be. This holds at any level—as an individual, as a team, as a community, as a nation. What do you want to stand for? What are your principles and values? Who do you wish to become?

These are big questions, and many people aren't sure where to begin—but they do know what kind of results they want: to get six-pack abs or to feel less anxious or to double their salary. That's fine. Start there and work backward from the results you want to the type of person who could get those results. Ask yourself, "Who is the type of person that could get the outcome I want?" Who is the type of person that could lose forty pounds? Who is the type of person that could learn a new language? Who is the type of person that could run a successful start-up?

For example, "Who is the type of person who could write a book?" It's probably someone who is consistent and reliable. Now your focus shifts from writing a book (outcome-based) to being the type of person who is consistent and reliable (identity-based).

This process can lead to beliefs like:

- "I'm the kind of teacher who stands up for her students."
- "I'm the kind of doctor who gives each patient the time and empathy they need."
- "I'm the kind of manager who advocates for her employees."

Once you have a handle on the type of person you want to be, you can begin taking small steps to reinforce your desired identity. I have a friend who lost over 100 pounds by asking herself, "What would a healthy person do?" All day long, she would use this question as a guide. Would a healthy person walk or take a cab? Would a healthy person order a burrito or a salad? She figured if she acted like a healthy person long enough, eventually she would become that person. She was right.

The concept of identity-based habits is our first introduction to another key theme in this book: feedback loops. Your habits shape your identity, and your identity shapes your habits. It's a two-way street. The formation of all habits is a feedback loop (a concept we will explore in depth in the next chapter), but it's important to let your values, principles, and identity drive the loop rather than your results. The focus should always be on becoming that type of person, not getting a particular outcome.

THE REAL REASON HABITS MATTER

Identity change is the North Star of habit change. The remainder of this book will provide you with step-by-step instructions on how to build better habits in yourself, your family, your team, your company, and anywhere else you wish. But the true question is: "Are you becoming the type of person you want to become?" The first step is not *what* or *how*, but *who*. You need to know who you want to be. Otherwise, your quest for change is like a boat without a rudder. And that's why we are starting here.

You have the power to change your beliefs about yourself. Your identity is not set in stone. You have a choice in every moment. You can choose the identity you want to reinforce today with the habits you choose today. And this brings us to the deeper purpose of this book and the real reason habits matter.

Building better habits isn't about littering your day with life hacks. It's not about flossing one tooth each night or taking a cold shower each morning or wearing the same outfit each day. It's not about achieving external measures of success like earning more money, losing weight, or reducing stress. Habits can help you achieve all of these things, but fundamentally they are not about *having* something. They are about *becoming* someone.

Ultimately, your habits matter because they help you become the type of person you wish to be. They are the channel through which you develop your deepest beliefs about yourself. Quite literally, you become your habits.

————————————— Chapter Summary —————————————

- There are three levels of change: outcome change, process change, and identity change.
- The most effective way to change your habits is to focus not on what you want to achieve, but on who you wish to become.
- Your identity emerges out of your habits. Every action is a vote for the type of person you wish to become.
- Becoming the best version of yourself requires you to continuously edit your beliefs, and to upgrade and expand your identity.
- The real reason habits matter is not because they can get you better results (although they can do that), but because they can change your beliefs about yourself.

3

How to Build Better Habits in 4 Simple Steps

I N 1898, A psychologist named Edward Thorndike conducted an experiment that would lay the foundation for our understanding of how habits form and the rules that guide our behavior. Thorndike was interested in studying the behavior of animals, and he started by working with cats.

He would place each cat inside a device known as a puzzle box. The box was designed so that the cat could escape through a door "by some simple act, such as pulling at a loop of cord, pressing a lever, or stepping on a platform." For example, one box contained a lever that, when pressed, would open a door on the side of the box. Once the door had been opened, the cat could dart out and run over to a bowl of food.

Most cats wanted to escape as soon as they were placed inside the box. They would poke their nose into the corners, stick their paws through openings, and claw at loose objects. After a few minutes of exploration, the cats would happen to press the magical lever, the door would open, and they would escape.

Thorndike tracked the behavior of each cat across many trials. In

the beginning, the animals moved around the box at random. But as soon as the lever had been pressed and the door opened, the process of learning began. Gradually, each cat learned to associate the action of pressing the lever with the reward of escaping the box and getting to the food.

After twenty to thirty trials, this behavior became so automatic and habitual that the cat could escape within a few seconds. For example, Thorndike noted, "Cat 12 took the following times to perform the act. 160 seconds, 30 seconds, 90 seconds, 60, 15, 28, 20, 30, 22, 11, 15, 20, 12, 10, 14, 10, 8, 8, 5, 10, 8, 6, 6, 7."

During the first three trials, the cat escaped in an average of 1.5 minutes. During the last three trials, it escaped in an average of 6.3 seconds. With practice, each cat made fewer errors and their actions became quicker and more automatic. Rather than repeat the same mistakes, the cat began to cut straight to the solution.

From his studies, Thorndike described the learning process by stating, "behaviors followed by satisfying consequences tend to be repeated and those that produce unpleasant consequences are less likely to be repeated." His work provides the perfect starting point for discussing how habits form in our own lives. It also provides answers to some fundamental questions like: What are habits? And why does the brain bother building them at all?

WHY YOUR BRAIN BUILDS HABITS

A habit is a behavior that has been repeated enough times to become automatic. The process of habit formation begins with trial and error. Whenever you encounter a new situation in life, your brain has to make a decision. *How do I respond to this?* The first time you come across a problem, you're not sure how to solve it. Like Thorndike's cat, you're just trying things out to see what works.

Neurological activity in the brain is high during this period. You are carefully analyzing the situation and making conscious decisions about how to act. You're taking in tons of new information and trying to make sense of it all. The brain is busy learning the most effective course of action.

Occasionally, like a cat pressing on a lever, you stumble across a solution. You're feeling anxious, and you discover that going for a run calms you down. You're mentally exhausted from a long day of work, and you learn that playing video games relaxes you. You're exploring, exploring, exploring, and then—BAM—a reward.

After you stumble upon an unexpected reward, you alter your strategy for next time. Your brain immediately begins to catalog the events that preceded the reward. *Wait a minute—that felt good. What did I do right before that?*

This is the feedback loop behind all human behavior: try, fail, learn, try differently. With practice, the useless movements fade away and the useful actions get reinforced. That's a habit forming.

Whenever you face a problem repeatedly, your brain begins to automate the process of solving it. Your habits are just a series of automatic solutions that solve the problems and stresses you face regularly. As behavioral scientist Jason Hreha writes, "Habits are, simply, reliable solutions to recurring problems in our environment."

As habits are created, the level of activity in the brain *decreases*. You learn to lock in on the cues that predict success and tune out everything else. When a similar situation arises in the future, you know exactly what to look for. There is no longer a need to analyze every angle of a situation. Your brain skips the process of trial and error and creates a mental rule: if this, then that. These cognitive scripts can be followed automatically whenever the situation is appropriate. Now, whenever you feel stressed, you get the itch to run. As soon as you walk in the door from work, you grab the video game controller. A

choice that once required effort is now automatic. A habit has been created.

Habits are mental shortcuts learned from experience. In a sense, a habit is just a memory of the steps you previously followed to solve a problem in the past. Whenever the conditions are right, you can draw on this memory and automatically apply the same solution. The primary reason the brain remembers the past is to better predict what will work in the future.

Habit formation is incredibly useful because the conscious mind is the bottleneck of the brain. It can only pay attention to one problem at a time. As a result, your brain is always working to preserve your conscious attention for whatever task is most essential. Whenever possible, the conscious mind likes to pawn off tasks to the nonconscious mind to do automatically. This is precisely what happens when a habit is formed. Habits reduce cognitive load and free up mental capacity, so you can allocate your attention to other tasks.

Despite their efficiency, some people still wonder about the benefits of habits. The argument goes like this: "Will habits make my life dull? I don't want to pigeonhole myself into a lifestyle I don't enjoy. Doesn't so much routine take away the vibrancy and spontaneity of life?" Hardly. Such questions set up a false dichotomy. They make you think that you have to choose between building habits and attaining freedom. In reality, the two complement each other.

Habits do not restrict freedom. They create it. In fact, the people who don't have their habits handled are often the ones with the *least* amount of freedom. Without good financial habits, you will always be struggling for the next dollar. Without good health habits, you will always seem to be short on energy. Without good learning habits, you will always feel like you're behind the curve. If you're always being forced to make decisions about simple tasks—when should I work out, where do

I go to write, when do I pay the bills—then you have less time for freedom. It's only by making the fundamentals of life easier that you can create the mental space needed for free thinking and creativity.

Conversely, when you have your habits dialed in and the basics of life are handled and done, your mind is free to focus on new challenges and master the next set of problems. Building habits in the present allows you to do more of what you want in the future.

THE SCIENCE OF HOW HABITS WORK

The process of building a habit can be divided into four simple steps: cue, craving, response, and reward.* Breaking it down into these fundamental parts can help us understand what a habit is, how it works, and how to improve it.

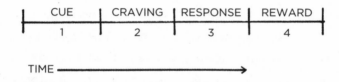

FIGURE 5: All habits proceed through four stages in the same order: cue, craving, response, and reward.

This four-step pattern is the backbone of every habit, and your brain runs through these steps in the same order each time.

First, there is the cue. The cue triggers your brain to initiate a be-

---

* Readers of *The Power of Habit* by Charles Duhigg will recognize these terms. Duhigg wrote a great book and my intention is to pick up where he left off by integrating these stages into four simple laws you can apply to build better habits in life and work.

havior. It is a bit of information that predicts a reward. Our prehistoric ancestors were paying attention to cues that signaled the location of primary rewards like food, water, and sex. Today, we spend most of our time learning cues that predict secondary rewards like money and fame, power and status, praise and approval, love and friendship, or a sense of personal satisfaction. (Of course, these pursuits also indirectly improve our odds of survival and reproduction, which is the deeper motive behind everything we do.)

Your mind is continuously analyzing your internal and external environment for hints of where rewards are located. Because the cue is the first indication that we're close to a reward, it naturally leads to a craving.

Cravings are the second step, and they are the motivational force behind every habit. Without some level of motivation or desire—without craving a change—we have no reason to act. What you crave is not the habit itself but the change in state it delivers. You do not crave smoking a cigarette, you crave the feeling of relief it provides. You are not motivated by brushing your teeth but rather by the feeling of a clean mouth. You do not want to turn on the television, you want to be entertained. Every craving is linked to a desire to change your internal state. This is an important point that we will discuss in detail later.

Cravings differ from person to person. In theory, any piece of information could trigger a craving, but in practice, people are not motivated by the same cues. For a gambler, the sound of slot machines can be a potent trigger that sparks an intense wave of desire. For someone who rarely gambles, the jingles and chimes of the casino are just background noise. Cues are meaningless until they are interpreted. The thoughts, feelings, and emotions of the observer are what transform a cue into a craving.

The third step is the response. The response is the actual habit you perform, which can take the form of a thought or an action. Whether

a response occurs depends on how motivated you are and how much friction is associated with the behavior. If a particular action requires more physical or mental effort than you are willing to expend, then you won't do it. Your response also depends on your ability. It sounds simple, but a habit can occur only if you are capable of doing it. If you want to dunk a basketball but can't jump high enough to reach the hoop, well, you're out of luck.

Finally, the response delivers a reward. Rewards are the end goal of every habit. The cue is about noticing the reward. The craving is about wanting the reward. The response is about obtaining the reward. We chase rewards because they serve two purposes: (1) they satisfy us and (2) they teach us.

The first purpose of rewards is to *satisfy your craving*. Yes, rewards provide benefits on their own. Food and water deliver the energy you need to survive. Getting a promotion brings more money and respect. Getting in shape improves your health and your dating prospects. But the more immediate benefit is that rewards satisfy your craving to eat or to gain status or to win approval. At least for a moment, rewards deliver contentment and relief from craving.

Second, rewards teach us which actions are worth remembering in the future. Your brain is a reward detector. As you go about your life, your sensory nervous system is continuously monitoring which actions satisfy your desires and deliver pleasure. Feelings of pleasure and disappointment are part of the feedback mechanism that helps your brain distinguish useful actions from useless ones. Rewards close the feedback loop and complete the habit cycle.

If a behavior is insufficient in any of the four stages, it will not become a habit. Eliminate the cue and your habit will never start. Reduce the craving and you won't experience enough motivation to act. Make the behavior difficult and you won't be able to do it. And if the reward fails to satisfy your desire, then you'll have no reason to do it again in

the future. Without the first three steps, a behavior will not occur. Without all four, a behavior will not be repeated.

THE HABIT LOOP

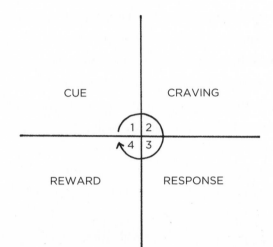

FIGURE 6: The four stages of habit are best described as a feedback loop. They form an endless cycle that is running every moment you are alive. This "habit loop" is continually scanning the environment, predicting what will happen next, trying out different responses, and learning from the results.*

In summary, the cue triggers a craving, which motivates a response, which provides a reward, which satisfies the craving and, ultimately, becomes associated with the cue. Together, these four steps form a neurological feedback loop—cue, craving, response, reward;

---

* Charles Duhigg and Nir Eyal deserve special recognition for their influence on this image. This representation of the habit loop is a combination of language that was popularized by Duhigg's book, *The Power of Habit*, and a design that was popularized by Eyal's book, *Hooked*.

cue, craving, response, reward—that ultimately allows you to create automatic habits. This cycle is known as the habit loop.

This four-step process is not something that happens occasionally, but rather it is an endless feedback loop that is running and active during every moment you are alive—even now. The brain is continually scanning the environment, predicting what will happen next, trying out different responses, and learning from the results. The entire process is completed in a split second, and we use it again and again without realizing everything that has been packed into the previous moment.

We can split these four steps into two phases: the problem phase and the solution phase. The problem phase includes the cue and the craving, and it is when you realize that something needs to change. The solution phase includes the response and the reward, and it is when you take action and achieve the change you desire.

Problem phase		Solution phase	
1. Cue	2. Craving	3. Response	4. Reward

All behavior is driven by the desire to solve a problem. Sometimes the problem is that you notice something good and you want to obtain it. Sometimes the problem is that you are experiencing pain and you want to relieve it. Either way, the purpose of every habit is to solve the problems you face.

In the table on the following page, you can see a few examples of what this looks like in real life.

Imagine walking into a dark room and flipping on the light switch. You have performed this simple habit so many times that it occurs without thinking. You proceed through all four stages in the fraction of a second. The urge to act strikes you without thinking.

By the time we become adults, we rarely notice the habits that are

Problem phase		Solution phase	
1. Cue	2. Craving	3. Response	4. Reward
Your phone buzzes with a new text message.	You want to learn the contents of the message.	You grab your phone and read the text.	You satisfy your craving to read the message. Grabbing your phone becomes associated with your phone buzzing.
You are answering emails.	You begin to feel stressed and overwhelmed by work. You want to feel in control.	You bite your nails.	You satisfy your craving to reduce stress. Biting your nails becomes associated with answering email.
You wake up.	You want to feel alert.	You drink a cup of coffee.	You satisfy your craving to feel alert. Drinking coffee becomes associated with waking up.
You smell a doughnut shop as you walk down the street near your office.	You begin to crave a doughnut.	You buy a doughnut and eat it.	You satisfy your craving to eat a doughnut. Buying a doughnut becomes associated with walking down the street near your office.

Problem phase		Solution phase	
1. Cue	2. Craving	3. Response	4. Reward
You hit a stumbling block on a project at work.	You feel stuck and want to relieve your frustration.	You pull out your phone and check social media.	You satisfy your craving to feel relieved. Checking social media becomes associated with feeling stalled at work.
You walk into a dark room.	You want to be able to see.	You flip the light switch.	You satisfy your craving to see. Turning on the light switch becomes associated with being in a dark room.

running our lives. Most of us never give a second thought to the fact that we tie the same shoe first each morning, or unplug the toaster after each use, or always change into comfortable clothes after getting home from work. After decades of mental programming, we automatically slip into these patterns of thinking and acting.

THE FOUR LAWS OF BEHAVIOR CHANGE

In the following chapters, we will see time and again how the four stages of cue, craving, response, and reward influence nearly everything we do each day. But before we do that, we need to transform these four steps into a practical framework that we can use to design good habits and eliminate bad ones.

I refer to this framework as the *Four Laws of Behavior Change*, and it provides a simple set of rules for creating good habits and breaking bad

ones. You can think of each law as a lever that influences human behavior. When the levers are in the right positions, creating good habits is effortless. When they are in the wrong positions, it is nearly impossible.

	How to Create a Good Habit
The 1st law (Cue)	Make it obvious.
The 2nd law (Craving)	Make it attractive.
The 3rd law (Response)	Make it easy.
The 4th law (Reward)	Make it satisfying.

We can invert these laws to learn how to break a bad habit.

	How to Break a Bad Habit
Inversion of the 1st law (Cue)	Make it invisible.
Inversion of the 2nd law (Craving)	Make it unattractive.
Inversion of the 3rd law (Response)	Make it difficult.
Inversion of the 4th law (Reward)	Make it unsatisfying.

It would be irresponsible for me to claim that these four laws are an exhaustive framework for changing *any* human behavior, but I think they're close. As you will soon see, the Four Laws of Behavior Change apply to nearly every field, from sports to politics, art to medicine, comedy to management. These laws can be used no matter what challenge you are facing. There is no need for completely different strategies for each habit.

Whenever you want to change your behavior, you can simply ask yourself:

1. How can I make it obvious?
2. How can I make it attractive?
3. How can I make it easy?
4. How can I make it satisfying?

If you have ever wondered, "Why don't I do what I say I'm going to do? Why don't I lose the weight or stop smoking or save for retirement or start that side business? Why do I say something is important but never seem to make time for it?" The answers to those questions can be found somewhere in these four laws. The key to creating good habits and breaking bad ones is to understand these fundamental laws and how to alter them to your specifications. Every goal is doomed to fail if it goes against the grain of human nature.

Your habits are shaped by the systems in your life. In the chapters that follow, we will discuss these laws one by one and show how you can use them to create a system in which good habits emerge naturally and bad habits wither away.

--------------------- Chapter Summary ---------------------

- A habit is a behavior that has been repeated enough times to become automatic.
- The ultimate purpose of habits is to solve the problems of life with as little energy and effort as possible.
- Any habit can be broken down into a feedback loop that involves four steps: cue, craving, response, and reward.
- The Four Laws of Behavior Change are a simple set of rules we can use to build better habits. They are (1) make it obvious, (2) make it attractive, (3) make it easy, and (4) make it satisfying.

THE 1ST LAW

Make It Obvious

ATOMIC HABITS

An Easy & Proven Way
to Build Good Habits &
Break Bad Ones

JAMES CLEAR

AVERY

an imprint of Penguin Random House

New York

a·tom·ic

ə'tämik

1. an extremely small amount of a thing; the single irreducible unit of a larger system.

2. the source of immense energy or power.

hab·it

'habət

1. a routine or practice performed regularly; an automatic response to a specific situation.

AVERY

AN IMPRINT OF PENGUIN RANDOM HOUSE LLC
375 Hudson Street
New York, New York 10014

Most Avery books are available at special quantity discounts for bulk
purchase for sales promotions, premiums, fund-raising, and educational
needs. Special books or book excerpts also can be created to fit specific
needs. For details, write SpecialMarkets@penguinrandomhouse.com.

ISBN 9780735211292

Printed in the United States of America
31 29 32 30 28

ATOMIC HABITS

An Easy & Proven Way
to Build Good Habits &
Break Bad Ones

Tiny Changes, Remarkable Results

4

The Man Who
Didn't Look Right

THE PSYCHOLOGIST GARY Klein once told me a story about a woman who attended a family gathering. She had spent years working as a paramedic and, upon arriving at the event, took one look at her father-in-law and got very concerned.

"I don't like the way you look," she said.

Her father-in-law, who was feeling perfectly fine, jokingly replied, "Well, I don't like your looks, either."

"No," she insisted. "You need to go to the hospital now."

A few hours later, the man was undergoing lifesaving surgery after an examination had revealed that he had a blockage to a major artery and was at immediate risk of a heart attack. Without his daughter-in-law's intuition, he could have died.

What did the paramedic see? How did she predict his impending heart attack?

When major arteries are obstructed, the body focuses on sending blood to critical organs and away from peripheral locations near the surface of the skin. The result is a change in the pattern of distribution of blood in the face. After many years of working with people with heart failure, the woman had unknowingly developed the ability to recognize this pattern on sight. She couldn't explain what it was that she noticed in her father-in-law's face, but she knew something was wrong.

Similar stories exist in other fields. For example, military analysts can identify which blip on a radar screen is an enemy missile and which one is a plane from their own fleet even though they are traveling at the same speed, flying at the same altitude, and look identical on radar in nearly every respect. During the Gulf War, Lieutenant Commander Michael Riley saved an entire battleship when he ordered a missile shot down—despite the fact that it looked exactly like the battleship's own planes on radar. He made the right call, but even his superior officers couldn't explain how he did it.

Museum curators have been known to discern the difference between an authentic piece of art and an expertly produced counterfeit even though they can't tell you precisely which details tipped them off. Experienced radiologists can look at a brain scan and predict the area where a stroke will develop before any obvious signs are visible to the untrained eye. I've even heard of hairdressers noticing whether a client is pregnant based only on the feel of her hair.

The human brain is a prediction machine. It is continuously taking in your surroundings and analyzing the information it comes across. Whenever you experience something repeatedly—like a paramedic seeing the face of a heart attack patient or a military analyst seeing a missile on a radar screen—your brain begins noticing what is important, sorting through the details and highlighting the relevant cues, and cataloging that information for future use.

With enough practice, you can pick up on the cues that predict certain outcomes without consciously thinking about it. Automatically, your brain encodes the lessons learned through experience. We can't always explain what it is we are learning, but learning is happening all along the way, and your ability to notice the relevant cues in a given situation is the foundation for every habit you have.

We underestimate how much our brains and bodies can do without thinking. You do not tell your hair to grow, your heart to pump, your lungs to breathe, or your stomach to digest. And yet your body handles all this and more on autopilot. You are much more than your conscious self.

Consider hunger. How do you know when you're hungry? You don't necessarily have to see a cookie on the counter to realize that it is time to eat. Appetite and hunger are governed nonconsciously. Your body has a variety of feedback loops that gradually alert you when it is time to eat again and that track what is going on around you and within you. Cravings can arise thanks to hormones and chemicals circulating through your body. Suddenly, you're hungry even though you're not quite sure what tipped you off.

This is one of the most surprising insights about our habits: you don't need to be aware of the cue for a habit to begin. You can notice an opportunity and take action without dedicating conscious attention to it. This is what makes habits useful.

It's also what makes them dangerous. As habits form, your actions come under the direction of your automatic and nonconscious mind. You fall into old patterns before you realize what's happening. Unless someone points it out, you may not notice that you cover your mouth with your hand whenever you laugh, that you apologize before asking a question, or that you have a habit of finishing other people's sentences. And the more you repeat these patterns, the less likely you become to question what you're doing and why you're doing it.

I once heard of a retail clerk who was instructed to cut up empty gift cards after customers had used up the balance on the card. One day, the clerk cashed out a few customers in a row who purchased with gift cards. When the next person walked up, the clerk swiped the customer's actual credit card, picked up the scissors, and then cut it in half—entirely on autopilot—before looking up at the stunned customer and realizing what had just happened.

Another woman I came across in my research was a former preschool teacher who had switched to a corporate job. Even though she was now working with adults, her old habits would kick in and she kept asking coworkers if they had washed their hands after going to the bathroom. I also found the story of a man who had spent years working as a lifeguard and would occasionally yell "Walk!" whenever he saw a child running.

Over time, the cues that spark our habits become so common that they are essentially invisible: the treats on the kitchen counter, the remote control next to the couch, the phone in our pocket. Our responses to these cues are so deeply encoded that it may feel like the urge to act comes from nowhere. For this reason, we must begin the process of behavior change with awareness.

Before we can effectively build new habits, we need to get a handle on our current ones. This can be more challenging than it sounds because once a habit is firmly rooted in your life, it is mostly nonconscious and automatic. If a habit remains mindless, you can't expect to improve it. As the psychologist Carl Jung said, "Until you make the unconscious conscious, it will direct your life and you will call it fate."

THE HABITS SCORECARD

The Japanese railway system is regarded as one of the best in the world. If you ever find yourself riding a train in Tokyo, you'll notice that the conductors have a peculiar habit.

As each operator runs the train, they proceed through a ritual of pointing at different objects and calling out commands. When the train approaches a signal, the operator will point at it and say, "Signal is green." As the train pulls into and out of each station, the operator will point at the speedometer and call out the exact speed. When it's time to leave, the operator will point at the timetable and state the time. Out on the platform, other employees are performing similar actions. Before each train departs, staff members will point along the edge of the platform and declare, "All clear!" Every detail is identified, pointed at, and named aloud.*

This process, known as *Pointing-and-Calling,* is a safety system designed to reduce mistakes. It seems silly, but it works incredibly well. Pointing-and-Calling reduces errors by up to 85 percent and cuts accidents by 30 percent. The MTA subway system in New York City adopted a modified version that is "point-only," and "within two years of implementation, incidents of incorrectly berthed subways fell 57 percent."

Pointing-and-Calling is so effective because it raises the level of awareness from a nonconscious habit to a more conscious level. Because the train operators must use their eyes, hands, mouth, and ears, they are more likely to notice problems before something goes wrong.

My wife does something similar. Whenever we are preparing to walk out the door for a trip, she verbally calls out the most essential

---

* When I visited Japan, I saw this strategy save a woman's life. Her young son stepped onto the Shinkansen, one of Japan's famous bullet trains that travel at over two hundred miles per hour, just as the doors were closing. She was left outside on the platform and jammed her arm through the door to grab him. With her arm stuck in the door, the train was about to take off, but right before it pulled away an employee performed a safety check by Pointing-and-Calling up and down the platform. In less than five seconds, he noticed the woman and managed to stop the train from leaving. The door opened, the woman—now in tears—ran to her son, and a minute later the train departed safely.

items in her packing list. "I've got my keys. I've got my wallet. I've got my glasses. I've got my husband."

The more automatic a behavior becomes, the less likely we are to consciously think about it. And when we've done something a thousand times before, we begin to overlook things. We assume that the next time will be just like the last. We're so used to doing what we've always done that we don't stop to question whether it's the right thing to do at all. Many of our failures in performance are largely attributable to a lack of self-awareness.

One of our greatest challenges in changing habits is maintaining awareness of what we are actually doing. This helps explain why the consequences of bad habits can sneak up on us. We need a "point-and-call" system for our personal lives. That's the origin of the Habits Scorecard, which is a simple exercise you can use to become more aware of your behavior. To create your own, make a list of your daily habits.

Here's a sample of where your list might start:

- Wake up
- Turn off alarm
- Check my phone
- Go to the bathroom
- Weigh myself
- Take a shower

- Brush my teeth
- Floss my teeth
- Put on deodorant
- Hang up towel to dry
- Get dressed
- Make a cup of tea

. . . and so on.

Once you have a full list, look at each behavior, and ask yourself, "Is this a good habit, a bad habit, or a neutral habit?" If it is a good habit, write "+" next to it. If it is a bad habit, write "–". If it is a neutral habit, write "=".

For example, the list above might look like this:

- ▪ Wake up =
- ▪ Turn off alarm =
- ▪ Check my phone –
- ▪ Go to the bathroom =
- ▪ Weigh myself +
- ▪ Take a shower +

- ▪ Brush my teeth +
- ▪ Floss my teeth +
- ▪ Put on deodorant +
- ▪ Hang up towel to dry =
- ▪ Get dressed =
- ▪ Make a cup of tea +

The marks you give to a particular habit will depend on your situation and your goals. For someone who is trying to lose weight, eating a bagel with peanut butter every morning might be a bad habit. For someone who is trying to bulk up and add muscle, the same behavior might be a good habit. It all depends on what you're working toward.*

Scoring your habits can be a bit more complex for another reason as well. The labels "good habit" and "bad habit" are slightly inaccurate. There are no good habits or bad habits. There are only effective habits. That is, effective at solving problems. All habits serve you in some way—even the bad ones—which is why you repeat them. For this exercise, categorize your habits by how they will benefit you in the long run. Generally speaking, good habits will have net positive outcomes. Bad habits have net negative outcomes. Smoking a cigarette may reduce stress right now (that's how it's serving you), but it's not a healthy long-term behavior.

If you're still having trouble determining how to rate a particular habit, here is a question I like to use: "Does this behavior help me become the type of person I wish to be? Does this habit cast a vote for or against my desired identity?" Habits that reinforce your desired identity are usually good. Habits that conflict with your desired identity are usually bad.

As you create your Habits Scorecard, there is no need to change anything at first. The goal is to simply notice what is actually going on. Observe your thoughts and actions without judgment or internal

---

* Interested readers can get a template to create their own Habits Scorecard at atomichabits .com/scorecard.

criticism. Don't blame yourself for your faults. Don't praise yourself for your successes.

If you eat a chocolate bar every morning, acknowledge it, almost as if you were watching someone else. *Oh, how interesting that they would do such a thing.* If you binge-eat, simply notice that you are eating more calories than you should. If you waste time online, notice that you are spending your life in a way that you do not want to.

The first step to changing bad habits is to be on the lookout for them. If you feel like you need extra help, then you can try Pointing-and-Calling in your own life. Say out loud the action that you are thinking of taking and what the outcome will be. If you want to cut back on your junk food habit but notice yourself grabbing another cookie, say out loud, "I'm about to eat this cookie, but I don't need it. Eating it will cause me to gain weight and hurt my health."

Hearing your bad habits spoken aloud makes the consequences seem more real. It adds weight to the action rather than letting yourself mindlessly slip into an old routine. This approach is useful even if you're simply trying to remember a task on your to-do list. Just saying out loud, "Tomorrow, I need to go to the post office after lunch," increases the odds that you'll actually do it. You're getting yourself to acknowledge the need for action—and that can make all the difference.

The process of behavior change always starts with awareness. Strategies like Pointing-and-Calling and the Habits Scorecard are focused on getting you to recognize your habits and acknowledge the cues that trigger them, which makes it possible to respond in a way that benefits you.

Chapter Summary

- With enough practice, your brain will pick up on the cues that predict certain outcomes without consciously thinking about it.

- Once our habits become automatic, we stop paying attention to what we are doing.
- The process of behavior change always starts with awareness. You need to be aware of your habits before you can change them.
- Pointing-and-Calling raises your level of awareness from a nonconscious habit to a more conscious level by verbalizing your actions.
- The Habits Scorecard is a simple exercise you can use to become more aware of your behavior.

5

The Best Way
to Start a New Habit

IN 2001, RESEARCHERS in Great Britain began working with 248 people to build better exercise habits over the course of two weeks. The
subjects were divided into three groups.

The first group was the control group. They were simply asked to
track how often they exercised.

The second group was the "motivation" group. They were asked not
only to track their workouts but also to read some material on the benefits of exercise. The researchers also explained to the group how exercise could reduce the risk of coronary heart disease and improve heart
health.

Finally, there was the third group. These subjects received the same
presentation as the second group, which ensured that they had equal
levels of motivation. However, they were also asked to formulate a plan
for when and where they would exercise over the following week. Specifically, each member of the third group completed the following sentence: "During the next week, I will partake in at least 20 minutes of
vigorous exercise on [DAY] at [TIME] in [PLACE]."

In the first and second groups, 35 to 38 percent of people exercised at least once per week. (Interestingly, the motivational presentation given to the second group seemed to have no meaningful impact on behavior.) But 91 percent of the third group exercised at least once per week—more than double the normal rate.

The sentence they filled out is what researchers refer to as an *implementation intention*, which is a plan you make beforehand about when and where to act. That is, how you *intend* to *implement* a particular habit.

The cues that can trigger a habit come in a wide range of forms— the feel of your phone buzzing in your pocket, the smell of chocolate chip cookies, the sound of ambulance sirens—but the two most common cues are time and location. Implementation intentions leverage both of these cues.

Broadly speaking, the format for creating
an implementation intention is:
"When situation X arises, I will perform response Y."

Hundreds of studies have shown that implementation intentions are effective for sticking to our goals, whether it's writing down the exact time and date of when you will get a flu shot or recording the time of your colonoscopy appointment. They increase the odds that people will stick with habits like recycling, studying, going to sleep early, and stopping smoking.

Researchers have even found that voter turnout increases when people are forced to create implementation intentions by answering questions like: "What route are you taking to the polling station? At what time are you planning to go? What bus will get you there?" Other successful government programs have prompted citizens to make a clear plan to send taxes in on time or provided directions on when and where to pay late traffic bills.

The punch line is clear: people who make a specific plan for when and where they will perform a new habit are more likely to follow through. Too many people try to change their habits without these basic details figured out. We tell ourselves, "I'm going to eat healthier" or "I'm going to write more," but we never say when and where these habits are going to happen. We leave it up to chance and hope that we will "just remember to do it" or feel motivated at the right time. An implementation intention sweeps away foggy notions like "I want to work out more" or "I want to be more productive" or "I should vote" and transforms them into a concrete plan of action.

Many people think they lack motivation when what they really lack is clarity. It is not always obvious when and where to take action. Some people spend their entire lives waiting for the time to be right to make an improvement.

Once an implementation intention has been set, you don't have to wait for inspiration to strike. *Do I write a chapter today or not? Do I meditate this morning or at lunch?* When the moment of action occurs, there is no need to make a decision. Simply follow your predetermined plan.

The simple way to apply this strategy to your habits
is to fill out this sentence:
I will [BEHAVIOR] at [TIME] in [LOCATION].

- Meditation. I will meditate for one minute at 7 a.m. in my kitchen.
- Studying. I will study Spanish for twenty minutes at 6 p.m. in my bedroom.
- Exercise. I will exercise for one hour at 5 p.m. in my local gym.
- Marriage. I will make my partner a cup of tea at 8 a.m. in the kitchen.

If you aren't sure when to start your habit, try the first day of the week, month, or year. People are more likely to take action at those times because hope is usually higher. If we have hope, we have a reason to take action. A fresh start feels motivating.

There is another benefit to implementation intentions. Being specific about what you want and how you will achieve it helps you say no to things that derail progress, distract your attention, and pull you off course. We often say yes to little requests because we are not clear enough about what we need to be doing instead. When your dreams are vague, it's easy to rationalize little exceptions all day long and never get around to the specific things you need to do to succeed.

Give your habits a time and a space to live in the world. The goal is to make the time and location so obvious that, with enough repetition, you get an urge to do the right thing at the right time, even if you can't say why. As the writer Jason Zweig noted, "Obviously you're never going to just work out without conscious thought. But like a dog salivating at a bell, maybe you start to get antsy around the time of day you normally work out."

There are many ways to use implementation intentions in your life and work. My favorite approach is one I learned from Stanford professor BJ Fogg and it is a strategy I refer to as *habit stacking*.

HABIT STACKING: A SIMPLE PLAN
TO OVERHAUL YOUR HABITS

The French philosopher Denis Diderot lived nearly his entire life in poverty, but that all changed one day in 1765.

Diderot's daughter was about to be married and he could not afford to pay for the wedding. Despite his lack of wealth, Diderot was well known for his role as the co-founder and writer of *Encyclopédie*, one of the most comprehensive encyclopedias of the time. When Catherine the Great, the Empress of Russia, heard of Diderot's financial troubles, her heart went out to him. She was a book lover and greatly enjoyed his encyclopedia. She offered to buy Diderot's personal library for

£1,000—more than $150,000 today.* Suddenly, Diderot had money to spare. With his new wealth, he not only paid for the wedding but also acquired a scarlet robe for himself.

Diderot's scarlet robe was beautiful. So beautiful, in fact, that he immediately noticed how out of place it seemed when surrounded by his more common possessions. He wrote that there was "no more co-ordination, no more unity, no more beauty" between his elegant robe and the rest of his stuff.

Diderot soon felt the urge to upgrade his possessions. He replaced his rug with one from Damascus. He decorated his home with expensive sculptures. He bought a mirror to place above the mantel, and a better kitchen table. He tossed aside his old straw chair for a leather one. Like falling dominoes, one purchase led to the next.

Diderot's behavior is not uncommon. In fact, the tendency for one purchase to lead to another one has a name: the Diderot Effect. The Diderot Effect states that obtaining a new possession often creates a spiral of consumption that leads to additional purchases.

You can spot this pattern everywhere. You buy a dress and have to get new shoes and earrings to match. You buy a couch and suddenly question the layout of your entire living room. You buy a toy for your child and soon find yourself purchasing all of the accessories that go with it. It's a chain reaction of purchases.

Many human behaviors follow this cycle. You often decide what to do next based on what you have just finished doing. Going to the bathroom leads to washing and drying your hands, which reminds you that you need to put the dirty towels in the laundry, so you add laundry detergent to the shopping list, and so on. No behavior happens in isolation. Each action becomes a cue that triggers the next behavior.

Why is this important?

---

* In addition to her payment for the library, Catherine the Great asked Diderot to keep the books until she needed them and offered to pay him a yearly salary to act as her librarian.

When it comes to building new habits, you can use the connectedness of behavior to your advantage. One of the best ways to build a new habit is to identify a current habit you already do each day and then stack your new behavior on top. This is called *habit stacking*.

Habit stacking is a special form of an implementation intention. Rather than pairing your new habit with a particular time and location, you pair it with a current habit. This method, which was created by BJ Fogg as part of his Tiny Habits program, can be used to design an obvious cue for nearly any habit.*

The habit stacking formula is:
"After [CURRENT HABIT], I will [NEW HABIT]."

For example:

- Meditation. After I pour my cup of coffee each morning, I will meditate for one minute.
- Exercise. After I take off my work shoes, I will immediately change into my workout clothes.
- Gratitude. After I sit down to dinner, I will say one thing I'm grateful for that happened today.
- Marriage. After I get into bed at night, I will give my partner a kiss.
- Safety. After I put on my running shoes, I will text a friend or family member where I am running and how long it will take.

The key is to tie your desired behavior into something you already do each day. Once you have mastered this basic structure, you can begin to create larger stacks by chaining small habits together. This allows you to

---

* Fogg refers to this strategy as the "Tiny Habits recipe," but I'll call it the habit stacking formula throughout the book.

HABIT STACKING

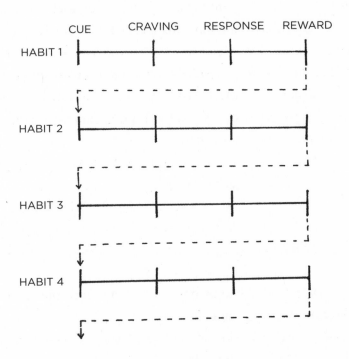

FIGURE 7: Habit stacking increases the likelihood that you'll stick with a habit by stacking your new behavior on top of an old one. This process can be repeated to chain numerous habits together, each one acting as the cue for the next.

take advantage of the natural momentum that comes from one behavior leading into the next—a positive version of the Diderot Effect.

Your morning routine habit stack might look like this:

1. After I pour my morning cup of coffee, I will meditate for sixty seconds.
2. After I meditate for sixty seconds, I will write my to-do list for the day.

3. After I write my to-do list for the day, I will immediately begin my first task.

Or, consider this habit stack in the evening:

1. After I finish eating dinner, I will put my plate directly into the dishwasher.
2. After I put my dishes away, I will immediately wipe down the counter.
3. After I wipe down the counter, I will set out my coffee mug for tomorrow morning.

You can also insert new behaviors into the middle of your current routines. For example, you may already have a morning routine that looks like this: Wake up > Make my bed > Take a shower. Let's say you want to develop the habit of reading more each night. You can expand your habit stack and try something like: Wake up > Make my bed > *Place a book on my pillow* > Take a shower. Now, when you climb into bed each night, a book will be sitting there waiting for you to enjoy.

Overall, habit stacking allows you to create a set of simple rules that guide your future behavior. It's like you always have a game plan for which action should come next. Once you get comfortable with this approach, you can develop general habit stacks to guide you whenever the situation is appropriate:

- Exercise. When I see a set of stairs, I will take them instead of using the elevator.
- Social skills. When I walk into a party, I will introduce myself to someone I don't know yet.
- Finances. When I want to buy something over $100, I will wait twenty-four hours before purchasing.

- Healthy eating. When I serve myself a meal, I will always put veggies on my plate first.
- Minimalism. When I buy a new item, I will give something away. ("One in, one out.")
- Mood. When the phone rings, I will take one deep breath and smile before answering.
- Forgetfulness. When I leave a public place, I will check the table and chairs to make sure I don't leave anything behind.

No matter how you use this strategy, the secret to creating a successful habit stack is selecting the right cue to kick things off. Unlike an implementation intention, which specifically states the time and location for a given behavior, habit stacking implicitly has the time and location built into it. When and where you choose to insert a habit into your daily routine can make a big difference. If you're trying to add meditation into your morning routine but mornings are chaotic and your kids keep running into the room, then that may be the wrong place and time. Consider when you are most likely to be successful. Don't ask yourself to do a habit when you're likely to be occupied with something else.

Your cue should also have the same frequency as your desired habit. If you want to do a habit every day, but you stack it on top of a habit that only happens on Mondays, that's not a good choice.

One way to find the right trigger for your habit stack is by brainstorming a list of your current habits. You can use your Habits Scorecard from the last chapter as a starting point. Alternatively, you can create a list with two columns. In the first column, write down the habits you do each day without fail.*

For example:

---

* If you're looking for more examples and guidance, you can download a Habit Stacking template at atomichabits.com/habitstacking.

- Get out of bed.
- Take a shower.
- Brush your teeth.
- Get dressed.
- Brew a cup of coffee.
- Eat breakfast.
- Take the kids to school.
- Start the work day.
- Eat lunch.
- End the work day.
- Change out of work clothes.
- Sit down for dinner.
- Turn off the lights.
- Get into bed.

Your list can be much longer, but you get the idea. In the second column, write down all of the things that happen to you each day without fail. For example:

- The sun rises.
- You get a text message.
- The song you are listening to ends.
- The sun sets.

Armed with these two lists, you can begin searching for the best place to layer your new habit into your lifestyle.

Habit stacking works best when the cue is highly specific and immediately actionable. Many people select cues that are too vague. I made this mistake myself. When I wanted to start a push-up habit, my habit stack was "When I take a break for lunch, I will do ten push-ups." At first glance, this sounded reasonable. But soon, I realized the trigger was unclear. Would I do my push-ups before I ate lunch? After I ate lunch? Where would I do them? After a few inconsistent days, I changed my habit stack to: "When I close my laptop for lunch, I will do ten push-ups next to my desk." Ambiguity gone.

Habits like "read more" or "eat better" are worthy causes, but these goals do not provide instruction on how and when to act. Be specific and clear: After I close the door. After I brush my teeth. After I sit down at the table. The specificity is important. The more tightly bound your new habit is to a specific cue, the better the odds are that you will notice when the time comes to act.

The 1st Law of Behavior Change is to *make it obvious*. Strategies like implementation intentions and habit stacking are among the most practical ways to create obvious cues for your habits and design a clear plan for when and where to take action.

Chapter Summary

- The 1st Law of Behavior Change is *make it obvious*.
- The two most common cues are time and location.
- Creating an implementation intention is a strategy you can use to pair a new habit with a specific time and location.
- The implementation intention formula is: I will [BEHAVIOR] at [TIME] in [LOCATION].
- Habit stacking is a strategy you can use to pair a new habit with a current habit.
- The habit stacking formula is: After [CURRENT HABIT], I will [NEW HABIT].

6

Motivation Is Overrated;
Environment Often Matters More

A NNE THORNDIKE, A primary care physician at Massachusetts
General Hospital in Boston, had a crazy idea. She believed she
could improve the eating habits of thousands of hospital staff and visitors without changing their willpower or motivation in the slightest
way. In fact, she didn't plan on talking to them at all.

Thorndike and her colleagues designed a six-month study to alter
the "choice architecture" of the hospital cafeteria. They started by
changing how drinks were arranged in the room. Originally, the refrigerators located next to the cash registers in the cafeteria were filled with
only soda. The researchers added water as an option to each one. Addi-
tionally, they placed baskets of bottled water next to the food stations
throughout the room. Soda was still in the primary refrigerators, but
water was now available at *all* drink locations.

Over the next three months, the number of soda sales at the hospital dropped by 11.4 percent. Meanwhile, sales of bottled water increased by 25.8 percent. They made similar adjustments—and saw
similar results—with the food in the cafeteria. Nobody had said a word
to anyone eating there.

BEFORE   **AFTER**

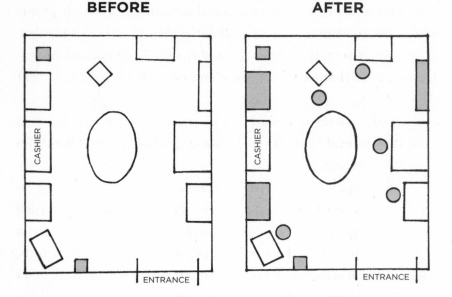

FIGURE 8: Here is a representation of what the cafeteria looked like before the environment design changes were made (left) and after (right). The shaded boxes indicate areas where bottled water was available in each instance. Because the amount of water in the environment was increased, behavior shifted naturally and without additional motivation.

People often choose products not because of *what* they are, but because of *where* they are. If I walk into the kitchen and see a plate of cookies on the counter, I'll pick up half a dozen and start eating, even if I hadn't been thinking about them beforehand and didn't necessarily feel hungry. If the communal table at the office is always filled with doughnuts and bagels, it's going to be hard not to grab one every now and then. Your habits change depending on the room you are in and the cues in front of you.

Environment is the invisible hand that shapes human behavior.

Despite our unique personalities, certain behaviors tend to arise again and again under certain environmental conditions. In church, people tend to talk in whispers. On a dark street, people act wary and guarded. In this way, the most common form of change is not internal, but external: we are changed by the world around us. Every habit is context dependent.

In 1936, psychologist Kurt Lewin wrote a simple equation that makes a powerful statement: Behavior is a function of the Person in their Environment, or $B = f(P,E)$.

It didn't take long for Lewin's Equation to be tested in business. In 1952, the economist Hawkins Stern described a phenomenon he called *Suggestion Impulse Buying*, which "is triggered when a shopper sees a product for the first time and visualizes a need for it." In other words, customers will occasionally buy products not because they *want* them but because of how they are *presented* to them.

For example, items at eye level tend to be purchased more than those down near the floor. For this reason, you'll find expensive brand names featured in easy-to-reach locations on store shelves because they drive the most profit, while cheaper alternatives are tucked away in harder-to-reach spots. The same goes for end caps, which are the units at the end of aisles. End caps are moneymaking machines for retailers because they are obvious locations that encounter a lot of foot traffic. For example, 45 percent of Coca-Cola sales come specifically from end-of-the-aisle racks.

The more obviously available a product or service is, the more likely you are to try it. People drink Bud Light because it is in every bar and visit Starbucks because it is on every corner. We like to think that we are in control. If we choose water over soda, we assume it is because we wanted to do so. The truth, however, is that many of the actions we take each day are shaped not by purposeful drive and choice but by the most obvious option.

Every living being has its own methods for sensing and understanding the world. Eagles have remarkable long-distance vision. Snakes can smell by "tasting the air" with their highly sensitive tongues. Sharks can detect small amounts of electricity and vibrations in the water caused by nearby fish. Even bacteria have chemoreceptors—tiny sensory cells that allow them to detect toxic chemicals in their environment.

In humans, perception is directed by the sensory nervous system. We perceive the world through sight, sound, smell, touch, and taste. But we also have other ways of sensing stimuli. Some are conscious, but many are nonconscious. For instance, you can "notice" when the temperature drops before a storm, or when the pain in your gut rises during a stomachache, or when you fall off balance while walking on rocky ground. Receptors in your body pick up on a wide range of internal stimuli, such as the amount of salt in your blood or the need to drink when thirsty.

The most powerful of all human sensory abilities, however, is vision. The human body has about eleven million sensory receptors. Approximately ten million of those are dedicated to sight. Some experts estimate that half of the brain's resources are used on vision. Given that we are more dependent on vision than on any other sense, it should come as no surprise that visual cues are the greatest catalyst of our behavior. For this reason, a small change in what you *see* can lead to a big shift in what you *do*. As a result, you can imagine how important it is to live and work in environments that are filled with productive cues and devoid of unproductive ones.

Thankfully, there is good news in this respect. You don't have to be the victim of your environment. You can also be the architect of it.

HOW TO DESIGN YOUR ENVIRONMENT FOR SUCCESS

During the energy crisis and oil embargo of the 1970s, Dutch research-ers began to pay close attention to the country's energy usage. In one suburb near Amsterdam, they found that some homeowners used 30 percent less energy than their neighbors—despite the homes being of similar size and getting electricity for the same price.

It turned out the houses in this neighborhood were nearly identical except for one feature: the location of the electrical meter. Some had one in the basement. Others had the electrical meter upstairs in the main hallway. As you may guess, the homes with the meters located in the main hallway used less electricity. When their energy use was ob-vious and easy to track, people changed their behavior.

Every habit is initiated by a cue, and we are more likely to notice cues that stand out. Unfortunately, the environments where we live and work often make it easy *not* to do certain actions because there is no obvious cue to trigger the behavior. It's easy *not* to practice the gui-tar when it's tucked away in the closet. It's easy *not* to read a book when the bookshelf is in the corner of the guest room. It's easy *not* to take your vitamins when they are out of sight in the pantry. When the cues that spark a habit are subtle or hidden, they are easy to ignore.

By comparison, creating obvious visual cues can draw your atten-tion toward a desired habit. In the early 1990s, the cleaning staff at Schiphol Airport in Amsterdam installed a small sticker that looked like a fly near the center of each urinal. Apparently, when men stepped up to the urinals, they aimed for what they thought was a bug. The stickers improved their aim and significantly reduced "spillage" around the urinals. Further analysis determined that the stickers cut bathroom cleaning costs by 8 percent per year.

I've experienced the power of obvious cues in my own life. I used to buy apples from the store, put them in the crisper in the bottom of the refrigerator, and forget all about them. By the time I remembered, the apples would have gone bad. I never saw them, so I never ate them.

Eventually, I took my own advice and redesigned my environment. I bought a large display bowl and placed it in the middle of the kitchen counter. The next time I bought apples, that was where they went—out in the open where I could see them. Almost like magic, I began eating a few apples each day simply because they were obvious rather than out of sight.

Here are a few ways you can redesign your environment and make the cues for your preferred habits more obvious:

- If you want to remember to take your medication each night, put your pill bottle directly next to the faucet on the bathroom counter.
- If you want to practice guitar more frequently, place your guitar stand in the middle of the living room.
- If you want to remember to send more thank-you notes, keep a stack of stationery on your desk.
- If you want to drink more water, fill up a few water bottles each morning and place them in common locations around the house.

If you want to make a habit a big part of your life, make the cue a big part of your environment. The most persistent behaviors usually have multiple cues. Consider how many different ways a smoker could be prompted to pull out a cigarette: driving in the car, seeing a friend smoke, feeling stressed at work, and so on.

The same strategy can be employed for good habits. By sprinkling triggers throughout your surroundings, you increase the odds that you'll think about your habit throughout the day. Make sure the best choice is the most obvious one. Making a better decision is easy and natural when the cues for good habits are right in front of you.

Environment design is powerful not only because it influences how we engage with the world but also because we rarely do it. Most people live in a world others have created for them. But you can alter the spaces where you live and work to increase your exposure to positive cues and reduce your exposure to negative ones. Environment design allows you to take back control and become the architect of your life. Be the designer of your world and not merely the consumer of it.

THE CONTEXT IS THE CUE

The cues that trigger a habit can start out very specific, but over time your habits become associated not with a single trigger but with the entire *context* surrounding the behavior.

For example, many people drink more in social situations than they would ever drink alone. The trigger is rarely a single cue, but rather the whole situation: watching your friends order drinks, hearing the music at the bar, seeing the beers on tap.

We mentally assign our habits to the locations in which they occur: the home, the office, the gym. Each location develops a connection to certain habits and routines. You establish a particular relationship with the objects on your desk, the items on your kitchen counter, the things in your bedroom.

Our behavior is not defined by the objects in the environment but by our relationship to them. In fact, this is a useful way to think about the influence of the environment on your behavior. Stop thinking about your environment as filled with objects. Start thinking about it as filled with relationships. Think in terms of how you interact with the spaces around you. For one person, her couch is the place where she reads for an hour each night. For someone else, the couch is where he watches television and eats a bowl of ice cream after work. Different people can have different memories—and thus different habits—associated with the same place.

The good news? You can train yourself to link a particular habit with a particular context.

In one study, scientists instructed insomniacs to get into bed only when they were tired. If they couldn't fall asleep, they were told to sit in a different room until they became sleepy. Over time, subjects began to associate the context of their bed with the action of sleeping, and it became easier to quickly fall asleep when they climbed in bed. Their brains learned that sleeping—not browsing on their phones, not watching television, not staring at the clock—was the only action that happened in that room.

The power of context also reveals an important strategy: habits can be easier to change in a new environment. It helps to escape the subtle triggers and cues that nudge you toward your current habits. Go to a new place—a different coffee shop, a bench in the park, a corner of your room you seldom use—and create a new routine there.

It is easier to associate a new habit with a new context than to build a new habit in the face of competing cues. It can be difficult to go to bed early if you watch television in your bedroom each night. It can be hard to study in the living room without getting distracted if that's where you always play video games. But when you step outside your normal environment, you leave your behavioral biases behind. You aren't battling old environmental cues, which allows new habits to form without interruption.

Want to think more creatively? Move to a bigger room, a rooftop patio, or a building with expansive architecture. Take a break from the space where you do your daily work, which is also linked to your current thought patterns.

Trying to eat healthier? It is likely that you shop on autopilot at your regular supermarket. Try a new grocery store. You may find it easier to avoid unhealthy food when your brain doesn't automatically know where it is located in the store.

When you can't manage to get to an entirely new environment, re-define or rearrange your current one. Create a separate space for work, study, exercise, entertainment, and cooking. The mantra I find useful is "One space, one use."

When I started my career as an entrepreneur, I would often work from my couch or at the kitchen table. In the evenings, I found it very difficult to stop working. There was no clear division between the end of work time and the beginning of personal time. Was the kitchen table my office or the space where I ate meals? Was the couch where I relaxed or where I sent emails? Everything happened in the same place.

A few years later, I could finally afford to move to a home with a separate room for my office. Suddenly, work was something that happened "in here" and personal life was something that happened "out there." It was easier for me to turn off the professional side of my brain when there was a clear dividing line between work life and home life. Each room had one primary use. The kitchen was for cooking. The office was for working.

Whenever possible, avoid mixing the context of one habit with another. When you start mixing contexts, you'll start mixing habits—and the easier ones will usually win out. This is one reason why the versatility of modern technology is both a strength and a weakness. You can use your phone for all sorts of tasks, which makes it a powerful device. But when you can use your phone to do nearly anything, it becomes hard to associate it with one task. You want to be productive, but you're also conditioned to browse social media, check email, and play video games whenever you open your phone. It's a mishmash of cues.

You may be thinking, "You don't understand. I live in New York City. My apartment is the size of a smartphone. I need each room to play multiple roles." Fair enough. If your space is limited, divide your room into activity zones: a chair for reading, a desk for writing, a table for eating. You can do the same with your digital spaces. I know a writer who uses his computer only for writing, his tablet only for reading, and his phone only for social media and texting. Every habit should have a home.

If you can manage to stick with this strategy, each context will become associated with a particular habit and mode of thought. Habits thrive under predictable circumstances like these. Focus comes automatically when you are sitting at your work desk. Relaxation is easier when you are in a space designed for that purpose. Sleep comes quickly when it is the only thing that happens in your bedroom. If you want behaviors that are stable and predictable, you need an environment that is stable and predictable.

A stable environment where everything has a place and a purpose is an environment where habits can easily form.

--- Chapter Summary ---

- Small changes in context can lead to large changes in behavior over time.
- Every habit is initiated by a cue. We are more likely to notice cues that stand out.
- Make the cues of good habits obvious in your environment.
- Gradually, your habits become associated not with a single trigger but with the entire context surrounding the behavior. The context becomes the cue.
- It is easier to build new habits in a new environment because you are not fighting against old cues.

7

The Secret to Self-Control

I N 1971, as the Vietnam War was heading into its sixteenth year, con-
gressmen Robert Steele from Connecticut and Morgan Murphy from
Illinois made a discovery that stunned the American public. While
visiting the troops, they had learned that over 15 percent of U.S. soldiers stationed there were heroin addicts. Follow-up research revealed
that 35 percent of service members in Vietnam had tried heroin and as
many as 20 percent were addicted—the problem was even worse than
they had initially thought.

The discovery led to a flurry of activity in Washington, including
the creation of the Special Action Office of Drug Abuse Prevention
under President Nixon to promote prevention and rehabilitation and
to track addicted service members when they returned home.

Lee Robins was one of the researchers in charge. In a finding that
completely upended the accepted beliefs about addiction, Robins found
that when soldiers who had been heroin users returned home, only 5
percent of them became re-addicted within a year, and just 12 percent
relapsed within three years. In other words, approximately nine out of

ten soldiers who used heroin in Vietnam eliminated their addiction nearly overnight.

This finding contradicted the prevailing view at the time, which considered heroin addiction to be a permanent and irreversible condition. Instead, Robins revealed that addictions could spontaneously dissolve if there was a radical change in the environment. In Vietnam, soldiers spent all day surrounded by cues triggering heroin use: it was easy to access, they were engulfed by the constant stress of war, they built friendships with fellow soldiers who were also heroin users, and they were thousands of miles from home. Once a soldier returned to the United States, though, he found himself in an environment devoid of those triggers. When the context changed, so did the habit.

Compare this situation to that of a typical drug user. Someone becomes addicted at home or with friends, goes to a clinic to get clean—which is devoid of all the environmental stimuli that prompt their habit—then returns to their old neighborhood with all of their previous cues that caused them to get addicted in the first place. It's no wonder that usually you see numbers that are the exact opposite of those in the Vietnam study. Typically, 90 percent of heroin users become re-addicted once they return home from rehab.

The Vietnam studies ran counter to many of our cultural beliefs about bad habits because it challenged the conventional association of unhealthy behavior as a moral weakness. If you're overweight, a smoker, or an addict, you've been told your entire life that it is because you lack self-control—maybe even that you're a bad person. The idea that a little bit of discipline would solve all our problems is deeply embedded in our culture.

Recent research, however, shows something different. When scientists analyze people who appear to have tremendous self-control, it turns out those individuals aren't all that different from those who are struggling. Instead, "disciplined" people are better at structuring their lives in a way that *does not require* heroic willpower and self-control. In other words, they spend less time in tempting situations.

The people with the best self-control are typically the ones who need to use it the least. It's easier to practice self-restraint when you don't have to use it very often. So, yes, perseverance, grit, and willpower are essential to success, but the way to improve these qualities is not by wishing you were a more disciplined person, but by creating a more disciplined environment.

This counterintuitive idea makes even more sense once you understand what happens when a habit is formed in the brain. A habit that has been encoded in the mind is ready to be used whenever the relevant situation arises. When Patty Olwell, a therapist from Austin, Texas, started smoking, she would often light up while riding horses with a friend. Eventually, she quit smoking and avoided it for years. She had also stopped riding. Decades later, she hopped on a horse again and found herself craving a cigarette for the first time in forever. The cues were still internalized; she just hadn't been exposed to them in a long time.

Once a habit has been encoded, the urge to act follows whenever the environmental cues reappear. This is one reason behavior change techniques can backfire. Shaming obese people with weight-loss presentations can make them feel stressed, and as a result many people return to their favorite coping strategy: overeating. Showing pictures of blackened lungs to smokers leads to higher levels of anxiety, which drives many people to reach for a cigarette. If you're not careful about cues, you can cause the very behavior you want to stop.

Bad habits are autocatalytic: the process feeds itself. They foster the feelings they try to numb. You feel bad, so you eat junk food. Because you eat junk food, you feel bad. Watching television makes you feel sluggish, so you watch more television because you don't have the energy to do anything else. Worrying about your health makes you feel anxious, which causes you to smoke to ease your anxiety, which makes your health even worse and soon you're feeling more anxious. It's a downward spiral, a runaway train of bad habits.

Researchers refer to this phenomenon as "cue-induced wanting": an external trigger causes a compulsive craving to repeat a bad habit. Once you *notice* something, you begin to *want* it. This process is happening all the time—often without us realizing it. Scientists have found that showing addicts a picture of cocaine for just thirty-three milliseconds stimulates the reward pathway in the brain and sparks desire. This speed is too fast for the brain to consciously register—the addicts couldn't even tell you what they had seen—but they craved the drug all the same.

Here's the punch line: You can break a habit, but you're unlikely to forget it. Once the mental grooves of habit have been carved into your brain, they are nearly impossible to remove entirely—even if they go unused for quite a while. And that means that simply resisting temptation is an ineffective strategy. It is hard to maintain a Zen attitude in a life filled with interruptions. It takes too much energy. In the short-run, you can choose to overpower temptation. In the long-run, we become a product of the environment that we live in. To put it bluntly, I have never seen someone consistently stick to positive habits in a negative environment.

A more reliable approach is to cut bad habits off at the source. One of the most practical ways to eliminate a bad habit is to reduce exposure to the cue that causes it.

- If you can't seem to get any work done, leave your phone in another room for a few hours.
- If you're continually feeling like you're not enough, stop following social media accounts that trigger jealousy and envy.

- If you're wasting too much time watching television, move the TV out of the bedroom.
- If you're spending too much money on electronics, quit reading reviews of the latest tech gear.
- If you're playing too many video games, unplug the console and put it in a closet after each use.

This practice is an inversion of the 1st Law of Behavior Change. Rather than *make it obvious*, you can *make it invisible*. I'm often surprised by how effective simple changes like these can be. Remove a single cue and the entire habit often fades away.

Self-control is a short-term strategy, not a long-term one. You may be able to resist temptation once or twice, but it's unlikely you can muster the willpower to override your desires every time. Instead of summoning a new dose of willpower whenever you want to do the right thing, your energy would be better spent optimizing your environment. This is the secret to self-control. Make the cues of your good habits obvious and the cues of your bad habits invisible.

Chapter Summary

- The inversion of the 1st Law of Behavior Change is *make it invisible*.
- Once a habit is formed, it is unlikely to be forgotten.
- People with high self-control tend to spend less time in tempting situations. It's easier to avoid temptation than resist it.
- One of the most practical ways to eliminate a bad habit is to reduce exposure to the cue that causes it.
- Self-control is a short-term strategy, not a long-term one.

HOW TO CREATE A GOOD HABIT

The 1st Law	Make It Obvious
1.1	Fill out the Habits Scorecard. Write down your current habits to become aware of them.
1.2	Use implementation intentions: "I will [BEHAVIOR] at [TIME] in [LOCATION]."
1.3	Use habit stacking: "After [CURRENT HABIT], I will [NEW HABIT]."
1.4	Design your environment. Make the cues of good habits obvious and visible.
The 2nd Law	Make It Attractive
The 3rd Law	Make It Easy
The 4th Law	Make It Satisfying

HOW TO BREAK A BAD HABIT

Inversion of the 1st Law	Make It Invisible
1.5	Reduce exposure. Remove the cues of your bad habits from your environment.
Inversion of the 2nd Law	Make It Unattractive
Inversion of the 3rd Law	Make It Difficult
Inversion of the 4th Law	Make It Unsatisfying

You can download a printable version of this habits cheat sheet at:
atomichabits.com/cheatsheet

THE 2ND LAW

Make It Attractive

8

How to Make a Habit Irresistible

IN THE 1940s, a Dutch scientist named Niko Tinbergen performed a series of experiments that transformed our understanding of what motivates us. Tinbergen—who eventually won a Nobel Prize for his work—was investigating herring gulls, the gray and white birds often seen flying along the seashores of North America.

Adult herring gulls have a small red dot on their beak, and Tinbergen noticed that newly hatched chicks would peck this spot whenever they wanted food. To begin one experiment, he created a collection of fake cardboard beaks, just a head without a body. When the parents had flown away, he went over to the nest and offered these dummy beaks to the chicks. The beaks were obvious fakes, and he assumed the baby birds would reject them altogether.

However, when the tiny gulls saw the red spot on the cardboard beak, they pecked away just as if it were attached to their own mother. They had a clear preference for those red spots—as if they had been genetically programmed at birth. Soon Tinbergen discovered that the bigger the red spot, the faster the chicks pecked. Eventually, he created a beak with three large red dots on it. When he placed it over the nest, the baby birds went crazy with delight. They pecked at the little red patches as if it was the greatest beak they had ever seen.

Tinbergen and his colleagues discovered similar behavior in other animals. For example, the greylag goose is a ground-nesting bird. Occasionally, as the mother moves around on the nest, one of the eggs will roll out and settle on the grass nearby. Whenever this happens, the goose will waddle over to the egg and use its beak and neck to pull it back into the nest.

Tinbergen discovered that the goose will pull *any* nearby round object, such as a billiard ball or a lightbulb, back into the nest. The bigger the object, the greater their response. One goose even made a tremendous effort to roll a volleyball back and sit on top. Like the baby gulls automatically pecking at red dots, the greylag goose was following an instinctive rule: *When I see a round object nearby, I must roll it back into the nest. The bigger the round object, the harder I should try to get it.*

It's like the brain of each animal is preloaded with certain rules for behavior, and when it comes across an exaggerated version of that rule, it lights up like a Christmas tree. Scientists refer to these exaggerated cues as *supernormal stimuli*. A supernormal stimulus is a heightened version of reality—like a beak with three red dots or an egg the size of a volleyball—and it elicits a stronger response than usual.

Humans are also prone to fall for exaggerated versions of reality. Junk food, for example, drives our reward systems into a frenzy. After spending hundreds of thousands of years hunting and foraging for food in the wild, the human brain has evolved to place a high value on salt, sugar, and fat. Such foods are often calorie-dense and they were quite rare when our ancient ancestors were roaming the savannah. When you don't know where your next meal is coming from, eating as much as possible is an excellent strategy for survival.

Today, however, we live in a calorie-rich environment. Food is abundant, but your brain continues to crave it like it is scarce. Placing a high value on salt, sugar, and fat is no longer advantageous to our health, but the craving persists because the brain's reward centers have not changed for approximately fifty thousand years. The modern food industry relies on stretching our Paleolithic instincts beyond their evolutionary purpose.

A primary goal of food science is to create products that are more attractive to consumers. Nearly every food in a bag, box, or jar has been enhanced in some way, if only with additional flavoring. Companies spend millions of dollars to discover the most satisfying level of crunch in a potato chip or the perfect amount of fizz in a soda. Entire departments are dedicated to optimizing how a product feels in your mouth—a quality known as *orosensation*. French fries, for example, are a potent combination—golden brown and crunchy on the outside, light and smooth on the inside.

Other processed foods enhance *dynamic contrast*, which refers to items with a combination of sensations, like crunchy and creamy. Imagine the gooeyness of melted cheese on top of a crispy pizza crust, or the crunch of an Oreo cookie combined with its smooth center. With natural, unprocessed foods, you tend to experience the same sensations over and over—*how's that seventeenth bite of kale taste?* After a few minutes, your brain loses interest and you begin to feel full. But foods that are high in dynamic contrast keep the experience novel and interesting, encouraging you to eat more.

Ultimately, such strategies enable food scientists to find the "bliss point" for each product—the precise combination of salt, sugar, and fat that excites your brain and keeps you coming back for more. The result, of course, is that you overeat because hyperpalatable foods are more attractive to the human brain. As Stephan Guyenet, a neuroscientist who specializes in eating behavior and obesity, says, "We've gotten too good at pushing our own buttons."

The modern food industry, and the overeating habits it has spawned, is just one example of the 2nd Law of Behavior Change: *Make it attractive.* The more attractive an opportunity is, the more likely it is to become habit-forming.

Look around. Society is filled with highly engineered versions of reality that are more attractive than the world our ancestors evolved in. Stores feature mannequins with exaggerated hips and breasts to sell clothes. Social media delivers more "likes" and praise in a few minutes than we could ever get in the office or at home. Online porn splices together stimulating scenes at a rate that would be impossible to replicate in real life. Advertisements are created with a combination of ideal lighting, professional makeup, and Photoshopped edits—even the model doesn't look like the person in the final image. These are the supernormal stimuli of our modern world. They exaggerate features that are naturally attractive to us, and our instincts go wild as a result, driving us into excessive shopping habits, social media habits, porn habits, eating habits, and many others.

If history serves as a guide, the opportunities of the future will be more attractive than those of today. The trend is for rewards to become more concentrated and stimuli to become more enticing. Junk food is a more concentrated form of calories than natural foods. Hard liquor is a more concentrated form of alcohol than beer. Video games are a more concentrated form of play than board games. Compared to nature, these pleasure-packed experiences are hard to resist. We have the brains of our ancestors but temptations they never had to face.

If you want to increase the odds that a behavior will occur, then you need to make it attractive. Throughout our discussion of the 2nd Law, our goal is to learn how to make our habits irresistible. While it is not possible to transform every habit into a supernormal stimulus, we can make any habit more enticing. To do this, we must start by understanding what a craving is and how it works.

We begin by examining a biological signature that all habits share—the dopamine spike.

THE DOPAMINE-DRIVEN FEEDBACK LOOP

Scientists can track the precise moment a craving occurs by measuring a neurotransmitter called dopamine.* The importance of dopamine became apparent in 1954 when the neuroscientists James Olds and Peter Milner ran an experiment that revealed the neurological processes behind craving and desire. By implanting electrodes in the brains of rats, the researchers blocked the release of dopamine. To the surprise of the scientists, the rats lost all will to live. They wouldn't eat. They wouldn't have sex. They didn't crave anything. Within a few days, the animals died of thirst.

In follow-up studies, other scientists also inhibited the dopamine-releasing parts of the brain, but this time, they squirted little droplets of sugar into the mouths of the dopamine-depleted rats. Their little rat faces lit up with pleasurable grins from the tasty substance. Even though dopamine was blocked, they *liked* the sugar just as much as before; they just didn't *want* it anymore. The ability to experience pleasure remained, but without dopamine, desire died. And without desire, action stopped.

When other researchers reversed this process and flooded the reward system of the brain with dopamine, animals performed habits at breakneck speed. In one study, mice received a powerful hit of dopamine each time they poked their nose in a box. Within minutes, the

---

* Dopamine is not the *only* chemical that influences your habits. Every behavior involves multiple brain regions and neurochemicals, and anyone who claims that "habits are all about dopamine" is skipping over major portions of the process. It is just one of the important role players in habit formation. However, I will single out the dopamine circuit in this chapter because it provides a window into the biological underpinnings of desire, craving, and motivation that are behind every habit.

mice developed a craving so strong they began poking their nose into the box eight hundred times per hour. (Humans are not so different: the average slot machine player will spin the wheel six hundred times per hour.)

Habits are a dopamine-driven feedback loop. Every behavior that is highly habit-forming—taking drugs, eating junk food, playing video games, browsing social media—is associated with higher levels of dopamine. The same can be said for our most basic habitual behaviors like eating food, drinking water, having sex, and interacting socially.

For years, scientists assumed dopamine was all about pleasure, but now we know it plays a central role in many neurological processes, including motivation, learning and memory, punishment and aversion, and voluntary movement.

When it comes to habits, the key takeaway is this: dopamine is released not only when you *experience* pleasure, but also when you *anticipate* it. Gambling addicts have a dopamine spike right *before* they place a bet, not after they win. Cocaine addicts get a surge of dopamine when they *see* the powder, not after they take it. Whenever you predict that an opportunity will be rewarding, your levels of dopamine spike in anticipation. And whenever dopamine rises, so does your motivation to act.

It is the anticipation of a reward—not the fulfillment of it—that gets us to take action.

Interestingly, the reward system that is activated in the brain when you *receive* a reward is the same system that is activated when you *anticipate* a reward. This is one reason the anticipation of an experience can often feel better than the attainment of it. As a child, thinking about Christmas morning can be better than opening the gifts. As an adult, daydreaming about an upcoming vacation can be more enjoyable than actually being on vacation. Scientists refer to this as the difference between "wanting" and "liking."

THE DOPAMINE SPIKE

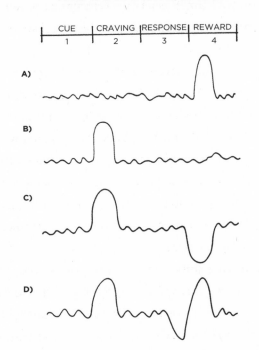

FIGURE 9: Before a habit is learned (A), dopamine is released when the reward is experienced for the first time. The next time around (B), dopamine rises *before* taking action, immediately after a cue is recognized. This spike leads to a feeling of desire and a craving to take action whenever the cue is spotted. Once a habit is learned, dopamine will not rise when a reward is experienced because you already expect the reward. However, if you see a cue and expect a reward, but do not get one, then dopamine will drop in disappointment (C). The sensitivity of the dopamine response can clearly be seen when a reward is provided late (D). First, the cue is identified and dopamine rises as a craving builds. Next, a response is taken but the reward does not come as quickly as expected and dopamine begins to drop. Finally, when the reward comes a little later than you had hoped, dopamine spikes again. It is as if the brain is saying, "See! I knew I was right. Don't forget to repeat this action next time."

Your brain has far more neural circuitry allocated for *wanting* rewards than for *liking* them. The wanting centers in the brain are large: the brain stem, the nucleus accumbens, the ventral tegmental area, the dorsal striatum, the amygdala, and portions of the prefrontal cortex. By comparison, the liking centers of the brain are much smaller. They are often referred to as "hedonic hot spots" and are distributed like tiny islands throughout the brain. For instance, researchers have found that 100 percent of the nucleus accumbens is activated during wanting. Meanwhile, only 10 percent of the structure is activated during liking.

The fact that the brain allocates so much precious space to the regions responsible for craving and desire provides further evidence of the crucial role these processes play. Desire is the engine that drives behavior. Every action is taken because of the anticipation that precedes it. It is the craving that leads to the response.

These insights reveal the importance of the 2nd Law of Behavior Change. We need to make our habits attractive because it is the expectation of a rewarding experience that motivates us to act in the first place. This is where a strategy known as temptation bundling comes into play.

HOW TO USE TEMPTATION BUNDLING TO MAKE YOUR HABITS MORE ATTRACTIVE

Ronan Byrne, an electrical engineering student in Dublin, Ireland, enjoyed watching Netflix, but he also knew that he should exercise more often than he did. Putting his engineering skills to use, Byrne hacked his stationary bike and connected it to his laptop and television. Then he wrote a computer program that would allow Netflix to run *only* if he was cycling at a certain speed. If he slowed down for too long, whatever show he was watching would pause until he started pedaling again. He was, in the words of one fan, "eliminating obesity one Netflix binge at a time."

He was also employing temptation bundling to make his exercise habit more attractive. Temptation bundling works by linking an action you want to do with an action you need to do. In Byrne's case, he bundled watching Netflix (the thing he wanted to do) with riding his stationary bike (the thing he needed to do).

Businesses are masters at temptation bundling. For instance, when the American Broadcasting Company, more commonly known as ABC, launched its Thursday-night television lineup for the 2014–2015 season, they promoted temptation bundling on a massive scale.

Every Thursday, the company would air three shows created by screenwriter Shonda Rhimes—*Grey's Anatomy, Scandal,* and *How to Get Away with Murder.* They branded it as "TGIT on ABC" (TGIT stands for Thank God It's Thursday). In addition to promoting the shows, ABC encouraged viewers to make popcorn, drink red wine, and enjoy the evening.

Andrew Kubitz, head of scheduling for ABC, described the idea behind the campaign: "We see Thursday night as a viewership opportunity, with either couples or women by themselves who want to sit down and escape and have fun and drink their red wine and have some popcorn." The brilliance of this strategy is that ABC was associating the thing they *needed* viewers to do (watch their shows) with activities their viewers already *wanted* to do (relax, drink wine, and eat popcorn).

Over time, people began to connect watching ABC with feeling relaxed and entertained. If you drink red wine and eat popcorn at 8 p.m. every Thursday, then eventually "8 p.m. on Thursday" *means* relaxation and entertainment. The reward gets associated with the cue, and the habit of turning on the television becomes more attractive.

You're more likely to find a behavior attractive if you get to do one of your favorite things at the same time. Perhaps you want to hear about the latest celebrity gossip, but you need to get in shape. Using temptation bundling, you could only read the tabloids and watch reality shows at the gym. Maybe you want to get a pedicure, but you need to clean out your email inbox. Solution: only get a pedicure while processing overdue work emails.

Temptation bundling is one way to apply a psychology theory known as Premack's Principle. Named after the work of professor David Premack, the principle states that "more probable behaviors will reinforce less probable behaviors." In other words, even if you don't really want to process overdue work emails, you'll become conditioned to do it if it means you get to do something you really want to do along the way.

You can even combine temptation bundling with the habit stacking strategy we discussed in Chapter 5 to create a set of rules to guide your behavior.

The habit stacking + temptation bundling formula is:

1. After [CURRENT HABIT], I will [HABIT I NEED].
2. After [HABIT I NEED], I will [HABIT I WANT].

If you want to read the news, but you need to express more gratitude:

1. After I get my morning coffee, I will say one thing I'm grateful for that happened yesterday (need).
2. After I say one thing I'm grateful for, I will read the news (want).

If you want to watch sports, but you need to make sales calls:

1. After I get back from my lunch break, I will call three potential clients (need).
2. After I call three potential clients, I will check ESPN (want).

If you want to check Facebook, but you need to exercise more:

1. After I pull out my phone, I will do ten burpees (need).
2. After I do ten burpees, I will check Facebook (want).

The hope is that eventually you'll look forward to calling three clients or doing ten burpees because it means you get to read the latest sports news or check Facebook. Doing the thing you need to do means you get to do the thing you want to do.

We began this chapter by discussing supernormal stimuli, which are heightened versions of reality that increase our desire to take action. Temptation bundling is one way to create a heightened version of any habit by connecting it with something you already want. Engineering a truly irresistible habit is a hard task, but this simple strategy can be employed to make nearly any habit more attractive than it would be otherwise.

Chapter Summary

- The 2nd Law of Behavior Change is *make it attractive.*
- The more attractive an opportunity is, the more likely it is to become habit-forming.
- Habits are a dopamine-driven feedback loop. When dopamine rises, so does our motivation to act.
- It is the anticipation of a reward—not the fulfillment of it—that gets us to take action. The greater the anticipation, the greater the dopamine spike.
- Temptation bundling is one way to make your habits more attractive. The strategy is to pair an action you *want* to do with an action you *need* to do.

9

The Role of Family and Friends in Shaping Your Habits

I N 1965, a Hungarian man named Laszlo Polgar wrote a series of strange letters to a woman named Klara.

Laszlo was a firm believer in hard work. In fact, it was all he believed in: he completely rejected the idea of innate talent. He claimed that with deliberate practice and the development of good habits, a child could become a genius in any field. His mantra was "A genius is not born, but is educated and trained."

Laszlo believed in this idea so strongly that he wanted to test it with his own children—and he was writing to Klara because he "needed a wife willing to jump on board." Klara was a teacher and, although she may not have been as adamant as Laszlo, she also believed that with proper instruction, anyone could advance their skills.

Laszlo decided chess would be a suitable field for the experiment, and he laid out a plan to raise his children to become chess prodigies. The kids would be home-schooled, a rarity in Hungary at the time. The house would be filled with chess books and pictures of famous chess players. The children would play against each other constantly and compete in the best tournaments they could find. The family would keep a meticulous file system of the tournament history of every competitor the children faced. Their lives would be dedicated to chess.

Laszlo successfully courted Klara, and within a few years, the Polgars were parents to three young girls: Susan, Sofia, and Judit.

Susan, the oldest, began playing chess when she was four years old. Within six months, she was defeating adults.

Sofia, the middle child, did even better. By fourteen, she was a world champion, and a few years later, she became a grandmaster.

Judit, the youngest, was the best of all. By age five, she could beat her father. At twelve, she was the youngest player ever listed among the top one hundred chess players in the world. At fifteen years and four months old, she became the youngest grandmaster of all time— younger than Bobby Fischer, the previous record holder. For twenty-seven years, she was the number-one-ranked female chess player in the world.

The childhood of the Polgar sisters was atypical, to say the least. And yet, if you ask them about it, they claim their lifestyle was attractive, even enjoyable. In interviews, the sisters talk about their childhood as entertaining rather than grueling. They loved playing chess. They couldn't get enough of it. Once, Laszlo reportedly found Sofia playing chess in the bathroom in the middle of the night. Encouraging her to go back to sleep, he said, "Sofia, leave the pieces alone!" To which she replied, "Daddy, *they* won't leave *me* alone!"

The Polgar sisters grew up in a culture that prioritized chess above all else—praised them for it, rewarded them for it. In their world, an obsession with chess was normal. And as we are about to see, whatever habits are normal in your culture are among the most attractive behaviors you'll find.

THE SEDUCTIVE PULL OF SOCIAL NORMS

Humans are herd animals. We want to fit in, to bond with others, and to earn the respect and approval of our peers. Such inclinations are essential to our survival. For most of our evolutionary history, our ancestors lived in tribes. Becoming separated from the tribe—or worse, being cast out—was a death sentence. "The lone wolf dies, but the pack survives."[*]

Meanwhile, those who collaborated and bonded with others enjoyed increased safety, mating opportunities, and access to resources. As Charles Darwin noted, "In the long history of humankind, those who learned to collaborate and improvise most effectively have prevailed." As a result, one of the deepest human desires is to belong. And this ancient preference exerts a powerful influence on our modern behavior.

We don't choose our earliest habits, we imitate them. We follow the script handed down by our friends and family, our church or school, our local community and society at large. Each of these cultures and groups comes with its own set of expectations and standards—when and whether to get married, how many children to have, which holidays to celebrate, how much money to spend on your child's birthday party. In many ways, these social norms are the invisible rules that guide your behavior each day. You're always keeping them in mind, even if they are at the not top of your mind. Often, you follow the habits of your culture without thinking, without questioning, and sometimes without remembering. As the French philosopher Michel de Montaigne wrote, "The customs and practices of life in society sweep us along."

Most of the time, going along with the group does not feel like a burden. Everyone wants to belong. If you grow up in a family that

---

[*] I'm so happy I was able to fit a *Game of Thrones* reference into this book.

rewards you for your chess skills, playing chess will seem like a very attractive thing to do. If you work in a job where everyone wears expensive suits, then you'll be inclined to splurge on one as well. If all of your friends are sharing an inside joke or using a new phrase, you'll want to do it, too, so they know that you "get it." Behaviors are attractive when they help us fit in.

We imitate the habits of three groups in particular:

1. The close.
2. The many.
3. The powerful.

Each group offers an opportunity to leverage the 2nd Law of Behavior Change and make our habits more attractive.

1. Imitating the Close

Proximity has a powerful effect on our behavior. This is true of the physical environment, as we discussed in Chapter 6, but it is also true of the social environment.

We pick up habits from the people around us. We copy the way our parents handle arguments, the way our peers flirt with one another, the way our coworkers get results. When your friends smoke pot, you give it a try, too. When your wife has a habit of double-checking that the door is locked before going to bed, you pick it up as well.

I find that I often imitate the behavior of those around me without realizing it. In conversation, I'll automatically assume the body posture of the other person. In college, I began to talk like my roommates. When traveling to other countries, I unconsciously imitate the local accent despite reminding myself to stop.

As a general rule, the closer we are to someone, the more likely we are to imitate some of their habits. One groundbreaking study tracked twelve thousand people for thirty-two years and found that "a person's chances of becoming obese increased by 57 percent if he or she had a friend who became obese." It works the other way, too. Another study found that if one person in a relationship lost weight, the other partner would also slim down about one third of the time. Our friends and family provide a sort of invisible peer pressure that pulls us in their direction.

Of course, peer pressure is bad only if you're surrounded by bad influences. When astronaut Mike Massimino was a graduate student at MIT, he took a small robotics class. Of the ten people in the class, *four* became astronauts. If your goal was to make it into space, then that room was about the best culture you could ask for. Similarly, one study found that the higher your best friend's IQ at age eleven or twelve, the higher your IQ would be at age fifteen, even after controlling for natural levels of intelligence. We soak up the qualities and practices of those around us.

One of the most effective things you can do to build better habits is to join a culture where your desired behavior is the normal behavior. New habits seem achievable when you see others doing them every day. If you are surrounded by fit people, you're more likely to consider working out to be a common habit. If you're surrounded by jazz lovers, you're more likely to believe it's reasonable to play jazz every day. Your culture sets your expectation for what is "normal." Surround yourself with people who have the habits you want to have yourself. You'll rise together.

To make your habits even more attractive, you can take this strategy one step further.

Join a culture where (1) your desired behavior is the normal behavior and (2) you already have something in common with the group. Steve Kamb, an entrepreneur in New York City, runs a company called

Nerd Fitness, which "helps nerds, misfits, and mutants lose weight, get strong, and get healthy." His clients include video game lovers, movie fanatics, and average Joes who want to get in shape. Many people feel out of place the first time they go to the gym or try to change their diet, but if you are already similar to the other members of the group in some way—say, your mutual love of *Star Wars*—change becomes more appealing because it feels like something people like you already do.

Nothing sustains motivation better than belonging to the tribe. It transforms a personal quest into a shared one. Previously, you were on your own. Your identity was singular. *You are a reader. You are a musician. You are an athlete.* When you join a book club or a band or a cycling group, your identity becomes linked to those around you. Growth and change is no longer an individual pursuit. *We are readers. We are musicians. We are cyclists.* The shared identity begins to reinforce your personal identity. This is why remaining part of a group after achieving a goal is crucial to maintaining your habits. It's friendship and community that embed a new identity and help behaviors last over the long run.

2. Imitating the Many

In the 1950s, psychologist Solomon Asch conducted a series of experiments that are now taught to legions of undergrads each year. To begin each experiment, the subject entered the room with a group of strangers. Unbeknownst to them, the other participants were actors planted by the researcher and instructed to deliver scripted answers to certain questions.

The group would be shown one card with a line on it and then a second card with a series of lines. Each person was asked to select the line on the second card that was similar in length to the line on the first card. It was a very simple task. Here is an example of two cards used in the experiment:

CONFORMING TO SOCIAL NORMS

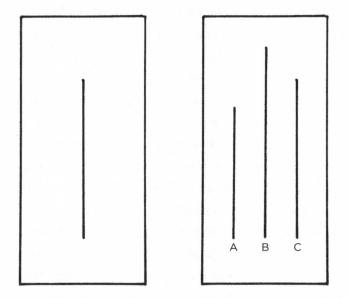

FIGURE 10: This is a representation of two cards used by Solomon Asch in his famous social conformity experiments. The length of the line on the first card (left) is obviously the same as line C, but when a group of actors claimed it was a different length the research subjects would often change their minds and go with the crowd rather than believe their own eyes.

The experiment always began the same. First, there would be some easy trials where everyone agreed on the correct line. After a few rounds, the participants were shown a test that was just as obvious as the previous ones, except the actors in the room would select an intentionally *incorrect* answer. For example, they would respond "A" to the comparison shown in Figure 10. Everyone would agree that the lines were the same even though they were clearly different.

The subject, who was unaware of the ruse, would immediately

become bewildered. Their eyes would open wide. They would laugh nervously to themselves. They would double-check the reactions of other participants. Their agitation would grow as one person after another delivered the same incorrect response. Soon, the subject began to doubt their own eyes. Eventually, they delivered the answer they knew in their heart to be incorrect.

Asch ran this experiment many times and in many different ways. What he discovered was that as the number of actors increased, so did the conformity of the subject. If it was just the subject and one actor, then there was no effect on the person's choice. They just assumed they were in the room with a dummy. When two actors were in the room with the subject, there was still little impact. But as the number of people increased to three actors and four and all the way to eight, the subject became more likely to second-guess themselves. By the end of the experiment, nearly 75 percent of the subjects had agreed with the group answer even though it was obviously incorrect.

Whenever we are unsure how to act, we look to the group to guide our behavior. We are constantly scanning our environment and wondering, "What is everyone else doing?" We check reviews on Amazon or Yelp or TripAdvisor because we want to imitate the "best" buying, eating, and travel habits. It's usually a smart strategy. There is evidence in numbers.

But there can be a downside.

The normal behavior of the tribe often overpowers the desired behavior of the individual. For example, one study found that when a chimpanzee learns an effective way to crack nuts open as a member of one group and then switches to a new group that uses a less effective strategy, it will avoid using the superior nut cracking method just to blend in with the rest of the chimps.

Humans are similar. There is tremendous internal pressure to comply with the norms of the group. The reward of being accepted is often greater than the reward of winning an argument, looking smart, or finding truth. Most days, we'd rather be wrong with the crowd than be right by ourselves.

The human mind knows how to get along with others. It *wants* to get along with others. This is our natural mode. You can override it— you can choose to ignore the group or to stop caring what other people think—but it takes work. Running against the grain of your culture requires extra effort.

When changing your habits means challenging the tribe, change is unattractive. When changing your habits means fitting in with the tribe, change is very attractive.

3. Imitating the Powerful

Humans everywhere pursue power, prestige, and status. We want pins and medallions on our jackets. We want President or Partner in our titles. We want to be acknowledged, recognized, and praised. This tendency can seem vain, but overall, it's a smart move. Historically, a person with greater power and status has access to more resources, worries less about survival, and proves to be a more attractive mate.

We are drawn to behaviors that earn us respect, approval, admiration, and status. We want to be the one in the gym who can do muscle-ups or the musician who can play the hardest chord progressions or the parent with the most accomplished children because these things separate us from the crowd. Once we fit in, we start looking for ways to stand out.

This is one reason we care so much about the habits of highly effective people. We try to copy the behavior of successful people because we desire success ourselves. Many of our daily habits are imitations of people we admire. You replicate the marketing strategies of the most successful firms in your industry. You make a recipe from your favorite baker. You borrow the storytelling strategies of your favorite writer. You mimic the communication style of your boss. We imitate people we envy.

High-status people enjoy the approval, respect, and praise of others. And that means if a behavior can get us approval, respect, and praise, we find it attractive.

We are also motivated to avoid behaviors that would lower our status. We trim our hedges and mow our lawn because we don't want to be the slob of the neighborhood. When our mother comes to visit, we clean up the house because we don't want to be judged. We are continually wondering "What will others think of me?" and altering our behavior based on the answer.

The Polgar sisters—the chess prodigies mentioned at the beginning of this chapter—are evidence of the powerful and lasting impact social influences can have on our behavior. The sisters practiced chess for many hours each day and continued this remarkable effort for decades. But these habits and behaviors maintained their attractiveness, in part, because they were valued by their culture. From the praise of their parents to the achievement of different status markers like becoming a grandmaster, they had many reasons to continue their effort.

Chapter Summary

- The culture we live in determines which behaviors are attractive to us.
- We tend to adopt habits that are praised and approved of by our culture because we have a strong desire to fit in and belong to the tribe.
- We tend to imitate the habits of three social groups: the close (family and friends), the many (the tribe), and the powerful (those with status and prestige).

- One of the most effective things you can do to build better habits is to join a culture where (1) your desired behavior is the normal behavior and (2) you already have something in common with the group.
- The normal behavior of the tribe often overpowers the desired behavior of the individual. Most days, we'd rather be wrong with the crowd than be right by ourselves.
- If a behavior can get us approval, respect, and praise, we find it attractive.

10

How to Find and Fix the Causes of Your Bad Habits

IN LATE 2012, I was sitting in an old apartment just a few blocks from Istanbul's most famous street, Istiklal Caddesi. I was in the middle of a four-day trip to Turkey and my guide, Mike, was relaxing in a worn-out armchair a few feet away.

Mike wasn't really a guide. He was just a guy from Maine who had been living in Turkey for five years, but he offered to show me around while I was visiting the country and I took him up on it. On this particular night, I had been invited to dinner with him and a handful of his Turkish friends.

There were seven of us, and I was the only one who hadn't, at some point, smoked at least one pack of cigarettes per day. I asked one of the Turks how he got started. "Friends," he said. "It always starts with your friends. One friend smokes, then you try it."

What was truly fascinating was that half of the people in the room had managed to *quit* smoking. Mike had been smoke-free for a few years at that point, and he swore up and down that he broke the habit because of a book called *Allen Carr's Easy Way to Stop Smoking*.

"It frees you from the mental burden of smoking," he said. "It tells you: 'Stop lying to yourself. You know you don't actually want to smoke. You know you don't really enjoy this.' It helps you feel like you're not the victim anymore. You start to realize that you don't *need* to smoke."

I had never tried a cigarette, but I took a look at the book afterward out of curiosity. The author employs an interesting strategy to help smokers eliminate their cravings. He systematically reframes each cue associated with smoking and gives it a new meaning.

He says things like:

- You think you are quitting something, but you're not quitting anything because cigarettes do nothing for you.
- You think smoking is something you need to do to be social, but it's not. You can be social without smoking at all.
- You think smoking is about relieving stress, but it's not. Smoking does not relieve your nerves, it destroys them.

Over and over, he repeats these phrases and others like them. "Get it clearly into your mind," he says. "You are losing nothing and you are making marvelous positive gains not only in health, energy and money but also in confidence, self-respect, freedom and, most important of all, in the length and quality of your future life."

By the time you get to the end of the book, smoking seems like the most ridiculous thing in the world to do. And if you no longer expect smoking to bring you any benefits, you have no reason to smoke. It is an inversion of the 2nd Law of Behavior Change: *make it unattractive*. Now, I know this idea might sound overly simplistic. Just change your mind and you can quit smoking. But stick with me for a minute.

WHERE CRAVINGS COME FROM

Every behavior has a surface level craving and a deeper, underlying motive. I often have a craving that goes something like this: "I want to eat tacos." If you were to ask me why I want to eat tacos, I wouldn't say, "Because I need food to survive." But the truth is, somewhere deep down, I am motivated to eat tacos because I have to eat to survive. The underlying motive is to obtain food and water even if my specific craving is for a taco.

Some of our underlying motives include:*

- Conserve energy
- Obtain food and water
- Find love and reproduce
- Connect and bond with others
- Win social acceptance and approval
- Reduce uncertainty
- Achieve status and prestige

A craving is just a specific manifestation of a deeper underlying motive. Your brain did not evolve with a desire to smoke cigarettes or to check Instagram or to play video games. At a deep level, you simply want to reduce uncertainty and relieve anxiety, to win social acceptance and approval, or to achieve status.

Look at nearly any product that is habit-forming and you'll see that it does not create a new motivation, but rather latches onto the underlying motives of human nature.

- Find love and reproduce = using Tinder
- Connect and bond with others = browsing Facebook

---

* This is just a partial list of underlying motives. I offer a more complete list and more examples of how to apply them to business at atomichabits.com/business.

- Win social acceptance and approval = posting on Instagram
- Reduce uncertainty = searching on Google
- Achieve status and prestige = playing video games

Your habits are modern-day solutions to ancient desires. New versions of old vices. The underlying motives behind human behavior remain the same. The specific habits we perform differ based on the period of history.

Here's the powerful part: there are many different ways to address the same underlying motive. One person might learn to reduce stress by smoking a cigarette. Another person learns to ease their anxiety by going for a run. Your current habits are not necessarily the best way to solve the problems you face; they are just the methods you learned to use. Once you associate a solution with the problem you need to solve, you keep coming back to it.

Habits are all about associations. These associations determine whether we predict a habit to be worth repeating or not. As we covered in our discussion of the 1st Law, your brain is continually absorbing information and noticing cues in the environment. Every time you perceive a cue, your brain runs a simulation and makes a prediction about what to do in the next moment.

Cue: You notice that the stove is hot.
Prediction: *If I touch it I'll get burned, so I should avoid touching it.*

Cue: You see that the traffic light turned green.
Prediction: *If I step on the gas, I'll make it safely through the intersection and get closer to my destination, so I should step on the gas.*

You see a cue, categorize it based on past experience, and determine the appropriate response.

This all happens in an instant, but it plays a crucial role in your habits because every action is preceded by a prediction. Life feels reactive, but it is actually predictive. All day long, you are making your best guess of how to act given what you've just seen and what has worked for you in the past. You are endlessly predicting what will happen in the next moment.

Our behavior is heavily dependent on these predictions. Put another way, our behavior is heavily dependent on how we interpret the events that happen to us, not necessarily the objective reality of the events themselves. Two people can look at the same cigarette, and one feels the urge to smoke while the other is repulsed by the smell. The same cue can spark a good habit or a bad habit depending on your prediction. The cause of your habits is actually the prediction that precedes them.

These predictions lead to feelings, which is how we typically describe a craving—a feeling, a desire, an urge. Feelings and emotions transform the cues we perceive and the predictions we make into a signal that we can apply. They help explain what we are currently sensing. For instance, whether or not you realize it, you are noticing how warm or cold you feel right now. If the temperature drops by one degree, you probably won't do anything. If the temperature drops ten degrees, however, you'll feel cold and put on another layer of clothing. Feeling cold was the signal that prompted you to act. You have been sensing the cues the entire time, but it is only when you predict that you would be better off in a different state that you take action.

A craving is the sense that something is missing. It is the desire to change your internal state. When the temperature falls, there is a gap between what your body is currently sensing and what it *wants* to be sensing. This gap between your current state and your desired state provides a reason to act.

Desire is the difference between where you are now and where you want to be in the future. Even the tiniest action is tinged with the motivation to feel differently than you do in the moment. When you binge-eat or light up or browse social media, what you really want is *not* a potato chip or a cigarette or a bunch of likes. What you really want is to *feel* different.

Our feelings and emotions tell us whether to hold steady in our current state or to make a change. They help us decide the best course of action. Neurologists have discovered that when emotions and feelings are impaired, we actually lose the ability to make decisions. We have no signal of what to pursue and what to avoid. As the neuroscientist Antonio Damasio explains, "It is emotion that allows you to mark things as good, bad, or indifferent."

To summarize, the specific cravings you feel and habits you perform are really an attempt to address your fundamental underlying motives. Whenever a habit successfully addresses a motive, you develop a craving to do it again. In time, you learn to predict that checking social media will help you feel loved or that watching YouTube will allow you to forget your fears. Habits are attractive when we associate them with positive feelings, and we can use this insight to our advantage rather than to our detriment.

HOW TO REPROGRAM YOUR BRAIN TO ENJOY HARD HABITS

You can make hard habits more attractive if you can learn to associate them with a positive experience. Sometimes, all you need is a slight mind-set shift. For instance, we often talk about everything we have to do in a given day. You have to wake up early for work. You have to make another sales call for your business. You have to cook dinner for your family.

Now, imagine changing just one word: You don't "have" to. You "get" to.

You *get* to wake up early for work. You *get* to make another sales call for your business. You *get* to cook dinner for your family. By simply changing one word, you shift the way you view each event. You transition from seeing these behaviors as burdens and turn them into opportunities.

The key point is that both versions of reality are true. You *have* to do those things, and you also *get* to do them. We can find evidence for whatever mind-set we choose.

I once heard a story about a man who uses a wheelchair. When asked if it was difficult being confined, he responded, "I'm not confined to my wheelchair—I am liberated by it. If it wasn't for my wheelchair, I would be bed-bound and never able to leave my house." This shift in perspective completely transformed how he lived each day.

Reframing your habits to highlight their *benefits* rather than their drawbacks is a fast and lightweight way to reprogram your mind and make a habit seem more attractive.

Exercise. Many people associate exercise with being a challenging task that drains energy and wears you down. You can just as easily view it as a way to develop skills and build you up. Instead of telling yourself "I need to go run in the morning," say "It's time to build endurance and get fast."

Finance. Saving money is often associated with sacrifice. However, you can associate it with freedom rather than limitation if you realize one simple truth: living below your current means *increases* your future means. The money you save this month increases your purchasing power next month.

Meditation. Anyone who has tried meditation for more than three seconds knows how frustrating it can be when the next distraction inevitably pops into your mind. You can transform frustration into delight when you realize that each interruption gives you a chance to practice returning to your breath. Distraction is a good thing because you need distractions to practice meditation.

Pregame jitters. Many people feel anxious before delivering a big presentation or competing in an important event. They experience quicker breathing, a faster heart rate, heightened arousal. If we interpret these feelings negatively, then we feel threatened and tense up. If we interpret these feelings positively, then we can respond with fluidity and grace. You can reframe "I am nervous" to "I am excited and I'm getting an adrenaline rush to help me concentrate."

These little mind-set shifts aren't magic, but they can help change the feelings you associate with a particular habit or situation.

If you want to take it a step further, you can create a *motivation ritual*. You simply practice associating your habits with something you enjoy, then you can use that cue whenever you need a bit of motivation. For instance, if you always play the same song before having sex, then you'll begin to link the music with the act. Whenever you want to get in the mood, just press play.

Ed Latimore, a boxer and writer from Pittsburgh, benefited from a similar strategy without knowing it. "Odd realization," he wrote. "My focus and concentration goes up just by putting my headphones [on] while writing. I don't even have to play any music." Without realizing it, he was conditioning himself. In the beginning, he put his headphones on, played some music he enjoyed, and did focused work. After doing it five, ten, twenty times, putting his headphones on became a cue that he automatically associated with increased focus. The craving followed naturally.

Athletes use similar strategies to get themselves in the mind-set to perform. During my baseball career, I developed a specific ritual of stretching and throwing before each game. The whole sequence took about ten minutes, and I did it the same way every single time. While it physically warmed me up to play, more importantly, it put me in the right mental state. I began to associate my pregame ritual with feeling competitive and focused. Even if I wasn't motivated beforehand, by the time I was done with my ritual, I was in "game mode."

You can adapt this strategy for nearly any purpose. Say you want to feel happier in general. Find something that makes you truly happy—like petting your dog or taking a bubble bath—and then create a short routine that you perform every time *before* you do the thing you love. Maybe you take three deep breaths and smile.

Three deep breaths. Smile. Pet the dog. Repeat.

Eventually, you'll begin to associate this breathe-and-smile routine with being in a good mood. It becomes a cue that *means* feeling happy. Once established, you can break it out anytime you need to change your emotional state. Stressed at work? Take three deep breaths and smile. Sad about life? Three deep breaths and smile. Once a habit has been built, the cue can prompt a craving, even if it has little to do with the original situation.

The key to finding and fixing the causes of your bad habits is to reframe the associations you have about them. It's not easy, but if you can reprogram your predictions, you can transform a hard habit into an attractive one.

———————————— Chapter Summary ————————————

- The inversion of the 2nd Law of Behavior Change is *make it unattractive.*
- Every behavior has a surface level craving and a deeper underlying motive.
- Your habits are modern-day solutions to ancient desires.
- The cause of your habits is actually the prediction that precedes them. The prediction leads to a feeling.

- Highlight the benefits of avoiding a bad habit to make it seem unattractive.

- Habits are attractive when we associate them with positive feelings and unattractive when we associate them with negative feelings. Create a motivation ritual by doing something you enjoy immediately before a difficult habit.

HOW TO CREATE A GOOD HABIT

The 1st Law	Make It Obvious
1.1	Fill out the Habits Scorecard. Write down your current habits to become aware of them.
1.2	Use implementation intentions: "I will [BEHAVIOR] at [TIME] in [LOCATION]."
1.3	Use habit stacking: "After [CURRENT HABIT], I will [NEW HABIT]."
1.4	Design your environment. Make the cues of good habits obvious and visible.
The 2nd Law	**Make It Attractive**
2.1	Use temptation bundling. Pair an action you *want* to do with an action you *need* to do.
2.2	Join a culture where your desired behavior is the normal behavior.
2.3	Create a motivation ritual. Do something you enjoy immediately before a difficult habit.
The 3rd Law	**Make It Easy**
The 4th Law	**Make It Satisfying**

HOW TO BREAK A BAD HABIT

Inversion of the 1st Law	Make It Invisible
1.5	Reduce exposure. Remove the cues of your bad habits from your environment.
Inversion of the 2nd Law	Make It Unattractive
2.4	Reframe your mind-set. Highlight the benefits of avoiding your bad habits.
Inversion of the 3rd Law	Make It Difficult
Inversion of the 4th Law	Make It Unsatisfying

You can download a printable version of this habits cheat sheet at:
atomichabits.com/cheatsheet

THE 3RD LAW

Make It Easy

11

Walk Slowly,
but Never Backward

ON THE FIRST day of class, Jerry Uelsmann, a professor at the University of Florida, divided his film photography students into two groups.

Everyone on the left side of the classroom, he explained, would be in the "quantity" group. They would be graded solely on the amount of work they produced. On the final day of class, he would tally the number of photos submitted by each student. One hundred photos would rate an A, ninety photos a B, eighty photos a C, and so on.

Meanwhile, everyone on the right side of the room would be in the "quality" group. They would be graded only on the excellence of their work. They would only need to produce one photo during the semester, but to get an A, it had to be a nearly perfect image.

At the end of the term, he was surprised to find that all the best photos were produced by the *quantity* group. During the semester, these students were busy taking photos, experimenting with composition and lighting, testing out various methods in the darkroom, and learning from their mistakes. In the process of creating hundreds of photos, they honed their skills. Meanwhile, the *quality* group sat around speculating about perfection. In the end, they had little to show for their efforts other than unverified theories and one mediocre photo.*

It is easy to get bogged down trying to find the optimal plan for change: the fastest way to lose weight, the best program to build muscle, the perfect idea for a side hustle. We are so focused on figuring out the best approach that we never get around to taking action. As Voltaire once wrote, "The best is the enemy of the good."

I refer to this as the difference between being in motion and taking action. The two ideas sound similar, but they're not the same. When you're in motion, you're planning and strategizing and learning. Those are all good things, but they don't produce a result.

Action, on the other hand, is the type of behavior that will deliver an outcome. If I outline twenty ideas for articles I want to write, that's motion. If I actually sit down and write an article, that's action. If I search for a better diet plan and read a few books on the topic, that's motion. If I actually eat a healthy meal, that's action.

Sometimes motion is useful, but it will never produce an outcome by itself. It doesn't matter how many times you go talk to the personal trainer, that motion will never get you in shape. Only the action of working out will get the result you're looking to achieve.

If motion doesn't lead to results, why do we do it? Sometimes we do it because we actually need to plan or learn more. But more often than not, we do it because motion allows us to feel like we're making progress without running the risk of failure. Most of us are experts at avoiding criticism. It doesn't feel good to fail or to be judged publicly, so we tend to avoid situations where that might happen. And that's the biggest reason why you slip into motion rather than taking action: you want to delay failure.

---

* A similar story is told in the book *Art & Fear* by David Bayles and Ted Orland. It has been adapted here with permission. See the endnotes for a full explanation.

It's easy to be in motion and convince yourself that you're still making progress. You think, *"I've got conversations going with four potential clients right now. This is good. We're moving in the right direction."* Or, *"I brainstormed some ideas for that book I want to write. This is coming together."*

Motion makes you feel like you're getting things done. But really, you're just preparing to get something done. When preparation becomes a form of procrastination, you need to change something. You don't want to merely be planning. You want to be practicing.

If you want to master a habit, the key is to start with repetition, not perfection. You don't need to map out every feature of a new habit. You just need to practice it. This is the first takeaway of the 3rd Law: you just need to get your reps in.

HOW LONG DOES IT ACTUALLY TAKE TO FORM A NEW HABIT?

Habit formation is the process by which a behavior becomes progressively more automatic through repetition. The more you repeat an activity, the more the structure of your brain changes to become efficient at that activity. Neuroscientists call this *long-term potentiation*, which refers to the strengthening of connections between neurons in the brain based on recent patterns of activity. With each repetition, cell-to-cell signaling improves and the neural connections tighten. First described by neuropsychologist Donald Hebb in 1949, this phenomenon is commonly known as Hebb's Law: "Neurons that fire together wire together."

Repeating a habit leads to clear physical changes in the brain. In musicians, the cerebellum—critical for physical movements like plucking a guitar string or pulling a violin bow—is larger than it is in nonmusicians. Mathematicians, meanwhile, have increased gray matter in the inferior parietal lobule, which plays a key role in computation and calculation. Its size is directly correlated with the amount of time spent in the field; the older and more experienced the mathematician, the greater the increase in gray matter.

When scientists analyzed the brains of taxi drivers in London, they found that the hippocampus—a region of the brain involved in spatial memory—was significantly larger in their subjects than in non–taxi drivers. Even more fascinating, the hippocampus decreased in size when a driver retired. Like the muscles of the body responding to regular weight training, particular regions of the brain adapt as they are used and atrophy as they are abandoned.

Of course, the importance of repetition in establishing habits was recognized long before neuroscientists began poking around. In 1860, the English philosopher George H. Lewes noted, "In learning to speak a new language, to play on a musical instrument, or to perform unaccustomed movements, great difficulty is felt, because the channels through which each sensation has to pass have not become established; but no sooner has frequent repetition cut a pathway, than this difficulty vanishes; the actions become so automatic that they can be performed while the mind is otherwise engaged." Both common sense and scientific evidence agree: repetition is a form of change.

Each time you repeat an action, you are activating a particular neural circuit associated with that habit. This means that simply putting in your reps is one of the most critical steps you can take to encoding a new habit. It is why the students who took tons of photos improved their skills while those who merely theorized about perfect photos did not. One group engaged in active practice, the other in passive learning. One in action, the other in motion.

All habits follow a similar trajectory from effortful practice to automatic behavior, a process known as *automaticity*. Automaticity is the ability to perform a behavior without thinking about each step, which occurs when the nonconscious mind takes over.

It looks something like this:

THE HABIT LINE

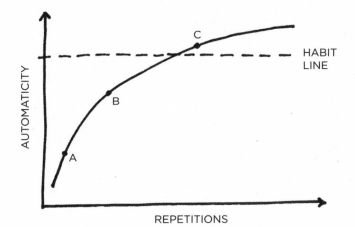

FIGURE 11: In the beginning (point A), a habit requires a good deal of effort and concentration to perform. After a few repetitions (point B), it gets easier, but still requires some conscious attention. With enough practice (point C), the habit becomes more automatic than conscious. Beyond this threshold—*the habit line*—the behavior can be done more or less without thinking. A new habit has been formed.

On the following page, you'll see what it looks like when researchers track the level of automaticity for an actual habit like walking for ten minutes each day. The shape of these charts, which scientists call *learning curves*, reveals an important truth about behavior change: habits form based on frequency, not time.

WALKING 10 MINUTES PER DAY

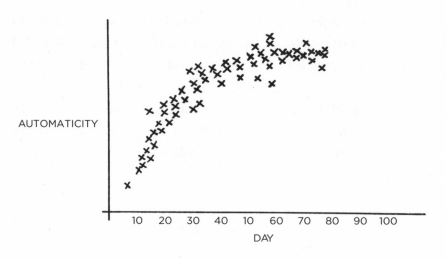

FIGURE 12: This graph shows someone who built the habit of walking for ten minutes after breakfast each day. Notice that as the repetitions increase, so does automaticity, until the behavior is as easy and automatic as it can be.

One of the most common questions I hear is, "How *long* does it take to build a new habit?" But what people really should be asking is, "How *many* does it take to form a new habit?" That is, how many repetitions are required to make a habit automatic?

There is nothing magical about time passing with regard to habit formation. It doesn't matter if it's been twenty-one days or thirty days or three hundred days. What matters is the rate at which you perform the behavior. You could do something twice in thirty days, or two hundred times. It's the frequency that makes the difference. Your current habits have been internalized over the course of hundreds, if not thousands, of repetitions. New habits require the same level of frequency. You need to string together enough successful attempts until the behavior is firmly embedded in your mind and you cross the Habit Line.

In practice, it doesn't really matter how long it takes for a habit to become automatic. What matters is that you take the actions you need to take to make progress. Whether an action is fully automatic is of less importance.

To build a habit, you need to practice it. And the most effective way to make practice happen is to adhere to the 3rd Law of Behavior Change: *make it easy*. The chapters that follow will show you how to do exactly that.

─────────── Chapter Summary ───────────

- The 3rd Law of Behavior Change is *make it easy*.
- The most effective form of learning is practice, not planning.
- Focus on taking action, not being in motion.
- Habit formation is the process by which a behavior becomes progressively more automatic through repetition.
- The amount of time you have been performing a habit is not as important as the number of times you have performed it.

12

The Law of Least Effort

I N HIS AWARD-WINNING BOOK, *Guns, Germs, and Steel*, anthropologist and biologist Jared Diamond points out a simple fact: different continents have different shapes. At first glance, this statement seems rather obvious and unimportant, but it turns out to have a profound impact on human behavior.

The primary axis of the Americas runs from north to south. That is, the landmass of North and South America tends to be tall and thin rather than wide and fat. The same is generally true for Africa. Meanwhile, the landmass that makes up Europe, Asia, and the Middle East is the opposite. This massive stretch of land tends to be more east-west in shape. According to Diamond, this difference in shape played a significant role in the spread of agriculture over the centuries.

When agriculture began to spread around the globe, farmers had an easier time expanding along east-west routes than along north-south ones. This is because locations along the same latitude generally share similar climates, amounts of sunlight and rainfall, and changes in season. These factors allowed farmers in Europe and Asia to domes-

THE SHAPE OF HUMAN BEHAVIOR

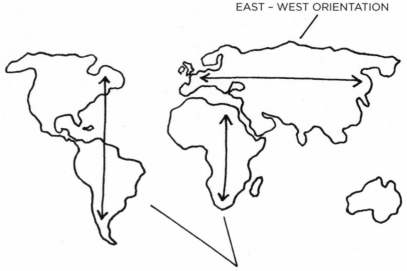

FIGURE 13: The primary axis of Europe and Asia is east-west. The primary axis of the Americas and Africa is north-south. This leads to a wider range of climates up-and-down the Americas than across Europe and Asia. As a result, agriculture spread nearly twice as fast across Europe and Asia than it did else-where. The behavior of farmers—even across hundreds or thousands of years—was constrained by the amount of friction in the environment.

ticate a few crops and grow them along the entire stretch of land from France to China.

By comparison, the climate varies greatly when traveling from north to south. Just imagine how different the weather is in Florida compared to Canada. You can be the most talented farmer in the world, but it won't help you grow Florida oranges in the Canadian winter. Snow is a poor substitute for soil. In order to spread crops along north-south routes, farmers would need to find and domesticate new plants whenever the climate changed.

As a result, agriculture spread two to three times faster across Asia and Europe than it did up and down the Americas. Over the span of centuries, this small difference had a very big impact. Increased food production allowed for more rapid population growth. With more people, these cultures were able to build stronger armies and were better equipped to develop new technologies. The changes started out small—a crop that spread slightly farther, a population that grew slightly faster—but compounded into substantial differences over time.

The spread of agriculture provides an example of the 3rd Law of Behavior Change on a global scale. Conventional wisdom holds that motivation is the key to habit change. Maybe if you *really* wanted it, you'd actually do it. But the truth is, our real motivation is to be lazy and to do what is convenient. And despite what the latest productivity best seller will tell you, this is a smart strategy, not a dumb one.

Energy is precious, and the brain is wired to conserve it whenever possible. It is human nature to follow the Law of Least Effort, which states that when deciding between two similar options, people will naturally gravitate toward the option that requires the least amount of work.* For example, expanding your farm to the east where you can grow the same crops rather than heading north where the climate is different. Out of all the possible actions we could take, the one that is realized is the one that delivers the most value for the least effort. We are motivated to do what is easy.

---

* This is a foundational principle in physics, where it is known as the Principle of Least Action. It states that the path followed between any two points will always be the path requiring the least energy. This simple principle underpins the laws of the universe. From this one idea, you can describe the laws of motion and relativity.

Every action requires a certain amount of energy. The more energy required, the less likely it is to occur. If your goal is to do a hundred push-ups per day, that's a lot of energy! In the beginning, when you're motivated and excited, you can muster the strength to get started. But after a few days, such a massive effort feels exhausting. Meanwhile, sticking to the habit of doing one push-up per day requires almost no energy to get started. And the less energy a habit requires, the more likely it is to occur.

Look at any behavior that fills up much of your life and you'll see that it can be performed with very low levels of motivation. Habits like scrolling on our phones, checking email, and watching television steal so much of our time because they can be performed almost without effort. They are remarkably convenient.

In a sense, every habit is just an obstacle to getting what you really want. Dieting is an obstacle to getting fit. Meditation is an obstacle to feeling calm. Journaling is an obstacle to thinking clearly. You don't actually want the habit itself. What you really want is the outcome the habit delivers. The greater the obstacle—that is, the more difficult the habit—the more friction there is between you and your desired end state. This is why it is crucial to make your habits so easy that you'll do them even when you don't feel like it. If you can make your good habits more convenient, you'll be more likely to follow through on them.

But what about all the moments when we seem to do the opposite? If we're all so lazy, then how do you explain people accomplishing hard things like raising a child or starting a business or climbing Mount Everest?

Certainly, you are capable of doing very hard things. The problem is that some days you feel like doing the hard work and some days you feel like giving in. On the tough days, it's crucial to have as many things working in your favor as possible so that you can overcome the challenges life naturally throws your way. The less friction you face, the easier it is for your stronger self to emerge. The idea behind *make it easy* is not to *only* do easy things. The idea is to make it as easy as possible in the moment to do things that payoff in the long run.

HOW TO ACHIEVE MORE WITH LESS EFFORT

Imagine you are holding a garden hose that is bent in the middle. Some water can flow through, but not very much. If you want to increase the rate at which water passes through the hose, you have two options. The first option is to crank up the valve and force more water out. The second option is to simply remove the bend in the hose and let water flow through naturally.

Trying to pump up your motivation to stick with a hard habit is like trying to force water through a bent hose. You can do it, but it requires a lot of effort and increases the tension in your life. Meanwhile, making your habits simple and easy is like removing the bend in the hose. Rather than trying to overcome the friction in your life, you reduce it.

One of the most effective ways to reduce the friction associated with your habits is to practice environment design. In Chapter 6, we discussed environment design as a method for making cues more obvious, but you can also optimize your environment to make actions easier. For example, when deciding where to practice a new habit, it is best to choose a place that is already along the path of your daily routine. Habits are easier to build when they fit into the flow of your life. You are more likely to go to the gym if it is on your way to work because stopping doesn't add much friction to your lifestyle. By comparison, if the gym is off the path of your normal commute—even by just a few blocks—now you're going "out of your way" to get there.

Perhaps even more effective is reducing the friction within your home or office. Too often, we try to start habits in high-friction environments. We try to follow a strict diet while we are out to dinner with friends. We try to write a book in a chaotic household. We try to concentrate while using a smartphone filled with distractions. It doesn't have to be this way. We can remove the points of friction that hold us back. This is precisely what electronics manufacturers in Japan began to do in the 1970s.

In an article published in the *New Yorker* titled "Better All the Time," James Suroweicki writes:

"Japanese firms emphasized what came to be known as 'lean production,' relentlessly looking to remove waste of all kinds from the production process, down to redesigning workspaces, so workers didn't have to waste time twisting and turning to reach their tools. The result was that Japanese factories were more efficient and Japanese products were more reliable than American ones. In 1974, service calls for American-made color televisions were five times as common as for Japanese televisions. By 1979, it took American workers three times as long to assemble their sets."

I like to refer to this strategy as *addition by subtraction*.* The Japanese companies looked for every point of friction in the manufacturing process and eliminated it. As they subtracted wasted effort, they added customers and revenue. Similarly, when we remove the points of friction that sap our time and energy, we can achieve more with less effort. (This is one reason tidying up can feel so good: we are simultaneously moving forward and lightening the cognitive load our environment places on us.)

If you look at the most habit-forming products, you'll notice that one of the things these goods and services do best is remove little bits of friction from your life. Meal delivery services reduce the friction of shopping for groceries. Dating apps reduce the friction of making

---

* The phrase *addition by subtraction* is also used by teams and businesses to describe removing people from a group in order to make the team stronger overall.

social introductions. Ride-sharing services reduce the friction of getting across town. Text messaging reduces the friction of sending a letter in the mail.

Like a Japanese television manufacturer redesigning their workspace to reduce wasted motion, successful companies design their products to automate, eliminate, or simplify as many steps as possible. They reduce the number of fields on each form. They pare down the number of clicks required to create an account. They deliver their products with easy-to-understand directions or ask their customers to make fewer choices.

When the first voice-activated speakers were released—products like Google Home, Amazon Echo, and Apple HomePod—I asked a friend what he liked about the product he had purchased. He said it was just easier to say "Play some country music" than to pull out his phone, open the music app, and pick a playlist. Of course, just a few years earlier, having unlimited access to music in your pocket was a remarkably frictionless behavior compared to driving to the store and buying a CD. Business is a never-ending quest to deliver the same result in an easier fashion.

Similar strategies have been used effectively by governments. When the British government wanted to increase tax collection rates, they switched from sending citizens to a web page where the tax form could be downloaded to linking directly to the form. Reducing that one step in the process increased the response rate from 19.2 percent to 23.4 percent. For a country like the United Kingdom, those percentage points represent millions in tax revenue.

The central idea is to create an environment where doing the right thing is as easy as possible. Much of the battle of building better habits comes down to finding ways to reduce the friction associated with our good habits and increase the friction associated with our bad ones.

PRIME THE ENVIRONMENT FOR FUTURE USE

Oswald Nuckols is an IT developer from Natchez, Mississippi. He is also someone who understands the power of priming his environment.

Nuckols dialed in his cleaning habits by following a strategy he refers to as "resetting the room." For instance, when he finishes watching television, he places the remote back on the TV stand, arranges the pillows on the couch, and folds the blanket. When he leaves his car, he throws any trash away. Whenever he takes a shower, he wipes down the toilet while the shower is warming up. (As he notes, the "perfect time to clean the toilet is right before you wash yourself in the shower anyway.") The purpose of resetting each room is not simply to clean up after the last action, but to prepare for the next action.

"When I walk into a room everything is in its right place," Nuckols wrote. "Because I do this every day in every room, stuff always stays in good shape. . . . People think I work hard but I'm actually really lazy. I'm just proactively lazy. It gives you so much time back."

Whenever you organize a space for its intended purpose, you are priming it to make the next action easy. For instance, my wife keeps a box of greeting cards that are presorted by occasion—birthday, sympathy, wedding, graduation, and more. Whenever necessary, she grabs an appropriate card and sends it off. She is incredibly good at remembering to send cards because she has reduced the friction of doing so. For years, I was the opposite. Someone would have a baby and I would think, "I should send a card." But then weeks would pass and by the time I remembered to pick one up at the store, it was too late. The habit wasn't easy.

There are many ways to prime your environment so it's ready for immediate use. If you want to cook a healthy breakfast, place the skillet on the stove, set the cooking spray on the counter, and lay out any plates and utensils you'll need the night before. When you wake up, making breakfast will be easy.

- Want to draw more? Put your pencils, pens, notebooks, and drawing tools on top of your desk, within easy reach.
- Want to exercise? Set out your workout clothes, shoes, gym bag, and water bottle ahead of time.
- Want to improve your diet? Chop up a ton of fruits and vegetables on weekends and pack them in containers, so you have easy access to healthy, ready-to-eat options during the week.

These are simple ways to make the good habit the path of least resistance.

You can also invert this principle and prime the environment to make bad behaviors difficult. If you find yourself watching too much television, for example, then unplug it after each use. Only plug it back in if you can say out loud the name of the show you want to watch. This setup creates just enough friction to prevent mindless viewing.

If that doesn't do it, you can take it a step further. Unplug the television and take the batteries out of the remote after each use, so it takes an extra ten seconds to turn it back on. And if you're really hard-core, move the television out of the living room and into a closet after each use. You can be sure you'll only take it out when you *really* want to watch something. The greater the friction, the less likely the habit.

Whenever possible, I leave my phone in a different room until lunch. When it's right next to me, I'll check it all morning for no reason at all. But when it is in another room, I rarely think about it. And the friction is high enough that I won't go get it without a reason. As a result, I get three to four hours each morning when I can work without interruption.

If sticking your phone in another room doesn't seem like enough, tell a friend or family member to hide it from you for a few hours. Ask a coworker to keep it at their desk in the morning and give it back to you at lunch.

It is remarkable how little friction is required to prevent unwanted behavior. When I hide beer in the back of the fridge where I can't see it, I drink less. When I delete social media apps from my phone, it can be weeks before I download them again and log in. These tricks are unlikely to curb a true addiction, but for many of us, a little bit of friction can be the difference between sticking with a good habit or sliding into a bad one. Imagine the cumulative impact of making dozens of these changes and living in an environment designed to make the good behaviors easier and the bad behaviors harder.

Whether we are approaching behavior change as an individual, a parent, a coach, or a leader, we should ask ourselves the same question: "How can we design a world where it's easy to do what's right?" Redesign your life so the actions that matter most are also the actions that are easiest to do.

Chapter Summary

- Human behavior follows the Law of Least Effort. We will naturally gravitate toward the option that requires the least amount of work.
- Create an environment where doing the right thing is as easy as possible.
- Reduce the friction associated with good behaviors. When friction is low, habits are easy.
- Increase the friction associated with bad behaviors. When friction is high, habits are difficult.
- Prime your environment to make future actions easier.

13

How to Stop Procrastinating
by Using the Two-Minute Rule

TWYLA THARP IS widely regarded as one of the greatest dancers and choreographers of the modern era. In 1992, she was awarded a MacArthur Fellowship, often referred to as the Genius Grant, and she has spent the bulk of her career touring the globe to perform her original works. She also credits much of her success to simple daily habits.

"I begin each day of my life with a ritual," she writes. "I wake up at 5:30 A.M., put on my workout clothes, my leg warmers, my sweat shirt, and my hat. I walk outside my Manhattan home, hail a taxi, and tell the driver to take me to the Pumping Iron gym at 91st Street and First Avenue, where I work out for two hours.

"The ritual is not the stretching and weight training I put my body through each morning at the gym; the ritual is the cab. The moment I tell the driver where to go I have completed the ritual.

"It's a simple act, but doing it the same way each morning habitualizes it—makes it repeatable, easy to do. It reduces the chance that I would skip it or do it differently. It is one more item in my arsenal of routines, and one less thing to think about."

Hailing a cab each morning may be a tiny action, but it is a splendid example of the 3rd Law of Behavior Change.

Researchers estimate that 40 to 50 percent of our actions on any given day are done out of habit. This is already a substantial percentage, but the true influence of your habits is even greater than these numbers suggest. Habits are automatic choices that influence the conscious decisions that follow. Yes, a habit can be completed in just a few seconds, but it can also shape the actions that you take for minutes or hours afterward.

Habits are like the entrance ramp to a highway. They lead you down a path and, before you know it, you're speeding toward the next behavior. It seems to be easier to continue what you are already doing than to start doing something different. You sit through a bad movie for two hours. You keep snacking even when you're already full. You check your phone for "just a second" and soon you have spent twenty minutes staring at the screen. In this way, the habits you follow without thinking often determine the choices you make when you are thinking.

Each evening, there is a tiny moment—usually around 5:15 p.m.—that shapes the rest of my night. My wife walks in the door from work and either we change into our workout clothes and head to the gym or we crash onto the couch, order Indian food, and watch *The Office.** Similar to Twyla Tharp hailing the cab, the ritual is changing into my workout clothes. If I change clothes, I know the workout will happen. Everything that follows—driving to the gym, deciding which exercises to do, stepping under the bar—is easy once I've taken the first step.

Every day, there are a handful of moments that deliver an outsized impact. I refer to these little choices as *decisive moments*. The moment you decide between ordering takeout or cooking dinner. The moment

---

* To be fair, this still sounds like an amazing night.

you choose between driving your car or riding your bike. The moment you decide between starting your homework or grabbing the video game controller. These choices are a fork in the road.

Decisive moments set the options available to your future self. For

DECISIVE MOMENTS

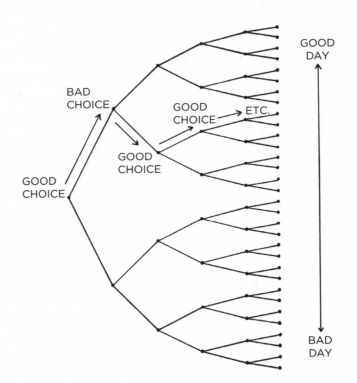

FIGURE 14: The difference between a good day and a bad day is often a few productive and healthy choices made at decisive moments. Each one is like a fork in the road, and these choices stack up throughout the day and can ultimately lead to very different outcomes.

instance, walking into a restaurant is a decisive moment because it determines what you'll be eating for lunch. Technically, you are in control of what you order, but in a larger sense, you can only order an item if it is on the menu. If you walk into a steakhouse, you can get a sirloin or a rib eye, but not sushi. Your options are constrained by what's available. They are shaped by the first choice.

We are limited by where our habits lead us. This is why mastering the decisive moments throughout your day is so important. Each day is made up of many moments, but it is really a few habitual choices that determine the path you take. These little choices stack up, each one setting the trajectory for how you spend the next chunk of time.

Habits are the entry point, not the end point. They are the cab, not the gym.

THE TWO-MINUTE RULE

Even when you know you should start small, it's easy to start too big. When you dream about making a change, excitement inevitably takes over and you end up trying to do too much too soon. The most effective way I know to counteract this tendency is to use the *Two-Minute Rule*, which states, "When you start a new habit, it should take less than two minutes to do."

You'll find that nearly any habit can be scaled down into a two-minute version:

- "Read before bed each night" becomes "Read one page."
- "Do thirty minutes of yoga" becomes "Take out my yoga mat."
- "Study for class" becomes "Open my notes."
- "Fold the laundry" becomes "Fold one pair of socks."
- "Run three miles" becomes "Tie my running shoes."

The idea is to make your habits as easy as possible to start. Anyone can meditate for one minute, read one page, or put one item of clothing away. And, as we have just discussed, this is a powerful strategy because once you've started doing the right thing, it is much easier to continue doing it. A new habit should not feel like a challenge. The actions that *follow* can be challenging, but the first two minutes should be easy. What you want is a "gateway habit" that naturally leads you down a more productive path.

You can usually figure out the gateway habits that will lead to your desired outcome by mapping out your goals on a scale from "very easy" to "very hard." For instance, running a marathon is very hard. Running a 5K is hard. Walking ten thousand steps is moderately difficult. Walking ten minutes is easy. And putting on your running shoes is very easy. Your goal might be to run a marathon, but your gateway habit is to put on your running shoes. That's how you follow the Two-Minute Rule.

Very easy	Easy	Moderate	Hard	Very hard
Put on your running shoes	Walk ten minutes	Walk ten thousand steps	Run a 5K	Run a marathon
Write one sentence	Write one paragraph	Write one thousand words	Write a five-thousand-word article	Write a book
Open your notes	Study for ten minutes	Study for three hours	Get straight A's	Earn a PhD

People often think it's weird to get hyped about reading one page or meditating for one minute or making one sales call. But the point is not to do one thing. The point is to master the habit of showing up. The truth is, a habit must be established before it can be improved. If you can't learn the basic skill of showing up, then you have little hope of mastering the finer details. Instead of trying to engineer a perfect habit from the start, do the easy thing on a more consistent basis. You have to standardize before you can optimize.

As you master the art of showing up, the first two minutes simply become a ritual at the beginning of a larger routine. This is not merely a hack to make habits easier but actually the ideal way to master a difficult skill. The more you ritualize the beginning of a process, the more likely it becomes that you can slip into the state of deep focus that is required to do great things. By doing the same warm-up before every workout, you make it easier to get into a state of peak performance. By following the same creative ritual, you make it easier to get into the hard work of creating. By developing a consistent power-down habit, you make it easier to get to bed at a reasonable time each night. You may not be able to automate the whole process, but you can make the first action mindless. Make it easy to start and the rest will follow.

The Two-Minute Rule can seem like a trick to some people. You know that the *real* goal is to do more than just two minutes, so it may feel like you're trying to fool yourself. Nobody is actually aspiring to read one page or do one push-up or open their notes. And if you know it's a mental trick, why would you fall for it?

If the Two-Minute Rule feels forced, try this: do it for two minutes and then stop. Go for a run, but you *must* stop after two minutes. Start meditating, but you *must* stop after two minutes. Study Arabic, but you *must* stop after two minutes. It's not a strategy for starting, it's the whole thing. Your habit can *only* last one hundred and twenty seconds.

One of my readers used this strategy to lose over one hundred pounds. In the beginning, he went to the gym each day, but he told himself he wasn't allowed to stay for more than five minutes. He would go to the gym, exercise for five minutes, and leave as soon as his time was up. After a few weeks, he looked around and thought, "Well, I'm always coming here anyway. I might as well start staying a little longer." A few years later, the weight was gone.

Journaling provides another example. Nearly everyone can benefit from getting their thoughts out of their head and onto paper, but most people give up after a few days or avoid it entirely because journaling feels like a chore.* The secret is to always stay below the point where it feels like work. Greg McKeown, a leadership consultant from the United Kingdom, built a daily journaling habit by specifically writing *less* than he felt like. He always stopped journaling before it seemed like a hassle. Ernest Hemingway believed in similar advice for any kind of writing. "The best way is to always stop when you are going good," he said.

Strategies like this work for another reason, too: they reinforce the identity you want to build. If you show up at the gym five days in a row—even if it's just for two minutes—you are casting votes for your new identity. You're not worried about getting in shape. You're focused on becoming the type of person who doesn't miss workouts. You're taking the smallest action that confirms the type of person you want to be.

We rarely think about change this way because everyone is consumed by the end goal. But one push-up is better than not exercising. One minute of guitar practice is better than none at all. One minute of reading is better than never picking up a book. It's better to do less than you hoped than to do nothing at all.

At some point, once you've established the habit and you're showing up each day, you can combine the Two-Minute Rule with a technique we call *habit shaping* to scale your habit back up toward your ultimate goal. Start by mastering the first two minutes of the smallest version of

---

* I designed a habit journal specifically to make journaling easier. It includes a "One Line Per Day" section where you simply write one sentence about your day. You can learn more at atomichabits.com/journal.

EXAMPLES OF HABIT SHAPING

Habit	Becoming an Early Riser	Becoming Vegan	Starting to Exercise
Phase 1	Be home by 10 p.m. every night.	Start eating vegetables at each meal.	Change into workout clothes.
Phase 2	Have all devices (TV, phone, etc.) turned off by 10 p.m. every night.	Stop eating animals with four legs (cow, pig, lamb, etc.).	Step out the door (try taking a walk).
Phase 3	Be in bed by 10 p.m. every night (reading a book, talking with your partner).	Stop eating animals with two legs (chicken, turkey, etc.).	Drive to the gym, exercise for five minutes, and leave.
Phase 4	Lights off by 10 p.m. every night.	Stop eating animals with no legs (fish, clams, scallops, etc.).	Exercise for fifteen minutes at least once per week.
Phase 5	Wake up at 6 a.m. every day.	Stop eating all animal products (eggs, milk, cheese).	Exercise three times per week.

the behavior. Then, advance to an intermediate step and repeat the process—focusing on just the first two minutes and mastering that stage before moving on to the next level. Eventually, you'll end up with the habit you had originally hoped to build while still keeping your focus where it should be: on the first two minutes of the behavior.

Nearly any larger life goal can be transformed into a two-minute behavior. I want to live a healthy and long life > I need to stay in shape > I need to exercise > I need to change into my workout clothes. I want to have a happy marriage > I need to be a good partner > I should do something each day to make my partner's life easier > I should meal plan for next week.

Whenever you are struggling to stick with a habit, you can employ the Two-Minute Rule. It's a simple way to make your habits easy.

Chapter Summary

- Habits can be completed in a few seconds but continue to impact your behavior for minutes or hours afterward.
- Many habits occur at decisive moments—choices that are like a fork in the road—and either send you in the direction of a productive day or an unproductive one.
- The Two-Minute Rule states, "When you start a new habit, it should take less than two minutes to do."
- The more you ritualize the beginning of a process, the more likely it becomes that you can slip into the state of deep focus that is required to do great things.
- Standardize before you optimize. You can't improve a habit that doesn't exist.

14

How to Make Good Habits Inevitable and Bad Habits Impossible

I N THE SUMMER OF 1830, Victor Hugo was facing an impossible deadline. Twelve months earlier, the French author had promised his publisher a new book. But instead of writing, he spent that year pursuing other projects, entertaining guests, and delaying his work. Frustrated, Hugo's publisher responded by setting a deadline less than six months away. The book had to be finished by February 1831.

Hugo concocted a strange plan to beat his procrastination. He collected all of his clothes and asked an assistant to lock them away in a large chest. He was left with nothing to wear except a large shawl. Lacking any suitable clothing to go outdoors, he remained in his study and wrote furiously during the fall and winter of 1830. *The Hunchback of Notre Dame* was published two weeks early on January 14, 1831.*

Sometimes success is less about making good habits easy and more about making bad habits hard. This is an inversion of the 3rd Law of Behavior Change: *make it difficult*. If you find yourself continually

---

* The irony of how closely this story matches my process of writing this book is not lost on me. Although my publisher was much more accommodating, and my closet remained full, I did feel like I had to place myself on house arrest to finish the manuscript.

struggling to follow through on your plans, then you can take a page from Victor Hugo and make your bad habits more difficult by creating what psychologists call a *commitment device.*

A commitment device is a choice you make in the present that controls your actions in the future. It is a way to lock in future behavior, bind you to good habits, and restrict you from bad ones. When Victor Hugo shut his clothes away so he could focus on writing, he was creating a commitment device.*

There are many ways to create a commitment device. You can reduce overeating by purchasing food in individual packages rather than in bulk size. You can voluntarily ask to be added to the banned list at casinos and online poker sites to prevent future gambling sprees. I've even heard of athletes who have to "make weight" for a competition choosing to leave their wallets at home during the week before weigh-in so they won't be tempted to buy fast food.

As another example, my friend and fellow habits expert Nir Eyal purchased an outlet timer, which is an adapter that he plugged in between his internet router and the power outlet. At 10 p.m. each night, the outlet timer cuts off the power to the router. When the internet goes off, everyone knows it is time to go to bed.

Commitment devices are useful because they enable you to take advantage of good intentions before you can fall victim to temptation. Whenever I'm looking to cut calories, for example, I will ask the waiter to split my meal and box half of it to go *before* the meal is served. If I waited until the meal came out and told myself "I'll just eat half," it would never work.

---

* This is also referred to as a "Ulysses pact" or a "Ulysses contract." Named after Ulysses, the hero of *The Odyssey*, who told his sailors to tie him to the mast of the ship so that he could hear the enchanting song of the Sirens but wouldn't be able to steer the ship toward them and crash on the rocks. Ulysses realized the benefits of locking in your future actions while your mind is in the right place rather than waiting to see where your desires take you in the moment.

The key is to change the task such that it requires more work to get *out* of the good habit than to get started on it. If you're feeling motivated to get in shape, schedule a yoga session and pay ahead of time. If you're excited about the business you want to start, email an entrepreneur you respect and set up a consulting call. When the time comes to act, the only way to bail is to cancel the meeting, which requires effort and may cost money.

Commitment devices increase the odds that you'll do the right thing in the future by making bad habits difficult in the present. However, we can do even better. We can make good habits inevitable and bad habits impossible.

HOW TO AUTOMATE A HABIT AND NEVER THINK ABOUT IT AGAIN

John Henry Patterson was born in Dayton, Ohio, in 1844. He spent his childhood doing chores on the family farm and working shifts at his father's sawmill. After attending college at Dartmouth, Patterson returned to Ohio and opened a small supply store for coal miners.

It seemed like a good opportunity. The store faced little competition and enjoyed a steady stream of customers, but still struggled to make money. That was when Patterson discovered his employees were stealing from him.

In the mid-1800s, employee theft was a common problem. Receipts were kept in an open drawer and could easily be altered or discarded. There were no video cameras to review behavior and no software to track transactions. Unless you were willing to hover over your employees every minute of the day, or to manage all transactions yourself, it was difficult to prevent theft.

As Patterson mulled over his predicament, he came across an advertisement for a new invention called Ritty's Incorruptible Cashier.

Designed by fellow Dayton resident James Ritty, it was the first cash register. The machine automatically locked the cash and receipts inside after each transaction. Patterson bought two for fifty dollars each.

Employee theft at his store vanished overnight. In the next six months, Patterson's business went from losing money to making $5,000 in profit—the equivalent of more than $100,000 today.

Patterson was so impressed with the machine that he changed businesses. He bought the rights to Ritty's invention and opened the National Cash Register Company. Ten years later, National Cash Register had over one thousand employees and was on its way to becoming one of the most successful businesses of its time.

The best way to break a bad habit is to make it impractical to do. Increase the friction until you don't even have the option to act. The brilliance of the cash register was that it automated ethical behavior by making stealing practically impossible. Rather than trying to change the employees, it made the preferred behavior automatic.

Some actions—like installing a cash register—pay off again and again. These onetime choices require a little bit of effort up front but create increasing value over time. I'm fascinated by the idea that a single choice can deliver returns again and again, and I surveyed my readers on their favorite onetime actions that lead to better long-term habits. The table on the following page shares some of the most popular answers.

I'd wager that if the average person were to simply do half of the onetime actions on this list—even if they didn't give another thought to their habits—most would find themselves living a better life a year from now. These onetime actions are a straightforward way to employ the 3rd Law of Behavior Change. They make it easier to sleep well, eat healthy, be productive, save money, and generally live better.

ONETIME ACTIONS THAT LOCK IN GOOD HABITS

Nutrition	Happiness
Buy a water filter to clean your drinking water.	Get a dog.
Use smaller plates to reduce caloric intake.	Move to a friendly, social neighborhood.
Sleep	**General Health**
Buy a good mattress.	Get vaccinated.
Get blackout curtains.	Buy good shoes to avoid back pain.
Remove your television from your bedroom.	Buy a supportive chair or standing desk.
Productivity	**Finance**
Unsubscribe from emails.	Enroll in an automatic savings plan.
Turn off notifications and mute group chats.	Set up automatic bill pay.
Set your phone to silent.	Cut cable service.
Use email filters to clear up your inbox.	Ask service providers to lower your bills.
Delete games and social media apps on your phone.	

Of course, there are many ways to automate good habits and eliminate bad ones. Typically, they involve putting technology to work for you. Technology can transform actions that were once hard, annoying, and complicated into behaviors that are easy, painless, and simple. It is the most reliable and effective way to guarantee the right behavior.

This is particularly useful for behaviors that happen too infrequently to become habitual. Things you have to do monthly or yearly—like rebalancing your investment portfolio—are never repeated frequently enough to become a habit, so they benefit in particular from technology "remembering" to do them for you.

Other examples include:

- Medicine: Prescriptions can be automatically refilled.
- Personal finance: Employees can save for retirement with an automatic wage deduction.
- Cooking: Meal-delivery services can do your grocery shopping.
- Productivity: Social media browsing can be cut off with a website blocker.

When you automate as much of your life as possible, you can spend your effort on the tasks machines cannot do yet. Each habit that we hand over to the authority of technology frees up time and energy to pour into the next stage of growth. As mathematician and philosopher Alfred North Whitehead wrote, "Civilization advances by extending the number of operations we can perform without thinking about them."

Of course, the power of technology can work against us as well. Binge-watching becomes a habit because you have to put more effort in to *stop* looking at the screen than to continue doing so. Instead of pressing a button to advance to the next episode, Netflix or YouTube will autoplay it for you. All you have to do is keep your eyes open.

Technology creates a level of convenience that enables you to act on your smallest whims and desires. At the mere suggestion of hunger, you can have food delivered to your door. At the slightest hint of boredom, you can get lost in the vast expanse of social media. When the effort required to act on your desires becomes effectively zero, you can find yourself slipping into whatever impulse arises at the moment. The downside of automation is that we can find ourselves jumping from easy task to easy task without making time for more difficult, but ultimately more rewarding, work.

I often find myself gravitating toward social media during any downtime. If I feel bored for just a fraction of a second, I reach for my phone. It's easy to write off these minor distractions as "just taking a break," but over time they can accumulate into a serious issue. The constant tug of "just one more minute" can prevent me from doing anything of consequence. (I'm not the only one. The average person spends over two hours per day on social media. What could you do with an extra six hundred hours per year?)

During the year I was writing this book, I experimented with a new time management strategy. Every Monday, my assistant would reset the passwords on all my social media accounts, which logged me out on each device. All week I worked without distraction. On Friday, she would send me the new passwords. I had the entire weekend to enjoy what social media had to offer until Monday morning when she would do it again. (If you don't have an assistant, team up with a friend or family member and reset each other's passwords each week.)

One of the biggest surprises was how quickly I adapted. Within the first week of locking myself out of social media, I realized that I didn't need to check it nearly as often as I had been, and I certainly didn't need it each day. It had simply been so easy that it had become the default. Once my bad habit became impossible, I discovered that I *did* actually have the motivation to work on more meaningful tasks. After I removed the mental candy from my environment, it became much easier to eat the healthy stuff.

When working in your favor, automation can make your good habits inevitable and your bad habits impossible. It is the ultimate way to lock in future behavior rather than relying on willpower in the moment. By utilizing commitment devices, strategic onetime decisions, and technology, you can create an environment of inevitability—a space where good habits are not just an outcome you hope for but an outcome that is virtually guaranteed.

—————————————— Chapter Summary ——————————————

- The inversion of the 3rd Law of Behavior Change is *make it difficult*.
- A commitment device is a choice you make in the present that locks in better behavior in the future.
- The ultimate way to lock in future behavior is to automate your habits.
- Onetime choices—like buying a better mattress or enrolling in an automatic savings plan—are single actions that automate your future habits and deliver increasing returns over time.
- Using technology to automate your habits is the most reliable and effective way to guarantee the right behavior.

HOW TO CREATE A GOOD HABIT

The 1st Law	Make It Obvious
1.1	Fill out the Habits Scorecard. Write down your current habits to become aware of them.
1.2	Use implementation intentions: "I will [BEHAVIOR] at [TIME] in [LOCATION]."
1.3	Use habit stacking: "After [CURRENT HABIT], I will [NEW HABIT]."
1.4	Design your environment. Make the cues of good habits obvious and visible.
The 2nd Law	**Make It Attractive**
2.1	Use temptation bundling. Pair an action you *want* to do with an action you *need* to do.
2.2	Join a culture where your desired behavior is the normal behavior.
2.3	Create a motivation ritual. Do something you enjoy immediately before a difficult habit.
The 3rd Law	**Make It Easy**
3.1	Reduce friction. Decrease the number of steps between you and your good habits.
3.2	Prime the environment. Prepare your environment to make future actions easier.
3.3	Master the decisive moment. Optimize the small choices that deliver outsized impact.
3.4	Use the Two-Minute Rule. Downscale your habits until they can be done in two minutes or less.
3.5	Automate your habits. Invest in technology and onetime purchases that lock in future behavior.
The 4th Law	**Make It Satisfying**

HOW TO BREAK A BAD HABIT

Inversion of the 1st Law	Make It Invisible
1.5	Reduce exposure. Remove the cues of your bad habits from your environment.
Inversion of the 2nd Law	Make It Unattractive
2.4	Reframe your mind-set. Highlight the benefits of avoiding your bad habits.
Inversion of the 3rd Law	Make It Difficult
3.6	Increase friction. Increase the number of steps between you and your bad habits.
3.7	Use a commitment device. Restrict your future choices to the ones that benefit you.
Inversion of the 4th Law	Make It Unsatisfying

You can download a printable version of this habits cheat sheet at:
atomichabits.com/cheatsheet

THE 4TH LAW

Make It Satisfying

15

The Cardinal Rule of
Behavior Change

I N THE LATE 1990S, a public health worker named Stephen Luby left his hometown of Omaha, Nebraska, and bought a one-way ticket to Karachi, Pakistan.

Karachi was one of the most populous cities in the world. By 1998, over nine million people called it home. It was the economic center of Pakistan and a transportation hub, with some of the most active airports and seaports in the region. In the commercial parts of town, you could find all of the standard urban amenities and bustling downtown streets. But Karachi was also one of the *least* livable cities in the world.

Over 60 percent of Karachi's residents lived in squatter settlements and slums. These densely packed neighborhoods were filled with makeshift houses cobbled together from old boards, cinder blocks, and other discarded materials. There was no waste removal system, no electricity grid, no clean water supply. When dry, the streets were a combination of dust and trash. When wet, they became a muddy pit of sewage. Mosquito colonies thrived in pools of stagnant water, and children played among the garbage.

The unsanitary conditions lead to widespread illness and disease.

Contaminated water sources caused epidemics of diarrhea, vomiting, and abdominal pain. Nearly one third of the children living there were malnourished. With so many people crammed into such a small space, viruses and bacterial infections spread rapidly. It was this public health crisis that had brought Stephen Luby to Pakistan.

Luby and his team realized that in an environment with poor sanitation, the simple habit of washing your hands could make a real difference in the health of the residents. But they soon discovered that many people were already aware that handwashing was important.

And yet, despite this knowledge, many residents were washing their hands in a haphazard fashion. Some people would just run their hands under the water quickly. Others would only wash one hand. Many would simply forget to wash their hands before preparing food. Everyone *said* handwashing was important, but few people made a habit out of it. The problem wasn't knowledge. The problem was consistency.

That was when Luby and his team partnered with Procter & Gamble to supply the neighborhood with Safeguard soap. Compared to your standard bar of soap, using Safeguard was a more enjoyable experience.

"In Pakistan, Safeguard was a premium soap," Luby told me. "The study participants commonly mentioned how much they liked it." The soap foamed easily, and people were able to lather their hands with suds. It smelled great. Instantly, handwashing became slightly more pleasurable.

"I see the goal of handwashing promotion not as behavior change but as habit adoption," Luby said. "It is a lot easier for people to adopt a product that provides a strong positive sensory signal, for example the mint taste of toothpaste, than it is to adopt a habit that does not provide pleasurable sensory feedback, like flossing one's teeth. The marketing team at Procter & Gamble talked about trying to create a positive handwashing experience."

Within months, the researchers saw a rapid shift in the health of children in the neighborhood. The rate of diarrhea fell by 52 percent; pneumonia by 48 percent; and impetigo, a bacterial skin infection, by 35 percent.

The long-term effects were even better. "We went back to some of the households in Karachi six years after," Luby told me. "Over 95 percent of households who had been given the soap for free and encouraged to wash their hands had a handwashing station with soap and water available when our study team visited. . . . We had not given any soap to the intervention group for over five years, but during the trial they had become so habituated to wash their hands, that they had maintained the practice." It was a powerful example of the fourth and final Law of Behavior Change: *make it satisfying.*

We are more likely to repeat a behavior when the experience is satisfying. This is entirely logical. Feelings of pleasure—even minor ones like washing your hands with soap that smells nice and lathers well—are signals that tell the brain: "This feels good. Do this again, next time." Pleasure teaches your brain that a behavior is worth remembering and repeating.

Take the story of chewing gum. Chewing gum had been sold commercially throughout the 1800s, but it wasn't until Wrigley launched in 1891 that it became a worldwide habit. Early versions were made from relatively bland resins—chewy, but not tasty. Wrigley revolutionized the industry by adding flavors like Spearmint and Juicy Fruit, which made the product flavorful and fun to use. Then they went a step further and began pushing chewing gum as a pathway to a clean mouth. Advertisements told readers to "Refresh Your Taste."

Tasty flavors and the feeling of a fresh mouth provided little bits of immediate reinforcement and made the product satisfying to use. Consumption skyrocketed, and Wrigley became the largest chewing gum company in the world.

Toothpaste had a similar trajectory. Manufacturers enjoyed great success when they added flavors like spearmint, peppermint, and cinnamon to their products. These flavors don't improve the effectiveness of toothpaste. They simply create a "clean mouth" feel and make the experience of brushing your teeth more pleasurable. My wife actually stopped using Sensodyne because she didn't like the aftertaste. She switched to a brand with a stronger mint flavor, which proved to be more satisfying.

Conversely, if an experience is not satisfying, we have little reason to repeat it. In my research, I came across the story of a woman who had a narcissistic relative who drove her nuts. In an attempt to spend less time with this egomaniac, she acted as dull and as boring as possible whenever he was around. Within a few encounters, *he* started avoiding *her* because he found her so uninteresting.

Stories like these are evidence of the Cardinal Rule of Behavior Change: *What is rewarded is repeated. What is punished is avoided.* You learn what to do in the future based on what you were rewarded for doing (or punished for doing) in the past. Positive emotions cultivate habits. Negative emotions destroy them.

The first three laws of behavior change—*make it obvious, make it attractive,* and *make it easy*—increase the odds that a behavior will be performed *this* time. The fourth law of behavior change—*make it satisfying*—increases the odds that a behavior will be repeated *next* time. It completes the habit loop.

But there is a trick. We are not looking for just any type of satisfaction. We are looking for immediate satisfaction.

THE MISMATCH BETWEEN IMMEDIATE
AND DELAYED REWARDS

Imagine you're an animal roaming the plains of Africa—a giraffe or an elephant or a lion. On any given day, most of your decisions have an immediate impact. You are always thinking about what to eat or where to sleep or how to avoid a predator. You are constantly focused on the present or the very near future. You live in what scientists call an *immediate-return environment* because your actions instantly deliver clear and immediate outcomes.

Now switch back to your human self. In modern society, many of the choices you make today will *not* benefit you immediately. If you do a good job at work, you'll get a paycheck in a few weeks. If you exercise today, perhaps you won't be overweight next year. If you save money now, maybe you'll have enough for retirement decades from now. You live in what scientists call a *delayed-return environment* because you can work for years before your actions deliver the intended payoff.

The human brain did not evolve for life in a delayed-return environment. The earliest remains of modern humans, known as *Homo sapiens sapiens*, are approximately two hundred thousand years old. These were the first humans to have a brain relatively similar to ours. In particular, the neocortex—the newest part of the brain and the region responsible for higher functions like language—was roughly the same size two hundred thousand years ago as today. You are walking around with the same hardware as your Paleolithic ancestors.

It is only recently—during the last five hundred years or so—that society has shifted to a predominantly delayed-return environment.*

---

* The shift to a delayed-return environment likely began around the advent of agriculture ten thousand years ago when farmers began planting crops in anticipation of a harvest months later. However, it was not until recent centuries that our lives became filled with delayed-return choices: career planning, retirement planning, vacation planning, and everything else that occupies our calendars.

Compared to the age of the brain, modern society is brand-new. In the last one hundred years, we have seen the rise of the car, the airplane, the television, the personal computer, the internet, the smartphone, and Beyoncé. The world has changed much in recent years, but human nature has changed little.

Similar to other animals on the African savannah, our ancestors spent their days responding to grave threats, securing the next meal, and taking shelter from a storm. It made sense to place a high value on instant gratification. The distant future was less of a concern. And after thousands of generations in an immediate-return environment, our brains evolved to prefer quick payoffs to long-term ones.

Behavioral economists refer to this tendency as *time inconsistency*. That is, the way your brain evaluates rewards is inconsistent across time.* You value the present more than the future. Usually, this tendency serves us well. A reward that is *certain* right now is typically worth more than one that is merely *possible* in the future. But occasionally, our bias toward instant gratification causes problems.

Why would someone smoke if they know it increases the risk of lung cancer? Why would someone overeat when they know it increases their risk of obesity? Why would someone have unsafe sex if they know it can result in sexually transmitted disease? Once you understand how the brain prioritizes rewards, the answers become clear: the consequences of bad habits are delayed while the rewards are immediate. Smoking might kill you in ten years, but it reduces stress and eases your nicotine cravings *now*. Overeating is harmful in the long run but appetizing in the moment. Sex—safe or not—provides pleasure right away. Disease and infection won't show up for days or weeks, even years.

Every habit produces multiple outcomes across time. Unfortunately,

---

* Time inconsistency is also referred to as *hyperbolic discounting*.

these outcomes are often misaligned. With our bad habits, the immediate outcome usually feels good, but the ultimate outcome feels bad. With good habits, it is the reverse: the immediate outcome is unenjoyable, but the ultimate outcome feels good. The French economist Frédéric Bastiat explained the problem clearly when he wrote, "It almost always happens that when the immediate consequence is favorable, the later consequences are disastrous, and vice versa. . . . Often, the sweeter the first fruit of a habit, the more bitter are its later fruits."

Put another way, the costs of your good habits are in the present. The costs of your bad habits are in the future.

The brain's tendency to prioritize the present moment means you can't rely on good intentions. When you make a plan—to lose weight, write a book, or learn a language—you are actually making plans for your future self. And when you envision what you want your life to be like, it is easy to see the value in taking actions with long-term benefits. We all want better lives for our future selves. However, when the moment of decision arrives, instant gratification usually wins. You are no longer making a choice for Future You, who dreams of being fitter or wealthier or happier. You are choosing for Present You, who wants to be full, pampered, and entertained. As a general rule, the more immediate pleasure you get from an action, the more strongly you should question whether it aligns with your long-term goals.*

With a fuller understanding of what causes our brain to repeat some behaviors and avoid others, let's update the Cardinal Rule of Behavior Change: What is *immediately* rewarded is repeated. What is *immediately* punished is avoided.

---

* This can derail our decision making as well. The brain overestimates the danger of anything that seems like an immediate threat but has almost no likelihood of actually occurring: your plane crashing during a bit of turbulence, a burglar breaking in while you're home alone, a terrorist blowing up the bus you're on. Meanwhile, it underestimates what appears to be a distant threat but is actually very likely: the steady accumulation of fat from eating unhealthy food, the gradual decay of your muscles from sitting at a desk, the slow creep of clutter when you fail to tidy up.

Our preference for instant gratification reveals an important truth about success: because of how we are wired, most people will spend all day chasing quick hits of satisfaction. The road less traveled is the road of delayed gratification. If you're willing to wait for the rewards, you'll face less competition and often get a bigger payoff. As the saying goes, the last mile is always the least crowded.

This is precisely what research has shown. People who are better at delaying gratification have higher SAT scores, lower levels of substance abuse, lower likelihood of obesity, better responses to stress, and superior social skills. We've all seen this play out in our own lives. If you delay watching television and get your homework done, you'll generally learn more and get better grades. If you don't buy desserts and chips at the store, you'll often eat healthier food when you get home. At some point, success in nearly every field requires you to ignore an immediate reward in favor of a delayed reward.

Here's the problem: most people *know* that delaying gratification is the wise approach. They want the benefits of good habits: to be healthy, productive, at peace. But these outcomes are seldom top-of-mind at the decisive moment. Thankfully, it's possible to train yourself to delay gratification—but you need to work with the grain of human nature, not against it. The best way to do this is to add a little bit of immediate pleasure to the habits that pay off in the long-run and a little bit of immediate pain to ones that don't.

HOW TO TURN INSTANT GRATIFICATION TO YOUR ADVANTAGE

The vital thing in getting a habit to stick is to feel successful—even if it's in a small way. The feeling of success is a signal that your habit paid off and that the work was worth the effort.

In a perfect world, the reward for a good habit is the habit itself. In the real world, good habits tend to feel worthwhile only after they have provided you with something. Early on, it's all sacrifice. You've gone to the gym a few times, but you're not stronger or fitter or faster—at least, not in any noticeable sense. It's only months later, once you shed a few pounds or your arms gain some definition, that it becomes easier to exercise for its own sake. In the beginning, you need a reason to stay on track. This is why immediate rewards are essential. They keep you excited while the delayed rewards accumulate in the background.

What we're really talking about here—when we're discussing immediate rewards—is the ending of a behavior. The ending of any experience is vital because we tend to remember it more than other phases. You want the ending of your habit to be satisfying. The best approach is to use *reinforcement*, which refers to the process of using an immediate reward to increase the rate of a behavior. Habit stacking, which we covered in Chapter 5, ties your habit to an immediate cue, which makes it obvious when to start. Reinforcement ties your habit to an immediate reward, which makes it satisfying when you finish.

Immediate reinforcement can be especially helpful when dealing with *habits of avoidance*, which are behaviors you want to stop doing. It can be challenging to stick with habits like "no frivolous purchases" or "no alcohol this month" because nothing happens when you skip happy hour drinks or don't buy that pair of shoes. It can be hard to feel satisfied when there is no action in the first place. All you're doing is resisting temptation, and there isn't much satisfying about that.

One solution is to turn the situation on its head. You want to make avoidance visible. Open a savings account and label it for something you want—maybe "Leather Jacket." Whenever you pass on a purchase, put the same amount of money in the account. Skip your morning latte? Transfer $5. Pass on another month of Netflix? Move $10 over. It's like creating a loyalty program for yourself. The immediate reward of seeing yourself save money toward the leather jacket feels a lot better than being deprived. You are making it satisfying to do nothing.

One of my readers and his wife used a similar setup. They wanted to stop eating out so much and start cooking together more. They labeled their savings account "Trip to Europe." Whenever they skipped going out to eat, they transferred $50 into the account. At the end of the year, they put the money toward the vacation.

It is worth noting that it is important to select short-term rewards that reinforce your identity rather than ones that conflict with it. Buying a new jacket is fine if you're trying to lose weight or read more books, but it doesn't work if you're trying to budget and save money. Instead, taking a bubble bath or going on a leisurely walk are good examples of rewarding yourself with free time, which aligns with your ultimate goal of more freedom and financial independence. Similarly, if your reward for exercising is eating a bowl of ice cream, then you're casting votes for conflicting identities, and it ends up being a wash. Instead, maybe your reward is a massage, which is both a luxury and a vote toward taking care of your body. Now the short-term reward is aligned with your long-term vision of being a healthy person.

Eventually, as intrinsic rewards like a better mood, more energy, and reduced stress kick in, you'll become less concerned with chasing the secondary reward. The identity itself becomes the reinforcer. You do it because it's who you are and it feels good to be you. The more a habit becomes part of your life, the less you need outside encouragement to follow through. Incentives can start a habit. Identity sustains a habit.

That said, it takes time for the evidence to accumulate and a new identity to emerge. Immediate reinforcement helps maintain motivation in the short term while you're waiting for the long-term rewards to arrive.

In summary, a habit needs to be enjoyable for it to last. Simple bits of reinforcement—like soap that smells great or toothpaste that has a refreshing mint flavor or seeing $50 hit your savings account—can offer the immediate pleasure you need to enjoy a habit. And change is easy when it is enjoyable.

—————— Chapter Summary ——————

- The 4th Law of Behavior Change is *make it satisfying.*
- We are more likely to repeat a behavior when the experience is satisfying.
- The human brain evolved to prioritize immediate rewards over delayed rewards.
- The Cardinal Rule of Behavior Change: *What is immediately rewarded is repeated. What is immediately punished is avoided.*
- To get a habit to stick you need to feel immediately successful—even if it's in a small way.
- The first three laws of behavior change—*make it obvious, make it attractive,* and *make it easy*—increase the odds that a behavior will be performed this time. The fourth law of behavior change—*make it satisfying*—increases the odds that a behavior will be repeated next time.

16

How to Stick with Good Habits Every Day

I N 1993, a bank in Abbotsford, Canada, hired a twenty-three-year-old stockbroker named Trent Dyrsmid. Abbotsford was a relatively small suburb, tucked away in the shadow of nearby Vancouver, where most of the big business deals were being made. Given the location, and the fact that Dyrsmid was a rookie, nobody expected too much of him. But he made brisk progress thanks to a simple daily habit.

Dyrsmid began each morning with two jars on his desk. One was filled with 120 paper clips. The other was empty. As soon as he settled in each day, he would make a sales call. Immediately after, he would move one paper clip from the full jar to the empty jar and the process would begin again. "Every morning I would start with 120 paper clips in one jar and I would keep dialing the phone until I had moved them all to the second jar," he told me.

Within eighteen months, Dyrsmid was bringing in $5 million to the firm. By age twenty-four, he was making $75,000 per year—the equivalent of $125,000 today. Not long after, he landed a six-figure job with another company.

I like to refer to this technique as the Paper Clip Strategy and, over the years, I've heard from readers who have employed it in a variety of ways. One woman shifted a hairpin from one container to another whenever she wrote a page of her book. Another man moved a marble from one bin to the next after each set of push-ups.

Making progress is satisfying, and visual measures—like moving paper clips or hairpins or marbles—provide clear evidence of your progress. As a result, they reinforce your behavior and add a little bit of immediate satisfaction to any activity. Visual measurement comes in many forms: food journals, workout logs, loyalty punch cards, the progress bar on a software download, even the page numbers in a book. But perhaps the best way to measure your progress is with a *habit tracker*.

HOW TO KEEP YOUR HABITS ON TRACK

A habit tracker is a simple way to measure whether you did a habit. The most basic format is to get a calendar and cross off each day you stick with your routine. For example, if you meditate on Monday, Wednesday, and Friday, each of those dates gets an *X*. As time rolls by, the calendar becomes a record of your habit streak.

Countless people have tracked their habits, but perhaps the most famous was Benjamin Franklin. Beginning at age twenty, Franklin carried a small booklet everywhere he went and used it to track thirteen personal virtues. This list included goals like "Lose no time. Be always employed in something useful" and "Avoid trifling conversation." At the end of each day, Franklin would open his booklet and record his progress.

Jerry Seinfeld reportedly uses a habit tracker to stick with his streak of writing jokes. In the documentary *Comedian*, he explains that his goal is simply to "never break the chain" of writing jokes every day. In other words, he is not focused on how good or bad a particular joke is or how inspired he feels. He is simply focused on showing up and adding to his streak.

"Don't break the chain" is a powerful mantra. Don't break the chain of sales calls and you'll build a successful book of business. Don't break the chain of workouts and you'll get fit faster than you'd expect. Don't break the chain of creating every day and you will end up with an impressive portfolio. Habit tracking is powerful because it leverages multiple Laws of Behavior Change. It simultaneously makes a behavior obvious, attractive, and satisfying.

Let's break down each one.

Benefit #1: Habit tracking is obvious.

Recording your last action creates a trigger that can initiate your next one. Habit tracking naturally builds a series of visual cues like the streak of *X*'s on your calendar or the list of meals in your food log. When you look at the calendar and see your streak, you'll be reminded to act again. Research has shown that people who track their progress on goals like losing weight, quitting smoking, and lowering blood pressure are all more likely to improve than those who don't. One study of more than sixteen hundred people found that those who kept a daily food log lost twice as much weight as those who did not. The mere act of tracking a behavior can spark the urge to change it.

Habit tracking also keeps you honest. Most of us have a distorted view of our own behavior. We think we act better than we do. Measurement offers one way to overcome our blindness to our own behavior and notice what's really going on each day. One glance at the paper clips in the container and you immediately know how much work you have (or haven't) been putting in. When the evidence is right in front of you, you're less likely to lie to yourself.

Benefit #2: Habit tracking is attractive.

The most effective form of motivation is progress. When we get a signal that we are moving forward, we become more motivated to continue down that path. In this way, habit tracking can have an addictive effect on motivation. Each small win feeds your desire.

This can be particularly powerful on a bad day. When you're feeling down, it's easy to forget about all the progress you have already made. Habit tracking provides visual proof of your hard work—a subtle reminder of how far you've come. Plus, the empty square you see each morning can motivate you to get started because you don't want to lose your progress by breaking the streak.

Benefit #3: Habit tracking is satisfying.

This is the most crucial benefit of all. Tracking can become its own form of reward. It is satisfying to cross an item off your to-do list, to complete an entry in your workout log, or to mark an X on the calendar. It feels good to watch your results grow—the size of your investment portfolio, the length of your book manuscript—and if it feels good, then you're more likely to endure.

Habit tracking also helps keep your eye on the ball: you're focused on the process rather than the result. You're not fixated on getting six-pack abs, you're just trying to keep the streak alive and become the type of person who doesn't miss workouts.

In summary, habit tracking (1) creates a visual cue that can remind you to act, (2) is inherently motivating because you see the progress you are making and don't want to lose it, and (3) feels satisfying whenever you record another successful instance of your habit. Furthermore, habit tracking provides visual proof that you are casting votes for the type of person you wish to become, which is a delightful form of immediate and intrinsic gratification.*

You may be wondering, if habit tracking is so useful, why have I waited so long to talk about it?

Despite all the benefits, I've left this discussion until now for a simple reason: many people resist the idea of tracking and measuring. It can feel like a burden because it forces you into *two* habits: the habit you're trying to build and the habit of tracking it. Counting calories sounds like a hassle when you're already struggling to follow a diet. Writing down every sales call seems tedious when you've got work to do. It feels easier to say, "I'll just eat less." Or, "I'll try harder." Or, "I'll remember to do it." People inevitably tell me things like, "I have a decision journal, but I wish I used it more." Or, "I recorded my workouts for a week, but then quit." I've been there myself. I once made a food log to track my calories. I managed to do it for *one meal* and then gave up.

Tracking isn't for everyone, and there is no need to measure your entire life. But nearly anyone can benefit from it in some form—even if it's only temporary.

What can we do to make tracking easier?

First, whenever possible, measurement should be automated. You'll probably be surprised by how much you're already tracking without knowing it. Your credit card statement tracks how often you go out to eat. Your Fitbit registers how many steps you take and how long you sleep. Your calendar records how many new places you travel to each year. Once you know where to get the data, add a note to your calendar to review it each week or each month, which is more practical than tracking it every day.

Second, manual tracking should be limited to your most important

---

* Interested readers can find a habit tracker template at atomichabits.com/tracker.

habits. It is better to consistently track one habit than to sporadically track ten.

Finally, record each measurement immediately after the habit occurs. The completion of the behavior is the cue to write it down. This approach allows you to combine the habit-stacking method mentioned in Chapter 5 with habit tracking.

The habit stacking + habit tracking formula is:
After [CURRENT HABIT], I will [TRACK MY HABIT].

- After I hang up the phone from a sales call, I will move one paper clip over.
- After I finish each set at the gym, I will record it in my workout journal.
- After I put my plate in the dishwasher, I will write down what I ate.

These tactics can make tracking your habits easier. Even if you aren't the type of person who enjoys recording your behavior, I think you'll find a few weeks of measurements to be insightful. It's always interesting to see how you've *actually* been spending your time.

That said, every habit streak ends at some point. And, more important than any single measurement, is having a good plan for when your habits slide off track.

HOW TO RECOVER QUICKLY WHEN YOUR HABITS BREAK DOWN

No matter how consistent you are with your habits, it is inevitable that life will interrupt you at some point. Perfection is not possible. Before long, an emergency will pop up—you get sick or you have to travel for work or your family needs a little more of your time.

Whenever this happens to me, I try to remind myself of a simple rule: never miss twice.

If I miss one day, I try to get back into it as quickly as possible. Missing one workout happens, but I'm not going to miss two in a row. Maybe I'll eat an entire pizza, but I'll follow it up with a healthy meal. I can't be perfect, but I can avoid a second lapse. As soon as one streak ends, I get started on the next one.

The first mistake is never the one that ruins you. It is the spiral of repeated mistakes that follows. Missing once is an accident. Missing twice is the start of a new habit.

This is a distinguishing feature between winners and losers. Anyone can have a bad performance, a bad workout, or a bad day at work. But when successful people fail, they rebound quickly. The breaking of a habit doesn't matter if the reclaiming of it is fast.

I think this principle is so important that I'll stick to it even if I can't do a habit as well or as completely as I would like. Too often, we fall into an all-or-nothing cycle with our habits. The problem is not slipping up; the problem is thinking that if you can't do something perfectly, then you shouldn't do it at all.

You don't realize how valuable it is to just show up on your bad (or busy) days. Lost days hurt you more than successful days help you. If you start with $100, then a 50 percent gain will take you to $150. But you only need a 33 percent loss to take you back to $100. In other words, avoiding a 33 percent loss is just as valuable as achieving a 50 percent gain. As Charlie Munger says, "The first rule of compounding: Never interrupt it unnecessarily."

This is why the "bad" workouts are often the most important ones. Sluggish days and bad workouts maintain the compound gains you accrued from previous good days. Simply doing something—ten squats, five sprints, a push-up, anything really—is huge. Don't put up a zero. Don't let losses eat into your compounding.

Furthermore, it's not always about what happens during the work-out. It's about being the type of person who doesn't miss workouts. It's easy to train when you feel good, but it's crucial to show up when you don't feel like it—even if you do less than you hope. Going to the gym for five minutes may not improve your performance, but it reaffirms your identity.

The all-or-nothing cycle of behavior change is just one pitfall that can derail your habits. Another potential danger—especially if you are using a habit tracker—is measuring the wrong thing.

KNOWING WHEN (AND WHEN NOT) TO TRACK A HABIT

Say you're running a restaurant and you want to know if your chef is doing a good job. One way to measure success is to track how many customers pay for a meal each day. If more customers come in, the food must be good. If fewer customers come in, something must be wrong.

However, this one measurement—daily revenue—only gives a limited picture of what's really going on. Just because someone pays for a meal doesn't mean they *enjoy* the meal. Even dissatisfied customers are unlikely to dine and dash. In fact, if you're only measuring revenue, the food might be getting worse but you're making up for it with marketing or discounts or some other method. Instead, it may be more effective to track how many customers *finish* their meal or perhaps the percentage of customers who leave a generous tip.

The dark side of tracking a particular behavior is that we become driven by the number rather than the purpose behind it. If your success is measured by quarterly earnings, you will optimize sales, revenue, and accounting for quarterly earnings. If your success is measured by a lower number on the scale, you will optimize for a lower number on the scale, even if that means embracing crash diets, juice cleanses, and fat-loss pills. The human mind wants to "win" whatever game is being played.

This pitfall is evident in many areas of life. We focus on working long hours instead of getting meaningful work done. We care more about getting ten thousand steps than we do about being healthy. We teach for standardized tests instead of emphasizing learning, curiosity, and critical thinking. In short, we optimize for what we measure. When we choose the wrong measurement, we get the wrong behavior.

This is sometimes referred to as Goodhart's Law. Named after the economist Charles Goodhart, the principle states, "When a measure becomes a target, it ceases to be a good measure." Measurement is only useful when it guides you and adds context to a larger picture, not when it consumes you. Each number is simply one piece of feedback in the overall system.

In our data-driven world, we tend to overvalue numbers and undervalue anything ephemeral, soft, and difficult to quantify. We mistakenly think the factors we can measure are the only factors that exist. But just because you can measure something doesn't mean it's the most important thing. And just because you *can't* measure something doesn't mean it's not important at all.

All of this to say, it's crucial to keep habit tracking in its proper place. It can feel satisfying to record a habit and track your progress, but the measurement is not the only thing that matters. Furthermore, there are many ways to measure progress, and sometimes it helps to shift your focus to something entirely different.

This is why *nonscale victories* can be effective for weight loss. The number on the scale may be stubborn, so if you focus solely on that number, your motivation will sag. But you may notice that your skin looks better or you wake up earlier or your sex drive got a boost. All of these are valid ways to track your improvement. If you're not feeling motivated by the number on the scale, perhaps it's time to focus on a different measurement—one that gives you more signals of progress.

No matter how you measure your improvement, habit tracking offers a simple way to make your habits more satisfying. Each measurement provides a little bit of evidence that you're moving in the right direction and a brief moment of immediate pleasure for a job well done.

Chapter Summary

- One of the most satisfying feelings is the feeling of making progress.
- A habit tracker is a simple way to measure whether you did a habit—like marking an X on a calendar.
- Habit trackers and other visual forms of measurement can make your habits satisfying by providing clear evidence of your progress.
- Don't break the chain. Try to keep your habit streak alive.
- Never miss twice. If you miss one day, try to get back on track as quickly as possible.
- Just because you can measure something doesn't mean it's the most important thing.

17

How an Accountability Partner Can Change Everything

AFTER SERVING AS a pilot in World War II, Roger Fisher attended Harvard Law School and spent thirty-four years specializing in negotiation and conflict management. He founded the Harvard Negotiation Project and worked with numerous countries and world leaders on peace resolutions, hostage crises, and diplomatic compromises. But it was in the 1970s and 1980s, as the threat of nuclear war escalated, that Fisher developed perhaps his most interesting idea.

At the time, Fisher was focused on designing strategies that could prevent nuclear war, and he had noticed a troubling fact. Any sitting president would have access to launch codes that could kill millions of people but would never actually see anyone die because he would always be thousands of miles away.

"My suggestion was quite simple," he wrote in 1981. "Put that [nuclear] code number in a little capsule, and then implant that capsule right next to the heart of a volunteer. The volunteer would carry with him a big, heavy butcher knife as he accompanied the President. If ever the President wanted to fire nuclear weapons, the only way he could do so would be for him first, with his own hands, to kill one human be-ing. The President says, 'George, I'm sorry but tens of millions must die.' He has to look at someone and realize what death is—what an innocent death is. Blood on the White House carpet. It's reality brought home.

"When I suggested this to friends in the Pentagon they said, 'My God, that's terrible. Having to kill someone would distort the Presi-dent's judgment. He might never push the button.'"

Throughout our discussion of the 4th Law of Behavior Change we have covered the importance of making good habits immediately sat-isfying. Fisher's proposal is an inversion of the 4th Law: *Make it imme-diately unsatisfying.*

Just as we are more likely to repeat an experience when the ending is satisfying, we are also more likely to avoid an experience when the ending is painful. Pain is an effective teacher. If a failure is painful, it gets fixed. If a failure is relatively painless, it gets ignored. The more immediate and more costly a mistake is, the faster you will learn from it. The threat of a bad review forces a plumber to be good at his job. The possibility of a customer never returning makes restaurants create good food. The cost of cutting the wrong blood vessel makes a surgeon master human anatomy and cut carefully. When the consequences are severe, people learn quickly.

The more immediate the pain, the less likely the behavior. If you want to prevent bad habits and eliminate unhealthy behaviors, then adding an instant cost to the action is a great way to reduce their odds.

We repeat bad habits because they serve us in some way, and that makes them hard to abandon. The best way I know to overcome this predicament is to increase the speed of the punishment associated with the behavior. There can't be a gap between the action and the consequences.

As soon as actions incur an immediate consequence, behavior begins to change. Customers pay their bills on time when they are charged a late fee. Students show up to class when their grade is linked to attendance. We'll jump through a lot of hoops to avoid a little bit of immediate pain.

There is, of course, a limit to this. If you're going to rely on punishment to change behavior, then the strength of the punishment must match the relative strength of the behavior it is trying to correct. To be productive, the cost of procrastination must be greater than the cost of action. To be healthy, the cost of laziness must be greater than the cost of exercise. Getting fined for smoking in a restaurant or failing to recycle adds consequence to an action. Behavior only shifts if the punishment is painful enough and reliably enforced.

In general, the more local, tangible, concrete, and immediate the consequence, the more likely it is to influence individual behavior. The more global, intangible, vague, and delayed the consequence, the less likely it is to influence individual behavior.

Thankfully, there is a straightforward way to add an immediate cost to any bad habit: create a *habit contract*.

THE HABIT CONTRACT

The first seat belt law was passed in New York on December 1, 1984. At the time, just 14 percent of people in the United States regularly wore a seat belt—but that was all about to change.

Within five years, over half of the nation had seat belt laws. Today, wearing a seat belt is enforceable by law in forty-nine of the fifty states. And it's not just the legislation, the number of people wearing seat belts has changed dramatically as well. In 2016, over 88 percent of Americans buckled up each time they got in a car. In just over thirty years, there was a complete reversal in the habits of millions of people.

Laws and regulations are an example of how government can change our habits by creating a social contract. As a society, we collectively agree to abide by certain rules and then enforce them as a group. Whenever a new piece of legislation impacts behavior—seat belt laws, banning smoking inside restaurants, mandatory recycling—it is an example of a social contract shaping our habits. The group agrees to act in a certain way, and if you don't follow along, you'll be punished.

Just as governments use laws to hold citizens accountable, you can create a habit contract to hold yourself accountable. A habit contract is a verbal or written agreement in which you state your commitment to a particular habit and the punishment that will occur if you don't follow through. Then you find one or two people to act as your accountability partners and sign off on the contract with you.

Bryan Harris, an entrepreneur from Nashville, Tennessee, was the first person I saw put this strategy into action. Shortly after the birth of his son, Harris realized he wanted to shed a few pounds. He wrote up a habit contract between himself, his wife, and his personal trainer. The first version read, "Bryan's #1 objective for Q1 of 2017 is to start eating correctly again so he feels better, looks better, and is able to hit his long-term goal of 200 pounds at 10% body fat."

Below that statement, Harris laid out a road map for achieving his ideal outcome:

- Phase #1: Get back to a strict "slow-carb" diet in Q1.
- Phase #2: Start a strict macronutrient tracking program in Q2.
- Phase #3: Refine and maintain the details of his diet and workout program in Q3.

Finally, he wrote out each of the daily habits that would get him to his goal. For example, "Write down all food that he consumes each day and weigh himself each day."

And then he listed the punishment if he failed: "If Bryan doesn't do these two items then the following consequence will be enforced: He will have to dress up each workday and each Sunday morning for the rest of the quarter. Dress up is defined as not wearing jeans, t-shirts, hoodies, or shorts. He will also give Joey (his trainer) $200 to use as he sees fit if he misses one day of logging food."

At the bottom of the page, Harris, his wife, and his trainer all signed the contract.

My initial reaction was that a contract like this seemed overly formal and unnecessary, especially the signatures. But Harris convinced me that signing the contract was an indication of seriousness. "Anytime I skip this part," he said, "I start slacking almost immediately."

Three months later, after hitting his targets for Q1, Harris upgraded his goals. The consequences escalated, too. If he missed his carbohydrate and protein targets, he had to pay his trainer $100. And if he failed to weigh himself, he had to give his wife $500 to use as she saw fit. Perhaps most painfully, if he forgot to run sprints, he had to dress up for work every day and wear an Alabama hat the rest of the quarter—the bitter rival of his beloved Auburn team.

The strategy worked. With his wife and trainer acting as accountability partners and with the habit contract clarifying exactly what to do each day, Harris lost the weight.*

To make bad habits unsatisfying, your best option is to make them painful in the moment. Creating a habit contract is a straightforward way to do exactly that.

Even if you don't want to create a full-blown habit contract, simply

---

* You can see the actual Habit Contracts used by Bryan Harris and get a blank template at atomichabits.com/contract.

having an accountability partner is useful. The comedian Margaret Cho writes a joke or song every day. She does the "song a day" challenge with a friend, which helps them both stay accountable. Knowing that someone is watching can be a powerful motivator. You are less likely to procrastinate or give up because there is an immediate cost. If you don't follow through, perhaps they'll see you as untrustworthy or lazy. Suddenly, you are not only failing to uphold your promises to yourself, but also failing to uphold your promises to others.

You can even automate this process. Thomas Frank, an entrepreneur in Boulder, Colorado, wakes up at 5:55 each morning. And if he doesn't, he has a tweet automatically scheduled that says, "It's 6:10 and I'm not up because I'm lazy! Reply to this for $5 via PayPal (limit 5), assuming my alarm didn't malfunction."

We are always trying to present our best selves to the world. We comb our hair and brush our teeth and dress ourselves carefully because we know these habits are likely to get a positive reaction. We want to get good grades and graduate from top schools to impress potential employers and mates and our friends and family. We care about the opinions of those around us because it helps if others like us. This is precisely why getting an accountability partner or signing a habit contract can work so well.

————————————— Chapter Summary —————————————

- The inversion of the 4th Law of Behavior Change is *make it unsatisfying.*
- We are less likely to repeat a bad habit if it is painful or unsatisfying.

- An accountability partner can create an immediate cost to inaction. We care deeply about what others think of us, and we do not want others to have a lesser opinion of us.
- A habit contract can be used to add a social cost to any behavior. It makes the costs of violating your promises public and painful.
- Knowing that someone else is watching you can be a powerful motivator.

HOW TO CREATE A GOOD HABIT

The 1st Law	Make It Obvious
1.1	Fill out the Habits Scorecard. Write down your current habits to become aware of them.
1.2	Use implementation intentions: "I will [BEHAVIOR] at [TIME] in [LOCATION]."
1.3	Use habit stacking: "After [CURRENT HABIT], I will [NEW HABIT]."
1.4	Design your environment. Make the cues of good habits obvious and visible.
The 2nd Law	**Make It Attractive**
2.1	Use temptation bundling. Pair an action you *want* to do with an action you *need* to do.
2.2	Join a culture where your desired behavior is the normal behavior.
2.3	Create a motivation ritual. Do something you enjoy immediately before a difficult habit.
The 3rd Law	**Make It Easy**
3.1	Reduce friction. Decrease the number of steps between you and your good habits.
3.2	Prime the environment. Prepare your environment to make future actions easier.
3.3	Master the decisive moment. Optimize the small choices that deliver outsized impact.
3.4	Use the Two-Minute Rule. Downscale your habits until they can be done in two minutes or less.
3.5	Automate your habits. Invest in technology and onetime purchases that lock in future behavior.
The 4th Law	**Make It Satisfying**
4.1	Use reinforcement. Give yourself an immediate reward when you complete your habit.
4.2	Make "doing nothing" enjoyable. When avoiding a bad habit, design a way to see the benefits.
4.3	Use a habit tracker. Keep track of your habit streak and "don't break the chain."
4.4	Never miss twice. When you forget to do a habit, make sure you get back on track immediately.

HOW TO BREAK A BAD HABIT

Inversion of the 1st Law	Make It Invisible
1.5	Reduce exposure. Remove the cues of your bad habits from your environment.
Inversion of the 2nd Law	**Make It Unattractive**
2.4	Reframe your mind-set. Highlight the benefits of avoiding your bad habits.
Inversion of the 3rd Law	**Make It Difficult**
3.6	Increase friction. Increase the number of steps between you and your bad habits.
3.7	Use a commitment device. Restrict your future choices to the ones that benefit you.
Inversion of the 4th Law	**Make It Unsatisfying**
4.5	Get an accountability partner. Ask someone to watch your behavior.
4.6	Create a habit contract. Make the costs of your bad habits public and painful.

You can download a printable version of this habits cheat sheet at:
atomichabits.com/cheatsheet

ADVANCED TACTICS

How to Go from Being Merely
Good to Being Truly Great

18

The Truth About Talent
(When Genes Matter and
When They Don't)

MANY PEOPLE ARE familiar with Michael Phelps, who is widely considered to be one of the greatest athletes in history. Phelps has won more Olympic medals not only than any swimmer but also more than any Olympian in *any* sport.

Fewer people know the name Hicham El Guerrouj, but he was a fantastic athlete in his own right. El Guerrouj is a Moroccan runner who holds two Olympic gold medals and is one of the greatest middle-distance runners of all time. For many years, he held the world record in the mile, 1,500-meter, and 2,000-meter races. At the Olympic Games in Athens, Greece, in 2004, he won gold in the 1,500-meter and 5,000-meter races.

These two athletes are wildly different in many ways. (For starters, one competed on land and the other in water.) But most notably, they differ significantly in height. El Guerrouj is five feet, nine inches tall. Phelps is six feet, four inches tall. Despite this seven-inch difference in height, the two men are identical in one respect: Michael Phelps and Hicham El Guerrouj wear the same length inseam on their pants.

How is this possible? Phelps has relatively short legs for his height and a very long torso, the perfect build for swimming. El Guerrouj has incredibly long legs and a short upper body, an ideal frame for distance running.

Now, imagine if these world-class athletes were to switch sports. Given his remarkable athleticism, could Michael Phelps become an Olympic-caliber distance runner with enough training? It's unlikely. At peak fitness, Phelps weighed 194 pounds, which is 40 percent heavier than El Guerrouj, who competed at an ultralight 138 pounds. Taller runners are heavier runners, and every extra pound is a curse when it comes to distance running. Against elite competition, Phelps would be doomed from the start.

Similarly, El Guerrouj might be one of the best runners in history, but it's doubtful he would ever qualify for the Olympics as a swimmer. Since 1976, the average height of Olympic gold medalists in the men's 1,500-meter run is five feet, ten inches. In comparison, the average height of Olympic gold medalists in the men's 100-meter freestyle swim is six feet, four inches. Swimmers tend to be tall and have long backs and arms, which are ideal for pulling through the water. El Guerrouj would be at a severe disadvantage before he ever touched the pool.

The secret to maximizing your odds of success is to choose the right field of competition. This is just as true with habit change as it is with sports and business. Habits are easier to perform, and more satisfying to stick with, when they align with your natural inclinations and abilities. Like Michael Phelps in the pool or Hicham El Guerrouj on the track, you want to play a game where the odds are in your favor.

Embracing this strategy requires the acceptance of the simple truth that people are born with different abilities. Some people don't like to discuss this fact. On the surface, your genes seem to be fixed, and it's no fun to talk about things you cannot control. Plus, phrases like *biological determinism* makes it sound like certain individuals are destined for success and others doomed to failure. But this is a shortsighted view of the influence of genes on behavior.

The strength of genetics is also their weakness. Genes cannot be easily changed, which means they provide a powerful advantage in favorable circumstances and a serious disadvantage in unfavorable circumstances. If you want to dunk a basketball, being seven feet tall is very useful. If you want to perform a gymnastics routine, being seven feet tall is a great hindrance. Our environment determines the suitability of our genes and the utility of our natural talents. When our environment changes, so do the qualities that determine success.

This is true not just for physical characteristics but for mental ones as well. I'm smart if you ask me about habits and human behavior; not so much when it comes to knitting, rocket propulsion, or guitar chords. Competence is highly dependent on context.

The people at the top of any competitive field are not only well trained, they are also well suited to the task. And this is why, if you want to be truly great, selecting the right place to focus is crucial.

In short: genes do not determine your destiny. They determine your areas of opportunity. As physician Gabor Mate notes, "Genes can predispose, but they don't predetermine." The areas where you are genetically predisposed to success are the areas where habits are more likely to be satisfying. The key is to direct your effort toward areas that both excite you and match your natural skills, to align your ambition with your ability.

The obvious question is, "How do I figure out where the odds are in my favor? How do I identify the opportunities and habits that are right for me?" The first place we will look for an answer is by understanding your personality.

HOW YOUR PERSONALITY INFLUENCES YOUR HABITS

Your genes are operating beneath the surface of every habit. Indeed, beneath the surface of every *behavior*. Genes have been shown to influence everything from the number of hours you spend watching television to your likelihood to marry or divorce to your tendency to get addicted to drugs, alcohol, or nicotine. There's a strong genetic component to how obedient or rebellious you are when facing authority, how vulnerable or resistant you are to stressful events, how proactive or reactive you tend to be, and even how captivated or bored you feel during sensory experiences like attending a concert. As Robert Plomin, a behavioral geneticist at King's College in London, told me, "It is now at the point where we have stopped testing to see if traits have a genetic component because we literally can't find a single one that isn't influenced by our genes."

Bundled together, your unique cluster of genetic traits predispose you to a particular personality. Your personality is the set of characteristics that is consistent from situation to situation. The most proven scientific analysis of personality traits is known as the "Big Five," which breaks them down into five spectrums of behavior.

1. Openness to experience: from curious and inventive on one end to cautious and consistent on the other.
2. Conscientiousness: organized and efficient to easygoing and spontaneous.
3. Extroversion: outgoing and energetic to solitary and reserved (you likely know them as extroverts vs. introverts).
4. Agreeableness: friendly and compassionate to challenging and detached.
5. Neuroticism: anxious and sensitive to confident, calm, and stable.

All five characteristics have biological underpinnings. Extroversion, for instance, can be tracked from birth. If scientists play a loud noise in the nursing ward, some babies turn toward it while others turn away. When the researchers tracked these children through life, they found that the babies who turned toward the noise were more likely to grow up to be extroverts. Those who turned away were more likely to become introverts.

People who are high in agreeableness are kind, considerate, and warm. They also tend to have higher natural oxytocin levels, a hormone that plays an important role in social bonding, increases feelings of trust, and can act as a natural antidepressant. You can easily imagine how someone with more oxytocin might be inclined to build habits like writing thank-you notes or organizing social events.

As a third example, consider neuroticism, which is a personality trait all people possess to various degrees. People who are high in neuroticism tend to be anxious and worry more than others. This trait has been linked to hypersensitivity of the amygdala, the portion of the brain responsible for noticing threats. In other words, people who are more sensitive to negative cues in their environment are more likely to score high in neuroticism.

Our habits are not solely determined by our personalities, but there is no doubt that our genes nudge us in a certain direction. Our deeply rooted preferences make certain behaviors easier for some people than for others. You don't have to apologize for these differences or feel guilty about them, but you do have to work with them. A person who scores lower on conscientiousness, for example, will be less likely to be orderly by nature and may need to rely more heavily on environment design to stick with good habits. (As a reminder for the less conscientious readers among us, environment design is a strategy we discussed in Chapters 6 and 12.)

The takeaway is that you should build habits that work for your personality.* People can get ripped working out like a bodybuilder, but if you prefer rock climbing or cycling or rowing, then shape your exercise habit around your interests. If your friend follows a low-carb diet but you find that low-fat works for you, then more power to you. If you want to read more, don't be embarrassed if you prefer steamy romance novels over nonfiction. Read whatever fascinates you.† You don't have to build the habits everyone tells you to build. Choose the habit that best suits you, not the one that is most popular.

There is a version of every habit that can bring you joy and satisfaction. Find it. Habits need to be enjoyable if they are going to stick. This is the core idea behind the 4th Law.

Tailoring your habits to your personality is a good start, but this is not the end of the story. Let's turn our attention to finding and designing situations where you're at a natural advantage.

HOW TO FIND A GAME WHERE THE ODDS ARE IN YOUR FAVOR

Learning to play a game where the odds are in your favor is critical for maintaining motivation and feeling successful. In theory, you can enjoy almost anything. In practice, you are more likely to enjoy the things that come easily to you. People who are talented in a particular area tend to be more competent at that task and are then praised for doing a good job. They stay energized because they are making progress where others have failed, and because they get rewarded with better pay and bigger opportunities, which not only makes them happier but also propels them to produce even higher-quality work. It's a virtuous cycle.

---

* If you are interested in taking a personality test, you can find links to the most reliable tests here: atomichabits.com/personality.
† If it's Harry Potter on repeat, I feel you.

Pick the right habit and progress is easy. Pick the wrong habit and life is a struggle.

How do you pick the right habit? The first step is something we covered in the 3rd Law: *make it easy*. In many cases, when people pick the wrong habit, it simply means they picked a habit that was too difficult. When a habit is easy, you are more likely to be successful. When you are successful, you are more likely to feel satisfied. However, there is another level to consider. In the long-run, if you continue to advance and improve, any area can become challenging. At some point, you need to make sure you're playing the right game for your skillset. How do you figure that out?

The most common approach is trial and error. Of course, there's a problem with this strategy: life is short. You don't have time to try every career, date every eligible bachelor, or play every musical instrument. Thankfully, there is an effective way to manage this conundrum, and it is known as the *explore/exploit trade-off.*

In the beginning of a new activity, there should be a period of exploration. In relationships, it's called dating. In college, it's called the liberal arts. In business, it's called split testing. The goal is to try out many possibilities, research a broad range of ideas, and cast a wide net.

After this initial period of exploration, shift your focus to the best solution you've found—but keep experimenting occasionally. The proper balance depends on whether you're winning or losing. If you are currently winning, you exploit, exploit, exploit. If you are currently losing, you continue to explore, explore, explore.

In the long-run it is probably most effective to work on the strategy that seems to deliver the best results about 80 to 90 percent of the time and keep exploring with the remaining 10 to 20 percent. Google famously asks employees to spend 80 percent of the workweek on their official job and 20 percent on projects of their choice, which has led to the creation of blockbuster products like AdWords and Gmail.

The optimal approach also depends on how much time you have. If you have a lot of time—like someone at the beginning of their career—it makes more sense to explore because once you find the right thing, you still have a good amount of time to exploit it. If you're pressed for time—say, as you come up on the deadline for a project—you should implement the best solution you've found so far and get some results.

As you explore different options, there are a series of questions you can ask yourself to continually narrow in on the habits and areas that will be most satisfying to you:

What feels like fun to me, but work to others? The mark of whether you are made for a task is not whether you love it but whether you can handle the pain of the task easier than most people. When are you enjoying yourself while other people are complaining? The work that hurts you less than it hurts others is the work you were made to do.

What makes me lose track of time? Flow is the mental state you enter when you are so focused on the task at hand that the rest of the world fades away. This blend of happiness and peak performance is what athletes and performers experience when they are "in the zone." It is nearly impossible to experience a flow state and not find the task satisfying at least to some degree.

Where do I get greater returns than the average person? We are continually comparing ourselves to those around us, and a behavior is more likely to be satisfying when the comparison is in our favor. When I started writing at jamesclear.com, my email list grew very quickly. I wasn't quite sure what I was doing well, but I knew that results seemed to be coming faster for me than for some of my colleagues, which motivated me to keep writing.

What comes naturally to me? For just a moment, ignore what you have been taught. Ignore what society has told you. Ignore what others expect of you. Look inside yourself and ask, "What feels natural to me? When have I felt alive? When have I felt like the real me?" No internal judgments or people-pleasing. No second-guessing or self-criticism. Just feelings of engagement and enjoyment. Whenever you feel authentic and genuine, you are headed in the right direction.

To be honest, some of this process is just luck. Michael Phelps and Hicham El Guerrouj were lucky to be born with a rare set of abilities that are highly valued by society and to be placed in the ideal environment for those abilities. We all have limited time on this planet, and the truly great among us are the ones who not only work hard but also have the good fortune to be exposed to opportunities that favor us.

But what if you don't want to leave it up to luck?

If you can't find a game where the odds are stacked in your favor, create one. Scott Adams, the cartoonist behind *Dilbert*, says, "Everyone has at least a few areas in which they could be in the top 25% with some effort. In my case, I can draw better than most people, but I'm hardly an artist. And I'm not any funnier than the average standup comedian who never makes it big, but I'm funnier than most people. The magic is that few people can draw well and write jokes. It's the combination of the two that makes what I do so rare. And when you add in my business background, suddenly I had a topic that few cartoonists could hope to understand without living it."

When you can't win by being better, you can win by being different. By combining your skills, you reduce the level of competition, which makes it easier to stand out. You can shortcut the need for a genetic advantage (or for years of practice) by rewriting the rules. A good player works hard to win the game everyone else is playing. A great player creates a new game that favors their strengths and avoids their weaknesses.

In college, I designed my own major, biomechanics, which was a combination of physics, chemistry, biology, and anatomy. I wasn't smart enough to stand out among the top physics or biology majors, so I created my own game. And because it suited me—I was only taking the courses I was interested in—studying felt like less of a chore. It was also easier to avoid the trap of comparing myself to everyone else. After all, nobody else was taking the same combination of classes, so who could say if they were better or worse?

Specialization is a powerful way to overcome the "accident" of bad genetics. The more you master a specific skill, the harder it becomes for others to compete with you. Many bodybuilders are stronger than the average arm wrestler, but even a massive bodybuilder may lose at arm wrestling because the arm wrestling champ has very specific strength. Even if you're not the most naturally gifted, you can often win by being the best in a very narrow category.

Boiling water will soften a potato but harden an egg. You can't control whether you're a potato or an egg, but you can decide to play a game where it's better to be hard or soft. If you can find a more favorable environment, you can transform the situation from one where the odds are against you to one where they are in your favor.

HOW TO GET THE MOST OUT OF YOUR GENES

Our genes do not eliminate the need for hard work. They clarify it. They tell us *what* to work hard on. Once we realize our strengths, we know where to spend our time and energy. We know which types of opportunities to look for and which types of challenges to avoid. The better we understand our nature, the better our strategy can be.

Biological differences matter. Even so, it's more productive to focus on whether you are fulfilling your own potential than comparing yourself to someone else. The fact that you have a natural limit to any specific ability has nothing to do with whether you are reaching the ceiling of your capabilities. People get so caught up in the fact that they *have* limits that they rarely exert the effort required to get close to them.

Furthermore, genes can't make you successful if you're not doing the work. Yes, it's possible that the ripped trainer at the gym has better genes, but if you haven't put in the same reps, it's impossible to say if you have been dealt a better or worse genetic hand. Until you work as hard as those you admire, don't explain away their success as luck.

In summary, one of the best ways to ensure your habits remain satisfying over the long-run is to pick behaviors that align with your personality and skills. Work hard on the things that come easy.

——————————— Chapter Summary ———————————

- The secret to maximizing your odds of success is to choose the right field of competition.
- Pick the right habit and progress is easy. Pick the wrong habit and life is a struggle.
- Genes cannot be easily changed, which means they provide a powerful advantage in favorable circumstances and a serious disadvantage in unfavorable circumstances.
- Habits are easier when they align with your natural abilities. Choose the habits that best suit you.
- Play a game that favors your strengths. If you can't find a game that favors you, create one.
- Genes do not eliminate the need for hard work. They clarify it. They tell us *what* to work hard on.

19

The Goldilocks Rule: How to Stay Motivated in Life and Work

I N 1955, Disneyland had just opened in Anaheim, California, when a ten-year-old boy walked in and asked for a job. Labor laws were loose back then and the boy managed to land a position selling guidebooks for $0.50 apiece.

Within a year, he had transitioned to Disney's magic shop, where he learned tricks from the older employees. He experimented with jokes and tried out simple routines on visitors. Soon he discovered that what he loved was not performing magic but performing in general. He set his sights on becoming a comedian.

Beginning in his teenage years, he started performing in little clubs around Los Angeles. The crowds were small and his act was short. He was rarely on stage for more than five minutes. Most of the people in the crowd were too busy drinking or talking with friends to pay attention. One night, he literally delivered his stand-up routine to an empty club.

It wasn't glamorous work, but there was no doubt he was getting better. His first routines would only last one or two minutes. By high school, his material had expanded to include a five-minute act and, a few years later, a ten-minute show. At nineteen, he was performing weekly for twenty minutes at a time. He had to read three poems during the show just to make the routine long enough, but his skills continued to progress.

He spent another decade experimenting, adjusting, and practicing. He took a job as a television writer and, gradually, he was able to land his own appearances on talk shows. By the mid-1970s, he had worked his way into being a regular guest on *The Tonight Show* and *Saturday Night Live*.

Finally, after nearly fifteen years of work, the young man rose to fame. He toured sixty cities in sixty-three days. Then seventy-two cities in eighty days. Then eighty-five cities in ninety days. He had 18,695 people attend one show in Ohio. Another 45,000 tickets were sold for his three-day show in New York. He catapulted to the top of his genre and became one of the most successful comedians of his time.

His name is Steve Martin.

Martin's story offers a fascinating perspective on what it takes to stick with habits for the long run. Comedy is not for the timid. It is hard to imagine a situation that would strike fear into the hearts of more people than performing alone on stage and failing to get a single laugh. And yet Steve Martin faced this fear every week for eighteen years. In his words, "10 years spent learning, 4 years spent refining, and 4 years as a wild success."

Why is it that some people, like Martin, stick with their habits—whether practicing jokes or drawing cartoons or playing guitar—while most of us struggle to stay motivated? How do we design habits that pull us in rather than ones that fade away? Scientists have been studying this question for many years. While there is still much to learn, one of the most consistent findings is that the way to maintain motivation and achieve peak levels of desire is to work on tasks of "just manageable difficulty."

The human brain loves a challenge, but only if it is within an optimal zone of difficulty. If you love tennis and try to play a serious match against a four-year-old, you will quickly become bored. It's too easy. You'll win every point. In contrast, if you play a professional tennis player like Roger Federer or Serena Williams, you will quickly lose motivation because the match is too difficult.

Now consider playing tennis against someone who is your equal. As the game progresses, you win a few points and you lose a few. You have a good chance of winning, but only if you really try. Your focus narrows, distractions fade away, and you find yourself fully invested in the task at hand. This is a challenge of just manageable difficulty and it is a prime example of the *Goldilocks Rule.*

The Goldilocks Rule states that humans experience peak motivation when working on tasks that are right on the edge of their current abilities. Not too hard. Not too easy. Just right.

Martin's comedy career is an excellent example of the Goldilocks Rule in practice. Each year, he expanded his comedy routine—but only by a minute or two. He was always adding new material, but he also kept a few jokes that were guaranteed to get laughs. There were just enough victories to keep him motivated and just enough mistakes to keep him working hard.

When you're starting a new habit, it's important to keep the behavior as easy as possible so you can stick with it even when conditions aren't perfect. This is an idea we covered in detail while discussing the 3rd Law of Behavior Change.

Once a habit has been established, however, it's important to continue to advance in small ways. These little improvements and new

THE GOLDILOCKS RULE

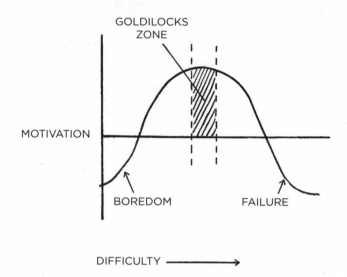

FIGURE 15: Maximum motivation occurs when facing a challenge of just manageable difficulty. In psychology research this is known as the Yerkes–Dodson law, which describes the optimal level of arousal as the midpoint between boredom and anxiety.

challenges keep you engaged. And if you hit the Goldilocks Zone just right, you can achieve a *flow state.**

---

* I have a pet theory about what happens when we achieve a flow state. This isn't confirmed. It's just my guess. Psychologists commonly refer to the brain as operating in two modes: System 1 and System 2. System 1 is fast and instinctual. Generally speaking, processes you can perform very quickly (like habits) are governed by System 1. Meanwhile, System 2 controls thinking processes that are more effortful and slow—like calculating the answer to a difficult math problem. With regard to flow, I like to imagine System 1 and System 2 as residing on opposite ends of the spectrum of thinking. The more automatic a cognitive process is, the more it slides toward the System 1 side of the spectrum. The more effortful a task is, the more it slides toward System 2. Flow, I believe, resides on the razor's edge between System 1 and System 2. You are fully using all of your automatic and implicit knowledge related to the task while also working hard to rise to a challenge beyond your ability. Both brain modes are fully engaged. The conscious and nonconscious are working perfectly in sync.

A flow state is the experience of being "in the zone" and fully immersed in an activity. Scientists have tried to quantify this feeling. They found that to achieve a state of flow, a task must be roughly 4 percent beyond your current ability. In real life it's typically not feasible to quantify the difficulty of an action in this way, but the core idea of the Goldilocks Rule remains: working on challenges of just manageable difficulty—something on the perimeter of your ability—seems crucial for maintaining motivation.

Improvement requires a delicate balance. You need to regularly search for challenges that push you to your edge while continuing to make enough progress to stay motivated. Behaviors need to remain novel in order for them to stay attractive and satisfying. Without variety, we get bored. And boredom is perhaps the greatest villain on the quest for self-improvement.

HOW TO STAY FOCUSED WHEN YOU GET BORED WORKING ON YOUR GOALS

After my baseball career ended, I was looking for a new sport. I joined a weightlifting team and one day an elite coach visited our gym. He had worked with thousands of athletes during his long career, including a few Olympians. I introduced myself and we began talking about the process of improvement.

"What's the difference between the best athletes and everyone else?" I asked. "What do the really successful people do that most don't?"

He mentioned the factors you might expect: genetics, luck, talent. But then he said something I wasn't expecting: "At some point it comes down to who can handle the boredom of training every day, doing the same lifts over and over and over."

His answer surprised me because it's a different way of thinking about work ethic. People talk about getting "amped up" to work on their goals. Whether it's business or sports or art, you hear people say things like, "It all comes down to passion." Or, "You have to really want it." As a result, many of us get depressed when we lose focus or motivation because we think that successful people have some bottomless reserve of passion. But this coach was saying that really successful people *feel* the same lack of motivation as everyone else. The difference is that they still find a way to show up despite the feelings of boredom.

Mastery requires practice. But the more you practice something, the more boring and routine it becomes. Once the beginner gains have been made and we learn what to expect, our interest starts to fade. Sometimes it happens even faster than that. All you have to do is hit the gym a few days in a row or publish a couple of blog posts on time and letting one day slip doesn't feel like much. Things are going well. It's easy to rationalize taking a day off because you're in a good place.

The greatest threat to success is not failure but boredom. We get bored with habits because they stop delighting us. The outcome becomes expected. And as our habits become ordinary, we start derailing our progress to seek novelty. Perhaps this is why we get caught up in a never-ending cycle, jumping from one workout to the next, one diet to the next, one business idea to the next. As soon as we experience the slightest dip in motivation, we begin seeking a new strategy—even if the old one was still working. As Machiavelli noted, "Men desire novelty to such an extent that those who are doing well wish for a change as much as those who are doing badly."

Perhaps this is why many of the most habit-forming products are those that provide continuous forms of novelty. Video games provide visual novelty. Porn provides sexual novelty. Junk foods provide culinary novelty. Each of these experiences offer continual elements of surprise.

In psychology, this is known as a *variable reward*.* Slot machines are the most common real-world example. A gambler hits the jackpot every now and then but not at any predictable interval. The pace of rewards varies. This variance leads to the greatest spike of dopamine, enhances memory recall, and accelerates habit formation.

Variable rewards won't *create* a craving—that is, you can't take a reward people are uninterested in, give it to them at a variable interval, and hope it will change their mind—but they are a powerful way to amplify the cravings we already experience because they reduce boredom.

The sweet spot of desire occurs at a 50/50 split between success and failure. Half of the time you get what you want. Half of the time you don't. You need just enough "winning" to experience satisfaction and just enough "wanting" to experience desire. This is one of the benefits of following the Goldilocks Rule. If you're already interested in a habit, working on challenges of just manageable difficulty is a good way to keep things interesting.

Of course, not all habits have a variable reward component, and you wouldn't want them to. If Google only delivered a useful search result some of the time, I would switch to a competitor pretty quickly. If Uber only picked up half of my trips, I doubt I'd be using that service much longer. And if I flossed my teeth each night and only sometimes ended up with a clean mouth, I think I'd skip it.

Variable rewards or not, no habit will stay interesting forever. At some point, everyone faces the same challenge on the journey of self-improvement: you have to fall in love with boredom.

We all have goals that we would like to achieve and dreams that we

---

* The discovery of variable rewards happened by accident. One day in the lab, the famous Harvard psychologist B. F. Skinner was running low on food pellets during one experiment and making more was a time-consuming process because he had to manually press the pellets in a machine. This situation led him to "ask myself why every press of the lever had to be reinforced." He decided to only give treats to the rats intermittently and, to his surprise, varying the delivery of food did not decrease behavior, but actually increased it.

would like to fulfill, but it doesn't matter what you are trying to become better at, if you only do the work when it's convenient or exciting, then you'll never be consistent enough to achieve remarkable results.

I can guarantee that if you manage to start a habit and keep sticking to it, there will be days when you feel like quitting. When you start a business, there will be days when you don't feel like showing up. When you're at the gym, there will be sets that you don't feel like finishing. When it's time to write, there will be days that you don't feel like typing. But stepping up when it's annoying or painful or draining to do so, that's what makes the difference between a professional and an amateur.

Professionals stick to the schedule; amateurs let life get in the way. Professionals know what is important to them and work toward it with purpose; amateurs get pulled off course by the urgencies of life.

David Cain, an author and meditation teacher, encourages his students to avoid being "fair-weather meditators." Similarly, you don't want to be a fair-weather athlete or a fair-weather writer or a fair-weather anything. When a habit is truly important to you, you have to be willing to stick to it in any mood. Professionals take action even when the mood isn't right. They might not enjoy it, but they find a way to put the reps in.

There have been a lot of sets that I haven't felt like finishing, but I've never regretted doing the workout. There have been a lot of articles I haven't felt like writing, but I've never regretted publishing on schedule. There have been a lot of days I've felt like relaxing, but I've never regretted showing up and working on something that was important to me.

The only way to become excellent is to be endlessly fascinated by doing the same thing over and over. You have to fall in love with boredom.

————————— **Chapter Summary** —————————

- The Goldilocks Rule states that humans experience peak motivation when working on tasks that are right on the edge of their current abilities.
- The greatest threat to success is not failure but boredom.
- As habits become routine, they become less interesting and less satisfying. We get bored.
- Anyone can work hard when they feel motivated. It's the ability to keep going when work isn't exciting that makes the difference.
- Professionals stick to the schedule; amateurs let life get in the way.

20

The Downside of Creating Good Habits

HABITS CREATE THE FOUNDATION FOR MASTERY. In chess, it is only after the basic movements of the pieces have become automatic that a player can focus on the next level of the game. Each chunk of information that is memorized opens up the mental space for more effortful thinking. This is true for any endeavor. When you know the simple movements so well that you can perform them without thinking, you are free to pay attention to more advanced details. In this way, habits are the backbone of any pursuit of excellence.

However, the benefits of habits come at a cost. At first, each repetition develops fluency, speed, and skill. But then, as a habit becomes automatic, you become less sensitive to feedback. You fall into mindless repetition. It becomes easier to let mistakes slide. When you can do it "good enough" on autopilot, you stop thinking about how to do it better.

The upside of habits is that we can do things without thinking. The downside of habits is that you get used to doing things a certain way and stop paying attention to little errors. You assume you're getting better because you're gaining experience. In reality, you are merely reinforcing your current habits—not improving them. In fact, some research has shown that once a skill has been mastered there is usually a slight *decline* in performance over time.

Usually, this minor dip in performance is no cause for worry. You don't need a system to continuously improve how well you brush your teeth or tie your shoes or make your morning cup of tea. With habits like these, good enough is usually good enough. The less energy you spend on trivial choices, the more you can spend it on what really matters.

However, when you want to maximize your potential and achieve elite levels of performance, you need a more nuanced approach. You can't repeat the same things blindly and expect to become exceptional. Habits are necessary, but not sufficient for mastery. What you need is a combination of automatic habits and deliberate practice.

Habits + Deliberate Practice = Mastery

To become great, certain skills *do* need to become automatic. Basketball players need to be able to dribble without thinking before they can move on to mastering layups with their nondominant hand. Surgeons need to repeat the first incision so many times that they could do it with their eyes closed, so that they can focus on the hundreds of variables that arise during surgery. But after one habit has been mastered, you have to return to the effortful part of the work and begin building the next habit.

Mastery is the process of narrowing your focus to a tiny element of success, repeating it until you have internalized the skill, and then using this new habit as the foundation to advance to the next frontier of your development. Old tasks become easier the second time around, but it doesn't get easier overall because now you're pouring your energy into the next challenge. Each habit unlocks the next level of performance. It's an endless cycle.

MASTERING ONE HABIT

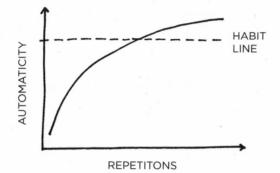

MASTERING A FIELD

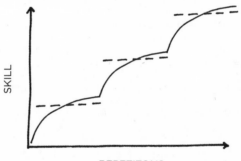

FIGURE 16: The process of mastery requires that you progressively layer improvements on top of one another, each habit building upon the last until a new level of performance has been reached and a higher range of skills has been internalized.

Although habits are powerful, what you need is a way to remain conscious of your performance over time, so you can continue to refine and improve. It is precisely at the moment when you begin to feel like you have mastered a skill—right when things are starting to feel automatic and you are becoming comfortable—that you must avoid slipping into the trap of complacency.

The solution? Establish a system for reflection and review.

HOW TO REVIEW YOUR HABITS
AND MAKE ADJUSTMENTS

In 1986, the Los Angeles Lakers had one of the most talented basketball teams ever assembled, but they are rarely remembered that way. The team started the 1985–1986 NBA season with an astounding 29–5 record. "The pundits were saying that we might be the best team in the history of basketball," head coach Pat Riley said after the season. Surprisingly, the Lakers stumbled in the 1986 playoffs and suffered a season-ending defeat in the Western Conference Finals. The "best team in the history of basketball" didn't even play for the NBA championship.

After that blow, Riley was tired of hearing about how much talent his players had and about how much promise his team held. He didn't want to see flashes of brilliance followed by a gradual fade in performance. He wanted the Lakers to play up to their potential, night after night. In the summer of 1986, he created a plan to do exactly that, a system that he called the Career Best Effort program or CBE.

"When players first join the Lakers," Riley explained, "we track their basketball statistics all the way back to high school. I call this Taking Their Number. We look for an accurate gauge of what a player can do, then build him into our plan for the team, based on the notion that he will maintain and then improve upon his averages."

After determining a player's baseline level of performance, Riley added a key step. He asked each player to "improve their output by at least 1 percent over the course of the season. If they succeeded, it would be a CBE, or Career Best Effort." Similar to the British Cycling team that we discussed in Chapter 1, the Lakers sought peak performance by getting slightly better each day.

Riley was careful to point out that CBE was not merely about points or statistics but about giving your "best effort spiritually and mentally and physically." Players got credit for "allowing an opponent to run into you when you know that a foul will be called against him, diving for loose balls, going after rebounds whether you are likely to get them or not, helping a teammate when the player he's guarding has surged past him, and other 'unsung hero' deeds."

As an example, let's say that Magic Johnson—the Lakers star player at the time—had 11 points, 8 rebounds, 12 assists, 2 steals, and 5 turnovers in a game. Magic also got credit for an "unsung hero" deed by diving after a loose ball (+1). Finally, he played a total of 33 minutes in this imaginary game.

The positive numbers (11 + 8 + 12 + 2 + 1) add up to 34. Then, we subtract the 5 turnovers (34–5) to get 29. Finally, we divide 29 by 33 minutes played.

$$29/33 = 0.879$$

Magic's CBE number here would be 879. This number was calculated for all of a player's games, and it was the average CBE that a player was asked to improve by 1 percent over the season. Riley compared each player's current CBE to not only their past performances but also those of other players in the league. As Riley put it, "We rank team members alongside league opponents who play the same position and have similar role definitions."

Sportswriter Jackie MacMullan noted, "Riley trumpeted the top performers in the league in bold lettering on the blackboard each week and measured them against the corresponding players on his own roster. Solid, reliable players generally rated a score in the 600s, while elite players scored at least 800. Magic Johnson, who submitted 138 triple-doubles in his career, often scored over 1,000."

The Lakers also emphasized year-over-year progress by making historical comparisons of CBE data. Riley said, "We stacked the month of November 1986, next to November 1985, and showed the players whether they were doing better or worse than at the same point last season. Then we showed them how their performance figures for December 1986, stacked up against November's."

The Lakers rolled out CBE in October 1986. Eight months later, they were NBA champions. The following year, Pat Riley led his team to another title as the Lakers became the first team in twenty years to win back-to-back NBA championships. Afterward, he said, "Sustaining an effort is the most important thing for any enterprise. The way to be successful is to learn how to do things right, then do them the same way every time."

The CBE program is a prime example of the power of reflection and review. The Lakers were already talented. CBE helped them get the most out of what they had, and made sure their habits improved rather than declined.

Reflection and review enables the long-term improvement of all habits because it makes you aware of your mistakes and helps you consider possible paths for improvement. Without reflection, we can make excuses, create rationalizations, and lie to ourselves. We have no process for determining whether we are performing better or worse compared to yesterday.

Top performers in all fields engage in various types of reflection and review, and the process doesn't have to be complex. Kenyan runner Eliud Kipchoge is one of the greatest marathoners of all time and an Olympic gold medalist. He still takes notes after every practice in which he reviews his training for the day and searches for areas that can be improved. Similarly, gold medal swimmer Katie Ledecky records her wellness on a scale of 1 to 10 and includes notes on her nutrition and how well she slept. She also records the times posted by other swimmers. At the end of each week, her coach goes over her notes and adds his thoughts.

It's not just athletes, either. When comedian Chris Rock is preparing fresh material, he will first appear at small nightclubs dozens of times and test hundreds of jokes. He brings a notepad on stage and records which bits go over well and where he needs to make adjustments. The few killer lines that survive will form the backbone of his new show.

I know of executives and investors who keep a "decision journal" in which they record the major decisions they make each week, why they made them, and what they expect the outcome to be. They review their choices at the end of each month or year to see where they were correct and where they went wrong.*

Improvement is not just about learning habits, it's also about fine-tuning them. Reflection and review ensures that you spend your time on the right things and make course corrections whenever necessary—like Pat Riley adjusting the effort of his players on a nightly basis. You don't want to keep practicing a habit if it becomes ineffective.

Personally, I employ two primary modes of reflection and review. Each December, I perform an *Annual Review*, in which I reflect on the previous year. I tally my habits for the year by counting up how many articles I published, how many workouts I put in, how many new places I visited, and more.† Then, I reflect on my progress (or lack thereof) by answering three questions:

---

* I created a template for readers interested in keeping a decision journal. It is included as part of the habit journal at atomichabits.com/journal.
† You can see my previous Annual Reviews at jamesclear.com/annual-review.

1. What went well this year?
2. What didn't go so well this year?
3. What did I learn?

Six months later, when summer rolls around, I conduct an *Integrity Report*. Like everyone, I make a lot of mistakes. My Integrity Report helps me realize where I went wrong and motivates me to get back on course. I use it as a time to revisit my core values and consider whether I have been living in accordance with them. This is when I reflect on my identity and how I can work toward being the type of person I wish to become.*

My yearly Integrity Report answers three questions:

1. What are the core values that drive my life and work?
2. How am I living and working with integrity right now?
3. How can I set a higher standard in the future?

These two reports don't take very long—just a few hours per year—but they are crucial periods of refinement. They prevent the gradual slide that happens when I don't pay close attention. They provide an annual reminder to revisit my desired identity and consider how my habits are helping me become the type of person I wish to be. They indicate when I should upgrade my habits and take on new challenges and when I should dial my efforts back and focus on the fundamentals.

Reflection can also bring a sense of perspective. Daily habits are powerful because of how they compound, but worrying too much about every daily choice is like looking at yourself in the mirror from an inch away. You can see every imperfection and lose sight of the

---

* You can see my previous Integrity Reports at jamesclear.com/integrity.

bigger picture. There is too much feedback. Conversely, never reviewing your habits is like never looking in the mirror. You aren't aware of easily fixable flaws—a spot on your shirt, a bit of food in your teeth. There is too little feedback. Periodic reflection and review is like viewing yourself in the mirror from a conversational distance. You can see the important changes you should make without losing sight of the bigger picture. You want to view the entire mountain range, not obsess over each peak and valley.

Finally, reflection and review offers an ideal time to revisit one of the most important aspects of behavior change: identity.

HOW TO BREAK THE BELIEFS THAT HOLD YOU BACK

In the beginning, repeating a habit is essential to build up evidence of your desired identity. As you latch on to that new identity, however, those same beliefs can hold you back from the next level of growth. When working against you, your identity creates a kind of "pride" that encourages you to deny your weak spots and prevents you from truly growing. This is one of the greatest downsides of building habits.

The more sacred an idea is to us—that is, the more deeply it is tied to our identity—the more strongly we will defend it against criticism. You see this in every industry. The schoolteacher who ignores innovative teaching methods and sticks with her tried-and-true lesson plans. The veteran manager who is committed to doing things "his way." The surgeon who dismisses the ideas of her younger colleagues. The band who produces a mind-blowing first album and then gets stuck in a rut. The tighter we cling to an identity, the harder it becomes to grow beyond it.

One solution is to avoid making any single aspect of your identity an overwhelming portion of who you are. In the words of investor Paul

Graham, "keep your identity small." The more you let a single belief define you, the less capable you are of adapting when life challenges you. If you tie everything up in being the point guard or the partner at the firm or whatever else, then the loss of that facet of your life will wreck you. If you're a vegan and then develop a health condition that forces you to change your diet, you'll have an identity crisis on your hands. When you cling too tightly to one identity, you become brittle. Lose that one thing and you lose yourself.

For most of my young life, being an athlete was a major part of my identity. After my baseball career ended, I struggled to find myself. When you spend your whole life defining yourself in one way and that disappears, who are you now?

Military veterans and former entrepreneurs report similar feelings. If your identity is wrapped up in a belief like "I'm a great soldier," what happens when your period of service ends? For many business owners, their identity is something along the lines of "I'm the CEO" or "I'm the founder." If you have spent every waking moment working on your business, how will you feel after you sell the company?

The key to mitigating these losses of identity is to redefine yourself such that you get to keep important aspects of your identity even if your particular role changes.

- "I'm an athlete" becomes "I'm the type of person who is mentally tough and loves a physical challenge."
- "I'm a great soldier" transforms into "I'm the type of person who is disciplined, reliable, and great on a team."
- "I'm the CEO" translates to "I'm the type of person who builds and creates things."

When chosen effectively, an identity can be flexible rather than brittle. Like water flowing around an obstacle, your identity works with the changing circumstances rather than against them.

The following quote from the *Tao Te Ching* encapsulates the ideas perfectly:

> *Men are born soft and supple;*
> *dead, they are stiff and hard.*
> *Plants are born tender and pliant;*
> *dead, they are brittle and dry.*
> *Thus whoever is stiff and inflexible*
> *is a disciple of death.*
> *Whoever is soft and yielding*
> *is a disciple of life.*
> *The hard and stiff will be broken.*
> *The soft and supple will prevail.*
>
> —Lao Tzu

Habits deliver numerous benefits, but the downside is that they can lock us into our previous patterns of thinking and acting—even when the world is shifting around us. Everything is impermanent. Life is constantly changing, so you need to periodically check in to see if your old habits and beliefs are still serving you.

A lack of self-awareness is poison. Reflection and review is the antidote.

Chapter Summary

- The upside of habits is that we can do things without thinking. The downside is that we stop paying attention to little errors.

- Habits + Deliberate Practice = Mastery
- Reflection and review is a process that allows you to remain conscious of your performance over time.
- The tighter we cling to an identity, the harder it becomes to grow beyond it.

Conclusion

The Secret to Results That Last

THERE IS AN ancient Greek parable known as the Sorites Paradox,* which talks about the effect one small action can have when repeated enough times. One formulation of the paradox goes as follows: Can one coin make a person rich? If you give a person a pile of ten coins, you wouldn't claim that he or she is rich. But what if you add another? And another? And another? At some point, you will have to admit that no one can be rich unless one coin can make him or her so.

We can say the same about atomic habits. Can one tiny change transform your life? It's unlikely you would say so. But what if you made another? And another? And another? At some point, you will have to admit that your life was transformed by one small change.

The holy grail of habit change is not a single 1 percent improvement, but a thousand of them. It's a bunch of atomic habits stacking up, each one a fundamental unit of the overall system.

In the beginning, small improvements can often seem meaningless because they get washed away by the weight of the system. Just as one

---

* Sorites is derived from the Greek word *sorós*, which means *heap* or *pile*.

coin won't make you rich, one positive change like meditating for one minute or reading one page each day is unlikely to deliver a noticeable difference.

Gradually, though, as you continue to layer small changes on top of one another, the scales of life start to move. Each improvement is like adding a grain of sand to the positive side of the scale, slowly tilting things in your favor. Eventually, if you stick with it, you hit a tipping point. Suddenly, it feels easier to stick with good habits. The weight of the system is working for you rather than against you.

Over the course of this book, we've looked at dozens of stories about top performers. We've heard about Olympic gold medalists, award-winning artists, business leaders, lifesaving physicians, and star comedians who have all used the science of small habits to master their craft and vault to the top of their field. Each of the people, teams, and companies we have covered has faced different circumstances, but ultimately progressed in the same way: through a commitment to tiny, sustainable, unrelenting improvements.

Success is not a goal to reach or a finish line to cross. It is a system to improve, an endless process to refine. In Chapter 1, I said, "If you're having trouble changing your habits, the problem isn't you. The problem is your system. Bad habits repeat themselves again and again not because you don't want to change, but because you have the wrong system for change."

As this book draws to a close, I hope the opposite is true. With the Four Laws of Behavior Change, you have a set of tools and strategies that you can use to build better systems and shape better habits. Sometimes a habit will be hard to remember and you'll need to *make it obvious*. Other times you won't feel like starting and you'll need to *make it attractive*. In many cases, you may find that a habit will be too difficult and you'll need to *make it easy*. And sometimes, you won't feel like sticking with it and you'll need to *make it satisfying*.

Behaviors are effortless here.   **Behaviors are difficult here.**

Obvious -------------------------- Invisible

Attractive -------------------- Unattractive

Easy ----------------------------------- Hard

Satisfying -------------------- Unsatisfying

You want to push your good habits toward the left side of the spectrum by making them obvious, attractive, easy, and satisfying. Meanwhile, you want to cluster your bad habits toward the right side by making them invisible, unattractive, hard, and unsatisfying.

This is a continuous process. There is no finish line. There is no permanent solution. Whenever you're looking to improve, you can rotate through the Four Laws of Behavior Change until you find the next bottleneck. *Make it obvious. Make it attractive. Make it easy. Make it satisfying.* Round and round. Always looking for the next way to get 1 percent better.

The secret to getting results that last is to never stop making improvements. It's remarkable what you can build if you just don't stop. It's remarkable the business you can build if you don't stop working. It's remarkable the body you can build if you don't stop training. It's remarkable the knowledge you can build if you don't stop learning. It's remarkable the fortune you can build if you don't stop saving. It's remarkable the friendships you can build if you don't stop caring. Small habits don't add up. They compound.

That's the power of atomic habits. Tiny changes. Remarkable results.

Appendix

What Should You Read Next?

THANK YOU SO much for taking the time to read this book. It has been a pleasure sharing my work with you. If you are looking for something to read next, allow me to offer a suggestion.

If you enjoyed *Atomic Habits*, then you may like my other writing as well. My latest articles are sent out in my free weekly newsletter. Subscribers are also the first to hear about my newest books and projects. Finally, in addition to my own work, each year I send out a reading list of my favorite books from other authors on a wide range of subjects.

You can sign up at:

atomichabits.com/newsletter

Little Lessons from the Four Laws

I N THIS BOOK, I have introduced a four-step model for human behavior: cue, craving, response, reward. This framework not only teaches us how to create new habits but also reveals some interesting insights about human behavior.

Problem phase		Solution phase	
1. Cue	2. Craving	3. Response	4. Reward

In this section, I have compiled some lessons (and a few bits of common sense) that are confirmed by the model. The purpose of these examples is to clarify just how useful and wide-ranging this framework is when describing human behavior. Once you understand the model, you'll see examples of it everywhere.

Awareness comes before desire. A craving is created when you assign meaning to a cue. Your brain constructs an emotion or feeling to describe your current situation, and that means a craving can only occur after you have noticed an opportunity.

Happiness is simply the absence of desire. When you observe a cue, but do not desire to change your state, you are content with the current situation. Happiness is not about the achievement of pleasure (which is joy or satisfaction), but about the lack of desire. It arrives when you have no urge to feel differently. Happiness is the state you enter when you no longer want to change your state.

However, happiness is fleeting because a new desire always comes along. As Caed Budris says, "Happiness is the space between one desire being fulfilled and a new desire forming." Likewise, suffering is the space between craving a change in state and getting it.

It is the *idea* of pleasure that we chase. We seek the image of pleasure that we generate in our minds. At the time of action, we do not know what it will be like to attain that image (or even if it will satisfy us). The feeling of satisfaction only comes afterward. This is what the Austrian neurologist Victor Frankl meant when he said that happiness cannot be pursued, it must ensue. Desire is pursued. Pleasure ensues from action.

Peace occurs when you don't turn your observations into problems. The first step in any behavior is observation. You notice a cue, a bit of information, an event. If you do not desire to act on what you observe, then you are at peace.

Craving is about wanting to fix everything. Observation without craving is the realization that you do not need to fix anything. Your desires are not running rampant. You do not crave a change in state. Your mind does not generate a problem for you to solve. You're simply observing and existing.

With a big enough *why* you can overcome any *how*. Friedrich Nietzsche, the German philosopher and poet, famously wrote, "He who has a why to live for can bear almost any how." This phrase harbors an important truth about human behavior. If your motivation and desire are great enough (that is, *why* you are acting), you'll take action even when it is quite difficult. Great craving can power great action—even when friction is high.

Being curious is better than being smart. Being motivated and curious counts for more than being smart because it leads to action. Being smart will never deliver results on its own because it doesn't get you to act. It is desire, not intelligence, that prompts behavior. As Naval Ravikant says, "The trick to doing anything is first cultivating a desire for it."

Emotions drive behavior. Every decision is an emotional decision at some level. Whatever your logical reasons are for taking action, you only feel compelled to act on them because of emotion. In fact, people with damage to emotional centers of the brain can list many reasons for taking action but still will not act because they do not have emotions to drive them. This is why craving comes *before* response. The feeling comes first, and then the behavior.

We can only be rational and logical *after* we have been emotional. The primary mode of the brain is to feel; the secondary mode is to think. Our first response—the fast, nonconscious portion of the brain—is optimized for feeling and anticipating. Our second response—the slow, conscious portion of the brain—is the part that does the "thinking."

Psychologists refer to this as System 1 (feelings and rapid judgments) versus System 2 (rational analysis). The feeling comes first (System 1); the rationality only intervenes later (System 2). This works great when the two are aligned, but it results in illogical and emotional thinking when they are not.

Your response tends to follow your emotions. Our thoughts and actions are rooted in what we find attractive, not necessarily in what is logical. Two people can notice the same set of facts and respond very differently because they run those facts through their unique emotional filter. This is one reason why appealing to emotion is typically more powerful than appealing to reason. If a topic makes someone feel emotional, they will rarely be interested in the data. This is why emotions can be such a threat to wise decision making.

Put another way: most people believe that the reasonable response is the one that benefits them: the one that satisfies their desires. To approach a situation from a more neutral emotional position allows you to base your response on the data rather than the emotion.

Suffering drives progress. The source of all suffering is the desire for a change in state. This is also the source of all progress. The desire to change your state is what powers you to take action. It is wanting more that pushes humanity to seek improvements, develop new technologies, and reach for a higher level. With craving, we are dissatisfied but driven. Without craving, we are satisfied but lack ambition.

Your actions reveal how badly you want something. If you keep saying something is a priority but you never act on it, then you don't really want it. It's time to have an honest conversation with yourself. Your actions reveal your true motivations.

Reward is on the other side of sacrifice. Response (sacrifice of energy) always precedes reward (the collection of resources). The "runner's high" only comes after the hard run. The reward only comes after the energy is spent.

Self-control is difficult because it is not satisfying. A reward is an outcome that satisfies your craving. This makes self-control ineffective because inhibiting our desires does not usually resolve them. Resisting temptation does not satisfy your craving; it just ignores it. It creates space for the craving to pass. Self-control requires you to release a desire rather than satisfy it.

Our expectations determine our satisfaction. The gap between our cravings and our rewards determines how satisfied we feel after taking action. If the mismatch between expectations and outcomes is positive (surprise and delight), then we are more likely to repeat a behavior in the future. If the mismatch is negative (disappointment and frustration), then we are less likely to do so.

For example, if you expect to get $10 and get $100, you feel great. If you expect to get $100 and get $10, you feel disappointed. Your expectation changes your satisfaction. An average experience preceded by high expectations is a disappointment. An average experience preceded by low expectations is a delight. When liking and wanting are approximately the same, you feel satisfied.

$$\text{Satisfaction} = \text{Liking} - \text{Wanting}$$

This is the wisdom behind Seneca's famous quote, "Being poor is not having too little, it is wanting more." If your wants outpace your likes, you'll always be unsatisfied. You're perpetually putting more weight on the problem than the solution.

Happiness is relative. When I first began sharing my writing publicly it took me three months to get one thousand subscribers. When I hit that milestone, I told my parents and my girlfriend. We celebrated. I felt excited and motivated. A few years later, I realized that one thousand people were signing up each day. And yet I didn't even think to tell anyone. It felt normal. I was getting results ninety times faster than before but experiencing little pleasure over it. It wasn't until a few days later that I realized how absurd it was that I wasn't celebrating something that would have seemed like a pipe dream just a few years before.

The pain of failure correlates to the height of expectation. When desire is high, it hurts to not *like* the outcome. Failing to attain something you want hurts more than failing to attain something you didn't think much about in the first place. This is why people say, "I don't want to get my hopes up."

Feelings come both before and after the behavior. Before acting, there is a feeling that motivates you to act—the craving. After acting, there is a feeling that teaches you to repeat the action in the future—the reward.

Cue > Craving (Feeling) > Response > Reward (Feeling)

How we feel influences how we act, and how we act influences how we feel.

Desire initiates. Pleasure sustains. Wanting and liking are the two drivers of behavior. If it's not desirable, you have no reason to do it. Desire and craving are what initiate a behavior. But if it's not enjoyable, you have no reason to repeat it. Pleasure and satisfaction are what sustain a behavior. Feeling motivated gets you to act. Feeling successful gets you to repeat.

Hope declines with experience and is replaced by acceptance. The first time an opportunity arises, there is hope of what could be. Your expectation (cravings) is based solely on *promise*. The second time around, your expectation is grounded in reality. You begin to understand how the process works and your hope is gradually traded for a more accurate prediction and acceptance of the likely outcome.

This is one reason why we continually grasp for the latest get-rich-quick or weight-loss scheme. New plans offer hope because we don't have any experiences to ground our expectations. New strategies seem more appealing than old ones because they can have unbounded hope. As Aristotle noted, "Youth is easily deceived because it is quick to hope." Perhaps this can be revised to "Youth is easily deceived because it only hopes." There is no experience to root the expectation in. In the beginning, hope is all you have.

How to Apply These Ideas
to Business

OVER THE YEARS, I've spoken at Fortune 500 companies and growing start-ups about how to apply the science of small habits to run more effective businesses and build better products. I've compiled many of the most practical strategies into a short bonus chapter. I think you'll find it to be an incredibly useful addition to the main ideas mentioned in *Atomic Habits*.

You can download this chapter at:
atomichabits.com/business

How to Apply These Ideas
to Parenting

ONE OF THE most common questions I hear from readers is something along the lines of, "How can I get my kids to do this stuff?" The ideas in *Atomic Habits* are intended to apply broadly to all of human behavior (teenagers are humans, too), which means you should find plenty of useful strategies in the main text. That said, parenting does face its own set of challenges. As a bonus chapter, I've put together a brief guide on how to apply these ideas specifically to parenting.

You can download this chapter at:
atomichabits.com/parenting

Acknowledgments

I HAVE RELIED HEAVILY on others during the creation of this book. Before anyone else, I must thank my wife, Kristy, who has been indispensable throughout this process. She has played every role a person can play in the writing of a book: spouse, friend, fan, critic, editor, researcher, therapist. It is no exaggeration to say this book would not be the same without her. It might not exist at all. Like everything in our life, we did it together.

Second, I am grateful to my family, not only for their support and encouragement on this book but also for believing in me no matter what project I happen to be working on. I have benefited from many years of support from my parents, grandparents, and siblings. In particular, I want my mom and dad to know that I love them. It is a special feeling to know that your parents are your greatest fans.

Third, to my assistant, Lyndsey Nuckols. At this point, her job defies description as she has been asked to do nearly everything one could imagine for a small business. Thankfully, her skills and talents are more powerful than my questionable management style. Some sections of this book are as much hers as they are mine. I am deeply grateful for her help.

As for the content and writing of the book, I have a long list of people to thank. To start, there are a few people from whom I have learned so much that it would be a crime to not mention them by name. Leo Babauta, Charles Duhigg, Nir Eyal, and BJ Fogg have each influenced my thoughts on habits in meaningful ways. Their work and ideas can be found sprinkled throughout this text. If you enjoyed this book, I'd encourage you to read their writing as well.

At various stages of writing, I benefited from the guidance of many fine editors. Thanks to Peter Guzzardi for walking me through the early stages of the writing process and for a kick in the pants when I really needed it. I am indebted to Blake Atwood and Robin Dellabough for transforming my ugly and insanely long first drafts into a tight, readable manuscript. And I am thankful to Anne Barngrover for her ability to add a little class and poetic style to my writing.

I'd like to thank the many people who read early versions of the manuscript, including Bruce Ammons, Darcey Ansell, Tim Ballard, Vishal Bhardwaj, Charlotte Blank, Jerome Burt, Sim Campbell, Al Carlos, Nicky Case, Julie Chang, Jason Collins, Debra Croy, Roger Dooley, Tiago Forte, Matt Gartland, Andrew Gierer, Randy Giffen, Jon Giganti, Adam Gilbert, Stephan Guyenet, Jeremy Hendon, Jane Horvath, Joakim Jansson, Josh Kaufman, Anne Kavanagh, Chris Klaus, Zeke Lopez, Cady Macon, Cyd Madsen, Kiera McGrath, Amy Mitchell, Anna Moise, Stacey Morris, Tara-Nicholle Nelson, Taylor Pearson, Max Shank, Trey Shelton, Jason Shen, Jacob Zangelidis, and Ari Zelmanow. The book benefited greatly from your feedback.

To the team at Avery and Penguin Random House who made this book a reality, thank you. I owe a debt of special thanks to my publisher, Megan Newman, for her endless patience as I continually pushed back deadlines. She gave me the space I needed to create a book I was proud of and championed my ideas at every step. To Nina, for her ability to transform my writing while still retaining my original message. To

Lindsay, Farin, Casey, and the rest of the PRH team for spreading the message of this book to more people than I could ever reach on my own. To Pete Garceau, for designing a beautiful cover for this book.

And to my agent, Lisa DiMona, for her guidance and insight at every step of the publishing process.

To the many friends and family members who asked "How's the book going?" and offered a word of encouragement when I inevitably replied "Slowly"—thank you. Every author faces a few dark moments when writing a book, and one kind word can be enough to get you to show up again the next day.

I am sure there are people I have forgotten, but I keep an updated list of anyone who has influenced my thinking in meaningful ways at jamesclear.com/thanks.

And finally, to you. Life is short and you have shared some of your precious time with me by reading this book. Thank you.

—May 2018

Notes

IN THIS SECTION, I have included a detailed list of notes, references, and citations for each chapter in the book. I trust that most readers will find this list to be sufficient. However, I also realize that scientific literature changes over time and the references for this book may need to be updated. Furthermore, I fully expect that I have made a mistake somewhere in this book—either in attributing an idea to the wrong person or not giving credit to someone where it is due. (If you believe this to be the case, please email me at james@jamesclear.com so I can fix the issue as soon as possible.)

In addition to the notes below, you can find a full list of updated endnotes and corrections at atomichabits.com/endnotes.

INTRODUCTION

7 **We all deal with setbacks:** What about luck, you might ask? Luck matters, certainly. Habits are not the only thing that influence your success, but they are probably the most important factor that is within your control. And the only self-improvement strategy that makes any sense is to focus on what you can control.

8 **The entrepreneur and investor Naval Ravikant:** Naval Ravikant (@naval), "To write a great book, you must first become the book," Twitter, May 15, 2018, https://twitter.com/naval/status/996460948029362176.

9 **"stimulus, response, reward":** B. F. Skinner, *The Behavior of Organisms* (New York: Appleton-Century-Crofts, 1938).

9 **"cue, routine, reward":** Charles Duhigg, *The Power of Habit: Why We Do What We Do in Life and Business* (New York: Random House, 2014).

CHAPTER 1

13 **just a single gold medal at the Olympic Games:** Matt Slater, "How GB Cycling Went from Tragic to Magic," BBC Sport, April 14, 2008, http://news.bbc.co.uk/sport2/hi/olympics/cycling/7534073.stm.

13 **the Tour de France:** Tom Fordyce, "Tour de France 2017: Is Chris Froome Britain's Least Loved Great Sportsman?" BBC Sport, July 23, 2017, https://www.bbc.com/sport/cycling/40692045.

13 **one of the top bike manufacturers in Europe refused to sell bikes:** Richard Moore, *Mastermind: How Dave Brailsford Reinvented the Wheel* (Glasgow: BackPage Press, 2013).

13 **"The whole principle came from the idea":** Matt Slater, "Olympics Cycling: Marginal Gains Underpin Team GB Dominance," BBC, August 8, 2012, https://www.bbc.com/sport/olympics/19174302.

14 **Brailsford and his coaches began by making small adjustments:** Tim Harford, "Marginal Gains Matter but Gamechangers Transform," Tim Harford, April 2017, http://timharford.com/2017/04/marginal-gains-matter-but-gamechangers-transform.

14 **they even painted the inside of the team truck white:** Eben Harrell, "How 1% Performance Improvements Led to Olympic Gold," *Harvard Business Review*, October 30, 2015, https://hbr.org/2015/10/how-1-performance-improvements-led-to-olympic-gold; Kevin Clark, "How a Cycling Team Turned the Falcons Into NFC Champions," The Ringer, September 12, 2017, https://www.theringer.com/nfl/2017/9/12/16293216/atlanta-falcons-thomas-dimitroff-cycling-team-sky.

14 **Just five years after Brailsford took over:** Technically, the British riders won 57 percent of the road and track cycling medals at the 2008 Olympics. Fourteen gold medals were available in road and track cycling events. The Brits won eight of them.

14 **the Brits raised the bar:** "World and Olympic Records Set at the 2012 Summer Olympics," Wikipedia, December 8, 2017, https://en.wikipedia.org/wiki/World_and_Olympic_records_set_at_the_2012_Summer_Olympics#Cycling.

14 **Bradley Wiggins became the first British cyclist:** Andrew Longmore, "Bradley Wiggins," *Encyclopaedia Britannica*, https://www.britannica.com/bio graphy/Bradley-Wiggins, last modified April 21, 2018.

14 **Chris Froome won:** Karen Sparks, "Chris Froome," *Encyclopaedia Britannica*, https://www.britannica.com/biography/Chris-Froome, last modified October 23, 2017.

15 **During the ten-year span from 2007 to 2017:** "Medals won by the Great Britain Cycling Team at world championships, Olympic Games and Paralympic Games since 2000," British Cycling, https://www.britishcycling.org.uk/gbcyclingteam /article/Gbrst_gb-cyclingteam-GB-Cycling-Team-Medal-History—0?c =EN#K0dWAPjq84CV8Wzw.99, accessed June 8, 2018.

15 **you'll end up thirty-seven times better:** Jason Shen, an entrepreneur and writer, received an early look at this book. After reading this chapter, he remarked: "If the gains were linear, you'd predict to be 3.65x better off. But because it is exponential, the improvement is actually 10x greater." April 3, 2018.

16 **Habits are the compound interest:** Many people have noted how habits multiply over time. Here are some of my favorite articles and books on the subject: Leo Babauta, "The Power of Habit Investments," Zen Habits, January 28, 2013, https://zenhabits.net/bank; Morgan Housel, "The Freakishly Strong Base," Collaborative Fund, October 31, 2017, http://www.collaborativefund.com/blog /the-freakishly-strong-base; Darren Hardy, *The Compound Effect* (New York: Vanguard Press, 2012).

18 **Accomplishing one extra task:** As Sam Altman says, "A small productivity gain, compounded over 50 years, is worth a lot." "Productivity," Sam Altman. April 10, 2018, http://blog.samaltman.com/productivity.

18 **Habits are a double-edged sword:** I'd like to credit Jason Hreha with originally describing habits to me in this way. Jason Hreha (@jhreha), "They're a double edged sword," Twitter, February 21, 2018, https://twitter.com/jhreha/status /966430907371433984.

19 **The more tasks you can handle without thinking:** Michael (@mmay3r), "The foundation of productivity is habits. The more you do automatically, the more you're subsequently freed to do. This effect compounds," Twitter, April 10, 2018, https://twitter.com/mmay3r/status/983837519274889216.

19 **each book you read not only teaches:** This idea—that learning new ideas increases the value of your old ideas—is something I first heard about from Patrick O'Shaughnessy, who writes, "This is why knowledge compounds. Old stuff that was a 4/10 in value can become a 10/10, unlocked by another book in the future." http://investorfieldguide.com/reading-tweet-storm.

20 **Cancer spends 80 percent of its life undetectable:** "How to Live a Longer, Higher Quality Life, with Peter Attia, M.D.," Investor's Field Guide, March 7, 2017, http://investorfieldguide.com/attia.

21 **The San Antonio Spurs:** Matt Moore, "NBA Finals: A Rock, Hammer and Cracking of Spurs' Majesty in Game 7," CBS Sports, June 21, 2013, https://www .cbssports.com/nba/news/nba-finals-a-rock-hammer-and-cracking-of-spurs -majesty-in-game-7.

22 Inspiration for this drawing came from a tweet titled "Deception of linear vs exponential" by @MlichaelW. May 19, 2018. https://twitter.com/MlichaelW /status/997878086132817920.

22 **The seed of every habit:** This paragraph was inspired by a quote from Mr. Mircea, an account on Twitter, who wrote, "each habit began its life as a single decision." https://twitter.com/mistermircea.

25 **the goal cannot be what differentiates the winners from the losers:** Hat tip to CrossFit coach Ben Bergeron for inspiring this quote during a conversation I had with him on February 28, 2017.

27 **You fall to the level of your systems:** This line was inspired by the following quote from Archilochus: "We don't rise to the level of our expectations, we fall to the level of our training."

CHAPTER 2

30 **You can imagine them like the layers of an onion:** Hat tip to Simon Sinek. His "Golden Circle" framework is similar in design, but discusses different topics. For more, see Simon Sinek, *Start with Why: How Great Leaders Inspire Everyone to Take Action* (London: Portfolio/Penguin, 2013), 37.

33 **I resolved to stop chewing my nails:** The quotes used in this section are presented as a conversation for reading clarity, but were originally written by Clark. See: Brian Clark, "The Powerful Psychological Boost that Helps You Make and Break Habits," Further, November 14, 2017, https://further.net/pride-habits.

34 **Research has shown that once a person:** Christopher J. Bryan et al., "Motivating Voter Turnout by Invoking the Self," *Proceedings of the National Academy of Sciences* 108, no. 31 (2011): 12653–12656.

35 **There is internal pressure:** Leon Festinger, *A Theory of Cognitive Dissonance* (Stanford, CA: Stanford University Press, 1957).

37 **Your identity is literally your "repeated beingness":** Technically, *identidem* is a word belonging to the Late Latin language. Also, thanks to Tamar Shippony, a reader of jamesclear.com, who originally told me about the etymology of the word *identity*, which she looked up in the American Heritage Dictionary.

38 **We change bit by bit:** This is another reason atomic habits are such an effective form of change. If you change your identity too quickly and become someone radically different overnight, then you feel as if you lose your sense of self. But if you update and expand your identity gradually, you will find yourself reborn into someone totally new and yet still familiar. Slowly—habit by habit, vote by vote—you become accustomed to your new identity. Atomic habits and gradual improvement are the keys to identity change without identity loss.

CHAPTER 3

43 **Edward Thorndike conducted an experiment:** Peter Gray, *Psychology*, 6th ed. (New York: Worth, 2011), 108–109.

43 **"by some simple act, such as pulling at a loop of cord":** Edward L. Thorndike, "Animal Intelligence: An Experimental Study of the Associative Processes in Animals," *Psychological Review: Monograph Supplements* 2, no. 4 (1898), doi:10.1037/h0092987.

44 **"behaviors followed by satisfying consequences":** This is an abbreviated version of the original quote from Thorndike, which reads: "responses that produce a satisfying effect in a particular situation become more likely to occur again in that situation, and responses that produce a discomforting effect become less

likely to occur again in that situation." For more, see Peter Gray, *Psychology*, 6th ed. (New York: Worth, 2011), 108–109.

45 **Neurological activity in the brain is high:** Charles Duhigg, *The Power of Habit: Why We Do What We Do in Life and Business* (New York: Random House, 2014), 15; Ann M. Graybiel, "Network-Level Neuroplasticity in Cortico-Basal Ganglia Pathways," *Parkinsonism and Related Disorders* 10, no. 5 (2004), doi:10.1016/j.parkreldis.2004.03.007.

45 **"Habits are, simply, reliable solutions":** Jason Hreha, "Why Our Conscious Minds Are Suckers for Novelty," *Revue*, https://www.getrevue.co/profile/jason /issues/why-our-conscious-minds-are-suckers-for-novelty-54131, accessed June 8, 2018.

45 **As habits are created:** John R. Anderson, "Acquisition of Cognitive Skill," *Psychological Review* 89, no. 4 (1982), doi:10.1037/0033–295X.89.4.369.

46 **the brain remembers the past:** Shahram Heshmat, "Why Do We Remember Certain Things, But Forget Others," *Psychology Today*, October 8, 2015, https: //www.psychologytoday.com/us/blog/science-choice/201510/why-do-we -remember-certain-things-forget-others.

46 **the conscious mind is the bottleneck:** William H. Gladstones, Michael A. Regan, and Robert B. Lee, "Division of Attention: The Single-Channel Hypothesis Revisited," *Quarterly Journal of Experimental Psychology Section A* 41, no. 1 (1989), doi:10.1080/14640748908402350.

46 **the conscious mind likes to pawn off tasks:** Daniel Kahneman, *Thinking, Fast and Slow* (New York: Farrar, Straus and Giroux, 2015).

46 **Habits reduce cognitive load:** John R. Anderson, "Acquisition of Cognitive Skill," *Psychological Review* 89, no. 4 (1982), doi:10.1037/0033–295X.89.4.369.

49 **Feelings of pleasure and disappointment:** Antonio R. Damasio, *The Strange Order of Things: Life, Feeling, and the Making of Cultures* (New York: Pantheon Books, 2018); Lisa Feldman Barrett, *How Emotions Are Made* (London: Pan Books, 2018).

CHAPTER 4

59 **The psychologist Gary Klein:** I originally heard about this story from Daniel Kahneman, but it was confirmed by Gary Klein in an email on March 30, 2017. Klein also covers the story in his own book, which uses slightly different quotes: Gary A. Klein, *Sources of Power: How People Make Decisions* (Cambridge, MA: MIT Press, 1998), 43–44.

60 **military analysts can identify which blip on a radar screen:** Gary A. Klein, *Sources of Power: How People Make Decisions* (Cambridge, MA: MIT Press, 1998), 38–40.

60 **Museum curators have been known to discern:** The story of the Getty kouros, covered in Malcolm Gladwell's book *Blink*, is a famous example. The sculpture, initially believed to be from ancient Greece, was purchased for $10 million. The controversy surrounding the sculpture happened later when one expert identified it as a forgery upon first glance.

60 **Experienced radiologists can look at a brain scan:** Siddhartha Mukherjee, "The Algorithm Will See You Now," *New Yorker,* April 3, 2017, https://www .newyorker.com/magazine/2017/04/03/ai-versus-md.

60 **The human brain is a prediction machine:** The German physician Hermann von Helmholtz developed the idea of the brain being a "prediction machine."

62 **the clerk swiped the customer's actual credit card:** Helix van Boron, "What's the Dumbest Thing You've Done While Your Brain Is on Autopilot," Reddit, August 21, 2017, https://www.reddit.com/r/AskReddit/comments/6v1t91 /whats_the_dumbest_thing_youve_done_while_your/dlxa5y9.

62 **she kept asking coworkers if they had washed their hands:** SwordOfTheLlama, "What Strange Habits Have You Picked Up from Your Line of Work," Reddit, January 4, 2016, https://www.reddit.com/r/AskReddit/comments/3zckq6/what _strange_habits_have_you_picked_up_from_your/cyl3nta.

62 **story of a man who had spent years working as a lifeguard:** SwearImaChick, "What Strange Habits Have You Picked Up from Your Line of Work," Reddit, January 4, 2016, https://www.reddit.com/r/AskReddit/comments/3zckq6/what _strange_habits_have_you_picked_up_from_your/cyl681q.

62 **"Until you make the unconscious conscious":** Although this quote by Jung is popular, I had trouble tracking down the original source. It's probably a paraphrase of this passage: "The psychological rule says that when an inner situation is not made conscious, it happens outside, as fate. That is to say, when the individual remains undivided and does not become conscious of his inner opposite, the world must perforce act out the conflict and be torn into opposing halves." For more, see C. G. Jung, *Aion: Researches into the Phenomenology of the Self* (Princeton, NJ: Princeton University Press, 1959), 71.

63 **Pointing-and-Calling reduces errors:** Alice Gordenker, "JR Gestures," *Japan Times,* October 21, 2008, https://www.japantimes.co.jp/news/2008/10/21/reference /jr-gestures/#.WvIG49Mvzu1.

63 **The MTA subway system in New York City:** Allan Richarz, "Why Japan's Rail Workers Can't Stop Pointing at Things," *Atlas Obscura,* March 29, 2017, https:// www.atlasobscura.com/articles/pointing-and-calling-japan-trains.

CHAPTER 5

69 **researchers in Great Britain began working:** Sarah Milne, Sheina Orbell, and Paschal Sheeran, "Combining Motivational and Volitional Interventions to Promote Exercise Participation: Protection Motivation Theory and Implementation Intentions," *British Journal of Health Psychology* 7 (May 2002): 163–184.

70 **implementation intentions are effective:** Peter Gollwitzer and Paschal Sheeran, "Implementation Intentions and Goal Achievement: A Meta-Analysis of Effects and Processes," *Advances in Experimental Social Psychology* 38 (2006): 69–119.

70 **writing down the exact time and date of when you will get a flu shot:** Katherine L. Milkman, John Beshears, James J. Choi, David Laibson, and Brigitte C. Madrian, "Using Implementation Intentions Prompts to Enhance Influenza Vaccination Rates," *Proceedings of the National Academy of Sciences* 108, no. 26 (June 2011): 10415–10420.

70 **recording the time of your colonoscopy appointment:** Katherine L. Milkman, John Beshears, James J. Choi, David Laibson, and Brigitte C. Madrian, "Planning Prompts as a Means of Increasing Preventive Screening Rates," *Preventive Medicine* 56, no. 1 (January 2013): 92–93.

70 **voter turnout increases:** David W. Nickerson and Todd Rogers, "Do You Have a Voting Plan? Implementation Intentions, Voter Turnout, and Organic Plan Making," *Psychological Science* 21, no. 2 (2010): 194–199.

70 **Other successful government programs:** "Policymakers around the World Are Embracing Behavioural Science," *The Economist*, May 18, 2017, https://www.economist.com/news/international/21722163-experimental-iterative-data-driven-approach-gaining-ground-policymakers-around.

70 **people who make a specific plan for when and where:** Edwin Locke and Gary Latham, "Building a Practically Useful Theory of Goal Setting and Task Motivation: A 35-Year Odyssey," *American Psychologist* 57, no. 9 (2002): 705–717, doi:10.1037//0003–066x.57.9.705.

72 **hope is usually higher:** Hengchen Dai, Katherine L. Milkman, and Jason Riis, "The Fresh Start Effect: Temporal Landmarks Motivate Aspirational Behavior," *PsycEXTRA Dataset*, 2014, doi:10.1037/e513702014–058.

72 **writer Jason Zweig noted:** Jason Zweig, "Elevate Your Financial IQ: A Value Packed Discussion with Jason Zweig," interview by Shane Parrish, *The Knowledge Project*, Farnam Street, audio, https://www.fs.blog/2015/10/jason-zweig-knowledge-project.

72 **many ways to use implementation intentions:** For the term *habit stacking*, I am indebted to S. J. Scott, who wrote a book by the same name. From what I understand, his concept is slightly different, but I like the term and thought it appropriate to use in this chapter. Previous writers such as Courtney Carver and Julien Smith have also used the term *habit stacking*, but in different contexts.

72 **The French philosopher Denis Diderot:** "Denis Diderot," *New World Encyclopedia*, http://www.newworldencyclopedia.org/entry/Denis_Diderot, last modified October 26, 2017.

73 **acquired a scarlet robe:** *Encyclopædia Britannica*, vol. 8 (1911), s.v. "Denis Diderot." Diderot's scarlet robe is frequently described as a gift from a friend. However, I could find no original source claiming it was a gift nor any mention of the friend who supplied the robe. If you happen to know any historians specializing in robe acquisitions, feel free to point them my way so we can clarify the mystery of the source of Diderot's famous scarlet robe.

73 **"no more coordination, no more unity, no more beauty":** Denis Diderot, "Regrets for My Old Dressing Gown," trans. Mitchell Abidor, 2005, https://www.marxists.org/reference/archive/diderot/1769/regrets.htm.

73 **The Diderot Effect states:** Juliet Schor, *The Overspent American: Why We Want What We Don't Need* (New York: HarperPerennial, 1999).

74 **which was created by BJ Fogg:** In this chapter, I used the term *habit stacking* to refer to linking a new habit to an old one. For this idea, I give credit to BJ Fogg. In his work, Fogg uses the term *anchoring* to describe this approach because your old habit acts as an "anchor" that keeps the new one in place. No matter what term you prefer, I believe it is a very effective strategy. You can learn more about Fogg's work and his Tiny Habits Method at https://www.tinyhabits.com.

77 **"One in, one out":** Dev Basu (@devbasu), "Have a one-in-one-out policy when buying things," Twitter, February 11, 2018, https://twitter.com/devbasu/status /962778141965000704.

CHAPTER 6

81 **Anne Thorndike:** Anne N. Thorndike et al., "A 2-Phase Labeling and Choice Architecture Intervention to Improve Healthy Food and Beverage Choices," *American Journal of Public Health* 102, no. 3 (2012), doi:10.2105/ajph.2011.300391.

82 **choose products not because of *what* they are:** Multiple research studies have shown that the mere sight of food can make us feel hungry even when we don't have actual physiological hunger. According to one researcher, "dietary behaviors are, in large part, the consequence of automatic responses to contextual food cues." For more, see D. A. Cohen and S. H. Babey, "Contextual Influences on Eating Behaviours: Heuristic Processing and Dietary Choices," *Obesity Reviews* 13, no. 9 (2012), doi:10.1111/j.1467–789x.2012.01001.x; and Andrew J. Hill, Lynn D. Magson, and John E. Blundell, "Hunger and Palatability: Tracking Ratings of Subjective Experience Before, during and after the Consumption of Preferred and Less Preferred Food," *Appetite* 5, no. 4 (1984), doi:10.1016/s0195 –6663(84)80008–2.

83 **Behavior is a function of their Person in the Environment:** Kurt Lewin, *Principles of Topological Psychology* (New York: McGraw-Hill, 1936).

83 ***Suggestion Impulse Buying*:** Hawkins Stern, "The Significance of Impulse Buying Today," *Journal of Marketing* 26, no. 2 (1962), doi:10.2307/1248439.

83 **45 percent of Coca-Cola sales:** Michael Moss, "Nudged to the Produce Aisle by a Look in the Mirror," *New York Times,* August 27, 2013, https://www.nytimes .com/2013/08/28/dining/wooing-us-down-the-produce-aisle.html?_r=0.

83 **People drink Bud Light because:** The more exposure people have to food, the more likely they are to purchase it and eat it. T. Burgoine et al., "Associations between Exposure to Takeaway Food Outlets, Takeaway Food Consumption, and Body Weight in Cambridgeshire, UK: Population Based, Cross Sectional Study," *British Medical Journal* 348, no. 5 (2014), doi:10.1136/bmj.g1464.

84 **The human body has about eleven million sensory receptors:** Timothy D. Wilson, *Strangers to Ourselves: Discovering the Adaptive Unconscious* (Cambridge, MA: Belknap Press, 2004), 24.

84 **half of the brain's resources are used on vision:** B. R. Sheth et al., "Orientation Maps of Subjective Contours in Visual Cortex," *Science* 274, no. 5295 (1996), doi:10.1126/science.274.5295.2110.

85 **When their energy use was obvious and easy to track:** This story was told to Donella Meadows at a conference in Kollekolle, Denmark, in 1973. For more, see Donella Meadows and Diana Wright, *Thinking in Systems: A Primer* (White River Junction, VT: Chelsea Green, 2015), 109.

85 **the stickers cut bathroom cleaning costs:** The actual estimate was 8 percent, but given the variables used, anywhere between 5 percent and 10 percent savings annually is a reasonable guess. Blake Evans-Pritchard, "Aiming to Reduce

Cleaning Costs," *Works That Work*, Winter 2013, https://worksthatwork.com/1/urinal-fly.

88 **sleeping . . . was the only action that happened in that room:** "Techniques involving stimulus control have even been successfully used to help people with insomnia. In short, those who had trouble falling asleep were told to only go to their room and lie in their bed when they were tired. If they couldn't fall asleep, they were told to get up and change rooms. Strange advice, but over time, researchers found that by associating the bed with 'It's time to go to sleep' and not with other activities (reading a book, just lying there, etc.), participants were eventually able to quickly fall asleep due to the repeated process: it became almost automatic to fall asleep in their bed because a successful trigger had been created." For more, see Charles M. Morin et al., "Psychological and Behavioral Treatment of Insomnia: Update of the Recent Evidence (1998–2004)," *Sleep* 29, no. 11 (2006), doi:10.1093/sleep/29.11.1398; and Gregory Ciotti, "The Best Way to Change Your Habits? Control Your Environment," Sparring Mind, https://www.sparringmind.com/changing-habits.

88 **habits can be easier to change in a new environment:** S. Thompson, J. Michaelson, S. Abdallah, V. Johnson, D. Morris, K. Riley, and A. Simms, *'Moments of Change' as Opportunities for Influencing Behaviour: A Report to the Department for Environment, Food and Rural Affairs* (London: Defra, 2011), http://randd.defra.gov.uk/Document.aspx?Document=MomentsofChangeEV0506FinalReportNov2011(2).pdf.

88 **when you step outside your normal environment:** Various research studies have found that it is easier to change your behavior when your environment changes. For example, students change their television watching habits when they transfer schools. Wendy Wood and David T. Neal, "Healthy through Habit: Interventions for Initiating and Maintaining Health Behavior Change," *Behavioral Science and Policy* 2, no. 1 (2016), doi:10.1353/bsp.2016.0008; W. Wood, L. Tam, and M. G. Witt, "Changing Circumstances, Disrupting Habits," *Journal of Personality and Social Psychology* 88, no. 6 (2005), doi:10.1037/0022-3514.88.6.918

88 **You aren't battling old environmental cues:** Perhaps this is why 36 percent of successful changes in behavior were associated with a move to a new place. Melissa Guerrero-Witt, Wendy Wood, and Leona Tam, "Changing Circumstances, Disrupting Habits," *PsycEXTRA Dataset* 88, no. 6 (2005), doi:10.1037/e529412014–144.

CHAPTER 7

91 **Follow-up research revealed that 35 percent of service members:** Lee N. Robins et al., "Vietnam Veterans Three Years after Vietnam: How Our Study Changed Our View of Heroin," *American Journal on Addictions* 19, no. 3 (2010), doi:10.1111/j.1521–0391.2010.00046.x.

91 **the creation of the Special Action Office of Drug Abuse Prevention:** "Excerpts from President's Message on Drug Abuse Control," *New York Times*, June 18, 1971, https://www.nytimes.com/1971/06/18/archives/excerpts-from-presidents-message-on-drug-abuse-control.html.

91 **nine out of ten soldiers who used heroin in Vietnam:** Lee N. Robins, Darlene H. Davis, and David N. Nurco, "How Permanent Was Vietnam Drug Addiction?" *American Journal of Public Health* 64, no. 12 (suppl.) (1974), doi:10.2105 /ajph.64.12_suppl.38.

92 **90 percent of heroin users become re-addicted:** Bobby P. Smyth et al., "Lapse and Relapse following Inpatient Treatment of Opiate Dependence," *Irish Medical Journal* 103, no. 6 (June 2010).

92 **"disciplined" people are better at structuring their lives:** Wilhelm Hofmann et al., "Everyday Temptations: An Experience Sampling Study on How People Control Their Desires," *PsycEXTRA Dataset* 102, no. 6 (2012), doi:10.1037/ e634112013–146.

93 **It's easier to practice self-restraint when you don't have to use it:** "Our prototypical model of self-control is angel on one side and devil on the other, and they battle it out. . . . We tend to think of people with strong willpower as people who are able to fight this battle effectively. Actually, the people who are really good at self-control never have these battles in the first place." For more, see Brian Resnick, "The Myth of Self-Control," *Vox*, November 24, 2016, https://www.vox .com/science-and-health/2016/11/3/13486940/self-control-psychology-myth.

93 **A habit that has been encoded in the mind is ready to be used:** Wendy Wood and Dennis Rünger, "Psychology of Habit," *Annual Review of Psychology* 67, no. 1 (2016), doi:10.1146/annurev-psych-122414–033417.

93 **The cues were still internalized:** "The Biology of Motivation and Habits: Why We Drop the Ball," *Therapist Uncensored)*, 20:00, http://www.therapistuncen sored.com/biology-of-motivation-habits, accessed June 8, 2018.

93 **Shaming obese people with weight-loss presentations:** Sarah E. Jackson, Rebecca J. Beeken, and Jane Wardle, "Perceived Weight Discrimination and Changes in Weight, Waist Circumference, and Weight Status," *Obesity*, 2014, doi:10.1002/oby.20891.

93 **Showing pictures of blackened lungs to smokers:** Kelly McGonigal, *The Upside of Stress: Why Stress Is Good for You, and How to Get Good at It* (New York: Avery, 2016), xv.

94 **showing addicts a picture of cocaine for just thirty-three milliseconds:** Fran Smith, "How Science Is Unlocking the Secrets of Addiction," *National Geographic*, September 2017, https://www.nationalgeographic.com/magazine/2017 /09/the-addicted-brain.

CHAPTER 8

101 **Niko Tinbergen performed a series of experiments:** Nikolaas Tinbergen, *The Herring Gull's World* (London: Collins, 1953); "Nikolaas Tinbergen," *New World Encyclopedia*, http://www.newworldencyclopedia.org/entry/Nikolaas_Tinber gen, last modified September 30, 2016.

102 **the goose will pull *any* nearby round object:** James L. Gould, *Ethology: The Mechanisms and Evolution of Behavior* (New York: Norton, 1982), 36–41.

103 **the modern food industry relies on stretching:** Steven Witherly, *Why Humans Like Junk Food* (New York: IUniverse, 2007).

103 **Nearly every food in a bag:** "Tweaking Tastes and Creating Cravings," *60 Minutes*, November 27, 2011. https://www.youtube.com/watch?v=a7Wh3uq1yTc.

103 **French fries . . . are a potent combination:** Steven Witherly, *Why Humans Like Junk Food* (New York: IUniverse, 2007).

103 **such strategies enable food scientists to find the "bliss point":** Michael Moss, *Salt, Sugar, Fat: How the Food Giants Hooked Us* (London: Allen, 2014).

103 **"We've gotten too good at pushing our own buttons":** This quote originally appeared in Stephan Guyenet, "Why Are Some People 'Carboholics'?" July 26, 2017, http://www.stephanguyenet.com/why-are-some-people-carboholics. The adapted version is given with permission granted in an email exchange with the author in April 2018.

105 **The importance of dopamine:** "The importance of dopamine was discovered by accident. In 1954, James Olds and Peter Milner, two neuroscientists at Mc-Gill University, decided to implant an electrode deep into the center of a rat's brain. The precise placement of the electrode was largely happenstance; at the time, the geography of the mind remained a mystery. But Olds and Milner got lucky. They inserted the needle right next to the nucleus accumbens (NAcc), a part of the brain that generates pleasurable feelings. Whenever you eat a piece of chocolate cake, or listen to a favorite pop song, or watch your favorite team win the World Series, it is your NAcc that helps you feel so happy. But Olds and Milner quickly discovered that too much pleasure can be fatal. They placed the electrodes in several rodents' brains and then ran a small current into each wire, making the NAccs continually excited. The scientists noticed that the rodents lost interest in everything. They stopped eating and drinking. All courtship behavior ceased. The rats would just huddle in the corners of their cages, transfixed by their bliss. Within days, all of the animals had perished. They died of thirst. For more, see Jonah Lehrer, *How We Decide* (Boston: Houghton Mifflin Harcourt, 2009).

105 **neurological processes behind craving and desire:** James Olds and Peter Milner, "Positive Reinforcement Produced by Electrical Stimulation of Septal Area and Other Regions of Rat Brain," *Journal of Comparative and Physiological Psychology* 47, no. 6 (1954), doi:10.1037/h0058775.

105 **rats lost all will to live:** Qun-Yong Zhou and Richard D. Palmiter, "Dopamine-Deficient Mice Are Severely Hypoactive, Adipsic, and Aphagic," *Cell* 83, no. 7 (1995), doi:10.1016/0092-8674(95)90145-0.

105 **without desire, action stopped:** Kent C. Berridge, Isabel L. Venier, and Terry E. Robinson, "Taste Reactivity Analysis of 6-Hydroxydopamine-Induced Aphagia: Implications for Arousal and Anhedonia Hypotheses of Dopamine Function," *Behavioral Neuroscience* 103, no. 1 (1989), doi:10.1037//0735-7044.103.1.36.

106 **the mice developed a craving so strong:** Ross A. Mcdevitt et al., "Serotonergic versus Nonserotonergic Dorsal Raphe Projection Neurons: Differential Participation in Reward Circuitry," *Cell Reports* 8, no. 6 (2014), doi:10.1016/j.celrep.2014.08.037.

106 **the average slot machine player:** Natasha Dow Schüll, *Addiction by Design: Machine Gambling in Las Vegas* (Princeton, NJ: Princeton University Press, 2014), 55.

106 **Habits are a dopamine-driven feedback loop:** I first heard the term *dopamine-driven feedback loop* from Chamath Palihapitiya. For more, see "Chamath Palihapitiya, Founder and CEO Social Capital, on Money as an Instrument of Change," Stanford Graduate School of Business, November 13, 2017, https://www.youtube.com/watch?v=PMotykw0SIk.

106 **dopamine . . . plays a central role in many neurological processes:** Researchers later discovered that endorphins and opioids were responsible for pleasure responses. For more, see V. S. Chakravarthy, Denny Joseph, and Raju S. Bapi, "What Do the Basal Ganglia Do? A Modeling Perspective," *Biological Cybernetics* 103, no. 3 (2010), doi:10.1007/s00422–010–0401-y.

106 **dopamine is released not only when you *experience* pleasure:** Wolfram Schultz, "Neuronal Reward and Decision Signals: From Theories to Data," *Physiological Reviews* 95, no. 3 (2015), doi:10.1152/physrev.00023.2014, fig. 8; Fran Smith, "How Science Is Unlocking the Secrets of Addiction," *National Geographic*, September 2017, https://www.nationalgeographic.com/magazine/2017/09/the-addicted-brain.

106 **whenever dopamine rises, so does your motivation:** Dopamine compels you to seek, explore, and take action: "Dopamine-energized, this mesolimbic SEEKING system, arising from the ventral tegmental area (VTA), encourages foraging, exploration, investigation, curiosity, interest and expectancy. Dopamine fires each time the rat (or human) explores its environment. . . . I can look at the animal and tell when I am tickling its SEEKING system because it is exploring and sniffing." For more, see Karin Badt, "Depressed? Your 'SEEKING' System Might Not Be Working: A Conversation with Neuroscientist Jaak Panksepp," Huffington Post, December 6, 2017, http://www.huffingtonpost.com/karin-badt/depressed-your-seeking-sy_b_3616967.html.

106 **the reward system that is activated in the brain:** Wolfram Schultz, "Multiple Reward Signals in the Brain," *Nature Reviews Neuroscience* 1, no. 3 (2000), doi:10.1038/35044563.

108 **100 percent of the nucleus accumbens is activated during wanting:** Kent Berridge, conversation with author, March 8, 2017.

108 **Byrne hacked his stationary bike:** Hackster Staff, "Netflix and Cycle!," Hackster, July 12, 2017, https://blog.hackster.io/netflix-and-cycle-1734d0179deb.

108 **"eliminating obesity one Netflix binge at a time":** "Cycflix: Exercise Powered Entertainment," Roboro, July 8, 2017, https://www.youtube.com/watch?v=-nc0irLB-iY.

109 **"We see Thursday night as a viewership opportunity":** Jeanine Poggi, "Shonda Rhimes Looks Beyond ABC's Nighttime Soaps," *AdAge*, May 16, 2016, http://adage.com/article/special-report-tv-upfront/shonda-rhimes-abc-soaps/303996.

110 **"more probable behaviors will reinforce less probable behaviors":** Jon E. Roeckelein, *Dictionary of Theories, Laws, and Concepts in Psychology* (Westport, CT: Greenwood Press, 1998), 384.

CHAPTER 9

113 **"A genius is not born, but is educated and trained":** Harold Lundstrom, "Father of 3 Prodigies Says Chess Genius Can Be Taught," *Deseret News*, December 25,

1992, https://www.deseretnews.com/article/266378/FATHER-OF-3-PRODIGIES -SAYS-CHESS-GENIUS-CAN-BE-TAUGHT.html?pg=all.

116 **We imitate the habits of three groups:** Peter J. Richerson and Robert Boyd, *Not by Genes Alone: How Culture Transformed Human Evolution* (Chicago: University of Chicago Press, 2006).

117 **"a person's chances of becoming obese increased by 57 percent":** Nicholas A. Christakis and James H. Fowler, "The Spread of Obesity in a Large Social Network over 32 Years," *New England Journal of Medicine* 357, no. 4 (2007), doi:10.1056/nejmsa066082. J. A. Stockman, "The Spread of Obesity in a Large Social Network over 32 Years," *Yearbook of Pediatrics 2009* (2009), doi:10.1016 /s0084–3954(08)79134–6.

117 **if one person in a relationship lost weight:** Amy A. Gorin et al., "Randomized Controlled Trial Examining the Ripple Effect of a Nationally Available Weight Management Program on Untreated Spouses," *Obesity* 26, no. 3 (2018), doi:10.1002/oby.22098.

117 **Of the ten people in the class, *four* became astronauts:** Mike Massimino, "Finding the Difference Between 'Improbable' and 'Impossible,'" interview by James Altucher, *The James Altucher Show*, January 2017, https://jamesaltucher .com/2017/01/mike-massimino-i-am-not-good-enough.

117 **the higher your best friend's IQ at age eleven or twelve:** Ryan Meldrum, Nicholas Kavish, and Brian Boutwell, "On the Longitudinal Association Between Peer and Adolescent Intelligence: Can Our Friends Make Us Smarter?," *PsyArXiv*, February 10, 2018, doi:10.17605/OSF.IO/TVJ9Z.

118 **Solomon Asch conducted a series of experiments:** Harold Steere Guetzkow, *Groups, Leadership and Men: Research in Human Relations* (Pittsburgh, PA: Carnegie Press, 1951), 177–190.

120 **By the end of the experiment, nearly 75 percent of the subjects:** Follow-up studies show that if there was just one actor in the group who disagreed with the group, then the subject was far more likely to state their true belief that the lines were different lengths. When you have an opinion that dissents from the tribe, it is much easier to stand by it if you have an ally. When you need the strength to stand up to the social norm, find a partner. For more, see Solomon E. Asch, "Opinions and Social Pressure," *Scientific American* 193, no. 5 (1955), doi:10.1038/scientifi-camerican1155–31; and William N. Morris and Robert S. Miller, "The Effects of Consensus-Breaking and Consensus-Preempting Partners on Reduction of Conformity," *Journal of Experimental Social Psychology* 11, no. 3 (1975), doi:10.1016 /s0022–1031(75)80023–0.
Nearly 75 percent of subjects made the incorrect choice at least once. However, considering the total number of responses throughout the experiment, about two thirds were correct. Either way, the point stands: group pressure can significantly alter our ability to make accurate decisions.

120 **a chimpanzee learns an effective way:** Lydia V. Luncz, Giulia Sirianni, Roger Mundry, and Christophe Boesch. "Costly culture: differences in nut-cracking efficiency between wild chimpanzee groups." *Animal Behaviour* 137 (2018): 63–73.

CHAPTER 10

127 **I wouldn't say, "Because I need food to survive":** I heard a similar example from the Twitter account, simpolism (@simpolism), "Let's extend this metaphor. If society is a human body, then the state is the brain. Humans are unaware of their motives. If asked 'why do you eat?' you might say 'bc food tastes good' and not 'bc I need food to survive.' What might a state's food be? (hint: are pills food?)," Twitter, May 7, 2018, https://twitter.com/simpolism/status/993632142700826624.

130 **when emotions and feelings are impaired:** Antoine Bechara et al., "Insensitivity to Future Consequences following Damage to Human Prefrontal Cortex," *Cognition* 50, no. 1–3 (1994), doi:10.1016/0010–0277(94)90018–3.

130 **As the neuroscientist Antonio Damasio:** "When Emotions Make Better Decisions—Antonio Damasio," August 11, 2009. https://www.youtube.com/watch?v=1wup _K2WN0I

131 **You don't "have" to. You "get" to:** I am indebted to my college strength and conditioning coach, Mark Watts, who originally shared this simple mind-set shift with me.

131 **"I'm not confined to my wheelchair":** RedheadBanshee, "What Is Something Someone Said That Forever Changed Your Way of Thinking," Reddit, October 22, 2014, https://www.reddit.com/r/AskReddit/comments/2jzn0j/what_is_something _someone_said_that_forever/clgm4s2.

131 **"It's time to build endurance and get fast":** WingedAdventurer, "Instead of Thinking 'Go Run in the Morning,' Think 'Go Build Endurance and Get Fast.' Make Your Habit a Benefit, Not a Task," Reddit, January 19, 2017, https://www .reddit.com/r/selfimprovement/comments/5ovrqf/instead_of_thinking_go _run_in_the_morning_think/?st=izmz9pks&sh=059312db.

132 **"I'm getting an adrenaline rush to help me concentrate":** Alison Wood Brooks, "Get Excited: Reappraising Pre-Performance Anxiety as Excitement with Minimal Cues," *PsycEXTRA Dataset*, June 2014, doi:10.1037/e578192014–321; Caroline Webb, *How to Have a Good Day* (London: Pan Books, 2017), 238. "Wendy Berry Mendes and Jeremy Jamieson have conducted a number of studies [that] show that people perform better when they decide to interpret their fast heartbeat and breathing as 'a resource that aids performance.'"

132 **Ed Latimore, a boxer and writer:** Ed Latimore (@EdLatimore), "Odd realization: My focus and concentration goes up just by putting my headphones [on] while writing. I don't even have to play any music," Twitter, May 7, 2018, https:// twitter.com/EdLatimore/status/993496493171662849.

CHAPTER 11

142 **In the end, they had little to show for their efforts:** This story comes from page 29 of *Art & Fear* by David Bayles and Ted Orland. In an email conversation with Orland on October 18, 2016, he explained the origins of the story. "Yes, the 'ceramics story' in 'Art & Fear' is indeed true, allowing for some literary license in the retelling. Its real-world origin was as a gambit employed by photographer Jerry Uelsmann to motivate his Beginning Photography students at the

University of Florida. As retold in 'Art & Fear' it faithfully captures the scene as Jerry told it to me—except I replaced photography with ceramics as the medium being explored. Admittedly, it would've been easier to retain photography as the art medium being discussed, but David Bayles (co-author) & I are both photographers ourselves, and at the time we were consciously trying to broaden the range of media being referenced in the text. The intriguing thing to me is that it hardly matters what art form was invoked—the moral of the story appears to hold equally true straight across the whole art spectrum (and even outside the arts, for that matter)." Later in that same email, Orland said, "You have our permission to reprint any or all of the 'ceramics' passage in your forthcoming book." In the end, I settled on publishing an adapted version, which combines their telling of the ceramics story with facts from the original source of Uelsmann's photography students. David Bayles and Ted Orland, *Art & Fear: Observations on the Perils (and Rewards) of Artmaking* (Santa Cruz, CA: Image Continuum Press, 1993), 29.

142 **As Voltaire once wrote:** Voltaire, *La Bégueule. Conte Moral* (1772).

143 *long-term potentiation:* Long-term potentiation was discovered by Terje Lømo in 1966. More precisely, he discovered that when a series of signals was repeatedly transmitted by the brain, there was a persistent effect that lasted afterward that made it easier for those signals to be transmitted in the future.

143 **"Neurons that fire together wire together":** Donald O. Hebb, *The Organization of Behavior: A Neuropsychological Theory* (New York: Wiley, 1949).

143 **In musicians, the cerebellum:** S. Hutchinson, "Cerebellar Volume of Musicians," *Cerebral Cortex* 13, no. 9 (2003), doi:10.1093/cercor/13.9.943.

143 **Mathematicians, meanwhile, have increased gray matter:** A. Verma, "Increased Gray Matter Density in the Parietal Cortex of Mathematicians: A Voxel-Based Morphometry Study," *Yearbook of Neurology and Neurosurgery 2008* (2008), doi:10.1016/s0513–5117(08)79083–5.

144 **When scientists analyzed the brains of taxi drivers in London:** Eleanor A. Maguire et al., "Navigation-Related Structural Change in the Hippocampi of Taxi Drivers," *Proceedings of the National Academy of Sciences* 97, no. 8 (2000), doi:10.1073/pnas.070039597; Katherine Woollett and Eleanor A. Maguire, "Acquiring 'the Knowledge' of London's Layout Drives Structural Brain Changes," *Current Biology* 21, no. 24 (December 2011), doi:10.1016/j.cub.2011.11.018; Eleanor A. Maguire, Katherine Woollett, and Hugo J. Spiers, "London Taxi Drivers and Bus Drivers: A Structural MRI and Neuropsychological Analysis," *Hippocampus* 16, no. 12 (2006), doi:10.1002/hipo.20233.

144 **"the actions become so automatic":** George Henry Lewes, *The Physiology of Common Life* (Leipzig: Tauchnitz, 1860).

144 **repetition is a form of change:** Apparently, Brian Eno says the same thing in his excellent, creatively inspiring Oblique Strategies card set, which I didn't know when I wrote this line! Great minds and all that.

144 **Automaticity is the ability to perform a behavior:** Phillippa Lally et al., "How Are Habits Formed: Modelling Habit Formation in the Real World," *European Journal of Social Psychology* 40, no. 6 (2009), doi:10.1002/ejsp.674.

145 **habits form based on frequency, not time:** Hermann Ebbinghaus was the first person to describe learning curves in his 1885 book *Über das Gedächtnis*. Hermann Ebbinghaus, *Memory: A Contribution to Experimental Psychology* (United States: Scholar Select, 2016).

CHAPTER 12

149 **this difference in shape played a significant role in the spread of agriculture:** Jared Diamond, *Guns, Germs, and Steel: The Fates of Human Societies* (New York: Norton, 1997).

151 **It is human nature to follow the Law of Least Effort:** Deepak Chopra uses the phrase "law of least effort" to describe one of his Seven Spiritual Laws of Yoga. This concept is not related to the principle I am discussing here.

153 **a garden hose that is bent in the middle:** This analogy is a modified version of an idea Josh Waitzkin mentioned in his interview with Tim Ferriss. "The Tim Ferriss Show, Episode 2: Josh Waitzkin," May 2, 2014, audio, https://sound cloud.com/tim-ferriss/the-tim-ferriss-show-episode-2-josh-waitzkin.

154 **"it took American workers three times as long to assemble their sets":** James Surowiecki, "Better All the Time," *New Yorker*, November 10, 2014, https://www.newyorker.com/magazine/2014/11/10/better-time.

154 *addition by subtraction:* Addition by subtraction is an example of a larger principle known as inversion, which I have written about previously at https://james clear.com/inversion. I'm indebted to Shane Parrish for priming my thoughts on this topic by writing about why "avoiding stupidity is easier than seeking brilliance." Shane Parrish, "Avoiding Stupidity Is Easier Than Seeking Brilliance," Farnam Street, June 2014, https://www.fs.blog/2014/06/avoiding-stupidity.

155 **those percentage points represent millions in tax revenue:** Owain Service et al., "East: Four Simple Ways to Apply Behavioural Insights," Behavioural Insights Team, 2015, http://38r8om2xjhhl25mw24492dir.wpengine.netdna-cdn.com/wp-content/uploads/2015/07/BIT-Publication-EAST_FA_WEB.pdf.

156 **Nuckols dialed in his cleaning habits:** Oswald Nuckols is an alias, used by request.

156 **"perfect time to clean the toilet":** Saul_Panzer_NY, "[Question] What One Habit Literally Changed Your Life?" Reddit, June 5, 2017, https://www.reddit.com/r/get disciplined/comments/6fgqbv/question_what_one_habit_literally_changed_your/diieswq.

CHAPTER 13

159 **"arsenal of routines":** Twyla Tharp and Mark Reiter, *The Creative Habit: Learn It and Use It for Life: A Practical Guide* (New York: Simon and Schuster, 2006).

160 **40 to 50 percent of our actions on any given day are done out of habit:** Wendy Wood, "Habits Across the Lifespan," 2006, https://www.researchgate.net/publication/315552294_Habits_Across_the_Lifespan.

160 **habits you follow without thinking:** Benjamin Gardner, "A Review and Analysis of the Use of 'Habit' in Understanding, Predicting and Influencing

Health-Related Behaviour," *Health Psychology Review* 9, no. 3 (2014), doi:10.1080 /17437199.2013.876238.

160 *decisive moments*: Shoutout to Henri Cartier-Bresson, one of the greatest street photographers of all time, who coined the term *decisive moment*, but for an entirely different purpose: capturing amazing images at just the right time.

162 the *Two-Minute Rule*: Hat tip to David Allen, whose version of the Two-Minute Rule states, "If it takes less than two minutes, then do it now." For more, see David Allen, *Getting Things Done* (New York: Penguin, 2015).

164 **power-down habit**: Author Cal Newport uses a shutdown ritual in which he does a last email inbox check, prepares his to-do list for the next day, and says "shutdown complete" to end work for the day. For more, see Cal Newport, *Deep Work* (Boston: Little, Brown, 2016).

165 **He always stopped journaling before it seemed like a hassle**: Greg McKeown, *Essentialism: The Disciplined Pursuit of Less* (New York: Crown, 2014), 78.

165 *habit shaping*: Gail B. Peterson, "A Day of Great Illumination: B. F. Skinner's Discovery of Shaping," *Journal of the Experimental Analysis of Behavior* 82, no. 3 (2004), doi:10.1901/jeab.2004.82–317.

CHAPTER 14

169 **he remained in his study and wrote furiously**: Adèle Hugo and Charles E. Wilbour, *Victor Hugo, by a Witness of His Life* (New York: Carleton, 1864).

170 **A commitment device is a choice you make in the present**: Gharad Bryan, Dean Karlan, and Scott Nelson, "Commitment Devices," *Annual Review of Economics* 2, no. 1 (2010), doi:10.1146/annurev.economics.102308.124324.

170 **outlet timer cuts off the power to router**: "Nir Eyal: Addictive Tech, Killing Bad Habits & Apps for Life Hacking—#260," interview by Dave Asprey, Bulletproof, November 13, 2015, https://blog.bulletproof.com/nir-eyal-life-hacking -260/.

170 **This is also referred to as a "Ulysses pact"**: Peter Ubel, "The Ulysses Strategy," *The New Yorker*, December 11, 2014, https://www.newyorker.com/business /currency/ulysses-strategy-self-control.

171 **Patterson's business went from losing money to making $5,000 in profit**: "John H. Patterson—Ringing Up Success with the Incorruptible Cashier," Dayton Innovation Legacy, http://www.daytoninnovationlegacy.org/patterson.html, accessed June 8, 2016.

172 **onetime actions that lead to better long-term habits**: James Clear (@james_clear), "What are one-time actions that pay off again and again in the future?" Twitter, February 11, 2018, https://twitter.com/james_clear/status/962694722702790659

174 **"Civilization advances by extending the number of operations"**: Alfred North Whitehead, *Introduction to Mathematics* (Cambridge, UK: Cambridge University Press, 1911), 166.

175 **The average person spends over two hours per day on social media**: "GWI Social," GlobalWebIndex, 2017, Q3, https://cdn2.hubspot.net/hubfs/304927 /Downloads/GWI%20Social%20Summary%20Q3%202017.pdf.

CHAPTER 15

183 **over nine million people called it home:** "Population Size and Growth of Major Cities, 1998 Census," Population Census Organization, http://www.statpak .gov.pk/depts/pco/statistics/pop_major_cities/pop_major_cities.html.

183 **Over 60 percent of Karachi's residents:** Sabiah Askari, *Studies on Karachi: Papers Presented at the Karachi Conference 2013* (Newcastle upon Tyne, UK: Cambridge Scholars, 2015).

184 **It was this public health crisis that had brought Luby to Pakistan:** Atul Gawande, *The Checklist Manifesto: How to Get Things Right* (Gurgaon, India: Penguin Random House, 2014).

184 **"In Pakistan, Safeguard was a premium soap":** All quotes in this section are from an email conversation with Stephen Luby on May 28, 2018.

185 **The rate of diarrhea fell by 52 percent:** Stephen P. Luby et al., "Effect of Handwashing on Child Health: A Randomised Controlled Trial," *Lancet* 366, no. 9481 (2005), doi:10.1016/s0140–6736(05)66912–7.

185 **"Over 95 percent of households":** Anna Bowen, Mubina Agboatwalla, Tracy Ayers, Timothy Tobery, Maria Tariq, and Stephen P. Luby. "Sustained improvements in handwashing indicators more than 5 years after a cluster-randomised, community-based trial of handwashing promotion in Karachi, Pakistan," *Tropical Medicine & International Health* 18, no. 3 (2013): 259–267. https://www .ncbi.nlm.nih.gov/pmc/articles/PMC4626884/

185 **Chewing gum had been sold commercially throughout the 1800s:** Mary Bellis, "How We Have Bubble Gum Today," ThoughtCo, October 16, 2017, https:// www.thoughtco.com/history-of-bubble-and-chewing-gum-1991856.

185 **Wrigley revolutionized the industry:** Jennifer P. Mathews, *Chicle: The Chewing Gum of the Americas, from the Ancient Maya to William Wrigley* (Tucson: University of Arizona Press, 2009), 44–46.

185 **Wrigley became the largest chewing gum company:** "William Wrigley, Jr.," *Encyclopædia Britannica*, https://www.britannica.com/biography/William-Wrigley -Jr, accessed June 8, 2018.

186 **Toothpaste had a similar trajectory:** Charles Duhigg, *The Power of Habit: Why We Do What We Do in Life and Business* (New York: Random House, 2014), chap. 2.

186 **he started avoiding her:** Sparkly_alpaca, "What Are the Coolest Psychology Tricks That You Know or Have Used?" Reddit, November 11, 2016, https://www .reddit.com/r/AskReddit/comments/5cgqbj/what_are_the_coolest_psychology _tricks_that_you/d9wcqsr/.

187 **The earliest remains of modern humans:** Ian Mcdougall, Francis H. Brown, and John G. Fleagle, "Stratigraphic Placement and Age of Modern Humans from Kibish, Ethiopia," *Nature* 433, no. 7027 (2005), doi:10.1038/nature03258.

187 **the neocortex . . . was roughly the same:** Some research indicates that the size of the human brain reached modern proportions around three hundred thousand years ago. Evolution never stops, of course, and the shape of the structure appears to have continued to evolve in meaningful ways until it reached both modern size and shape sometime between one hundred thousand and thirty-five

thousand years ago. Simon Neubauer, Jean-Jacques Hublin, and Philipp Gunz, "The Evolution of Modern Human Brain Shape," *Science Advances* 4, no. 1 (2018): eaao5961.

187 **society has shifted to a predominantly delayed-return environment:** The original research on this topic used the terms *delayed-return societies* and *immediate-return societies*. James Woodburn, "Egalitarian Societies," *Man* 17, no. 3 (1982), doi:10.2307/2801707. I first heard of the difference between immediate-return environments and delayed-return environments in a lecture from Mark Leary. Mark Leary, *Understanding the Mysteries of Human Behavior* (Chantilly, VA: Teaching, 2012).

188 **The world has changed much in recent years:** The rapid environmental changes of recent centuries have far outpaced our biological ability to adapt. On average, it takes about twenty-five thousand years for meaningful genetic changes to be selected for in a human population. For more, see Edward O. Wilson, *Sociobiology* (Cambridge, MA: Belknap Press, 1980), 151.

188 **our brains evolved to prefer quick payoffs to long-term ones:** Daniel Gilbert, "Humans Wired to Respond to Short-Term Problems," interview by Neal Conan, *Talk of the Nation*, NPR, July 3, 2006, https://www.npr.org/templates/story/story.php?storyId=5530483.

188 **Disease and infection won't show up for days or weeks, even years:** The topics of irrational behavior and cognitive biases have become quite popular in recent years. However, many actions that *seem* irrational on the whole have rational origins if you consider their immediate outcome.

189 **Frédéric Bastiat:** Frédéric Bastiat and W. B. Hodgson, *What Is Seen and What Is Not Seen: Or Political Economy in One Lesson* (London: Smith, 1859).

189 **Future You:** Hat tip to behavioral economist Daniel Goldstein, who said, "It's an unequal battle between the present self and the future self. I mean, let's face it, the present self is present. It's in control. It's in power right now. It has these strong, heroic arms that can lift doughnuts into your mouth. And the future self is not even around. It's off in the future. It's weak. It doesn't even have a lawyer present. There's nobody to stick up for the future self. And so the present self can trounce all over its dreams." For more, see Daniel Goldstein, "The Battle between Your Present and Future Self," TEDSalon NY2011, November 2011, video, https://www.ted.com/talks/daniel_goldstein_the_battle_between_your_present_and_future_self.

190 **People who are better at delaying gratification have higher SAT scores:** Walter Mischel, Ebbe B. Ebbesen, and Antonette Raskoff Zeiss, "Cognitive and Attentional Mechanisms in Delay of Gratification," *Journal of Personality and Social Psychology* 21, no. 2 (1972), doi:10.1037/h0032198; W. Mischel, Y. Shoda, and M. Rodriguez, "Delay of Gratification in Children," *Science* 244, no. 4907 (1989), doi:10.1126/science.2658056; Walter Mischel, Yuichi Shoda, and Philip K. Peake, "The Nature of Adolescent Competencies Predicted by Preschool Delay of Gratification," *Journal of Personality and Social Psychology* 54, no. 4 (1988), doi:10.1037//0022–3514.54.4.687; Yuichi Shoda, Walter Mischel, and Philip K. Peake, "Predicting Adolescent Cognitive and Self-Regulatory Competencies from Preschool Delay of Gratification: Identifying Diagnostic

Conditions," *Developmental Psychology* 26, no. 6 (1990), doi:10.1037//0012–1649 .26.6.978.

CHAPTER 16

195 **"I would start with 120 paper clips in one jar":** Trent Dyrsmid, email to author, April 1, 2015.

196 **Benjamin Franklin:** Benjamin Franklin and Frank Woodworth Pine, *Autobiography of Benjamin Franklin* (New York: Holt, 1916), 148.

197 **Don't break the chain of creating every day:** Shout-out to my friend Nathan Barry, who originally inspired me with the mantra, "Create Every Day."

197 **people who track their progress on goals like losing weight:** Benjamin Harkin et al., "Does Monitoring Goal Progress Promote Goal Attainment? A Meta-analysis of the Experimental Evidence," *Psychological Bulletin* 142, no. 2 (2016), doi:10.1037/bul0000025.

197 **those who kept a daily food log lost twice as much weight as those who did not:** Miranda Hitti, "Keeping Food Diary Helps Lose Weight," WebMD, July 8, 2008, http://www.webmd.com/diet/news/20080708/keeping-food-diary-helps-lose -weight; Kaiser Permanente, "Keeping a Food Diary Doubles Diet Weight Loss, Study Suggests," Science Daily, July 8, 2008, https://www.sciencedaily.com /releases/2008/07/080708080738.htm; Jack F. Hollis et al., "Weight Loss during the Intensive Intervention Phase of the Weight-Loss Maintenance Trial," *American Journal of Preventive Medicine* 35, no. 2 (2008), doi:10.1016/j.amepre.2008.04.013; Lora E. Burke, Jing Wang, and Mary Ann Sevick, "Self-Monitoring in Weight Loss: A Systematic Review of the Literature," *Journal of the American Dietetic Association* 111, no. 1 (2011), doi:10.1016/j.jada.2010.10.008.

198 **The most effective form of motivation is progress:** This line is paraphrased from Greg McKeown, who wrote, "Research has shown that of all forms of human motivation the most effective one is progress." Greg McKeown, *Essentialism: The Disciplined Pursuit of Less* (Currency, 2014).

201 **The first mistake is never the one that ruins you:** In fact, research has shown that missing a habit once has virtually no impact on the odds of developing a habit over the long-term, regardless of when the mistake occurs. As long as you get back on track, you're fine. See: Phillippa Lally et al., "How Are Habits Formed: Modelling Habit Formation in the Real World," *European Journal of Social Psychology* 40, no. 6 (2009), doi:10.1002/ejsp.674.

201 **Missing once is an accident:** "Missing once is an accident. Missing twice is the start of a new habit." I swear I read this line somewhere or perhaps paraphrased it from something similar, but despite my best efforts all of my searches for a source are coming up empty. Maybe I came up with it, but my best guess is it belongs to an unidentified genius instead.

203 **"When a measure becomes a target":** This definition of Goodhart's Law was actually formulated by the British anthropologist Marilyn Strathern. "'Improving Ratings': Audit in the British University System," *European Review* 5 (1997): 305–321, http://conferences.asucollegeoflaw.com/sciencepublicsphere/files/2014 /02/Strathern1997–2.pdf. Goodhart himself reportedly advanced the idea some-

time around 1975 and put it formally into writing in 1981. Charles Goodhart, "Problems of Monetary Management: The U.K. Experience," in Anthony S. Courakis (ed.), *Inflation, Depression, and Economic Policy in the West* (London: Rowman and Littlefield, 1981), 111–146.

CHAPTER 17

206 **"When I suggested this to friends in the Pentagon":** Roger Fisher, "Preventing Nuclear War," *Bulletin of the Atomic Scientists* 37, no. 3 (1981), doi:10.1080/00963402.1981.11458828.

207 **The first seat belt law:** Michael Goryl and Michael Cynecki, "Restraint System Usage in the Traffic Population," *Journal of Safety Research* 17, no. 2 (1986), doi:10.1016/0022–4375(86)90107–6.

207 **wearing a seat belt is enforceable by law:** New Hampshire is the lone exception, where seat belts are only required for children. "New Hampshire," Governors Highway Safety Association, https://www.ghsa.org/state-laws/states/new%20hampshire, accessed June 8, 2016.

207 **over 88 percent of Americans buckled up:** "Seat Belt Use in U.S. Reaches Historic 90 Percent," National Highway Traffic Safety Administration, November 21, 2016, https://www.nhtsa.gov/press-releases/seat-belt-use-us-reaches-historic-90-percent.

208 **Bryan Harris:** Bryan Harris, email conversation with author, October 24, 2017.

210 **She does the "song a day" challenge:** Courtney Shea, "Comedian Margaret Cho's Tips for Success: If You're Funny, Don't Do Comedy," *Globe and Mail*, July 1, 2013, https://www.theglobeandmail.com/life/comedian-margaret-chos-tips-for-success-if-youre-funny-dont-do-comedy/article12902304/?service=mobile.

210 **Thomas Frank, an entrepreneur in Boulder, Colorado:** Thomas Frank, "How Buffer Forces Me to Wake Up at 5:55 AM Every Day," College Info Geek, July 2, 2014, https://collegeinfogeek.com/early-waking-with-buffer/.

CHAPTER 18

217 **Phelps has won more Olympic medals:** "Michael Phelps Biography," Biography, https://www.biography.com/people/michael-phelps-345192, last modified March 29, 2018.

217 **El Guerrouj:** Doug Gillan, "El Guerrouj: The Greatest of All Time," IAFF, November 15, 2004, https://www.iaaf.org/news/news/el-guerrouj-the-greatest-of-all-time.

217 **they differ significantly in height:** Heights and weights for Michael Phelps and Hicham El Guerrouj were pulled from their athlete profiles during the 2008 Summer Olympics. "Michael Phelps," ESPN, 2008, http://www.espn.com/olympics/summer08/fanguide/athlete?athlete=29547l; "Hicham El Guerrouj," ESPN, 2008, http://www.espn.com/oly/summer08/fanguide/athlete?athlete=29886.

217 **same length inseam on their pants:** David Epstein, *The Sports Gene: Inside the Science of Extraordinary Athletic Performance* (St. Louis, MO: Turtleback Books, 2014).

218 **average height of Olympic gold medalists in the men's 1,500-meter run:** Alex Hutchinson, "The Incredible Shrinking Marathoner," *Runner's World*, No-

vember 12, 2013, https://www.runnersworld.com/sweat-science/the-incredible -shrinking-marathoner.

218 **average height of Olympic gold medalists in the men's 100-meter:** Alvin Chang, "Want to Win Olympic Gold? Here's How Tall You Should Be for Archery, Swimming, and More," *Vox*, August 9, 2016, http://www.vox.com/2016/8 /9/12387684/olympic-heights.

219 **"Genes can predispose, but they don't predetermine":** Gabor Maté, "Dr. Gabor Maté—New Paradigms, Ayahuasca, and Redefining Addiction," *The Tim Ferriss Show*, February 20, 2018, https://tim.blog/2018/02/20/gabor-mate/.

220 **Genes have been shown to influence everything:** "All traits are heritable" is a bit of an exaggeration, but not by much. Concrete behavioral traits that patently depend on content provided by the home or culture are, of course, not heritable at all; which language you speak, which religion you worship in, which political party you belong to. But behavioral traits that reflect the underlying talents and temperaments are heritable: how proficient with language you are, how religious, how liberal or conservative. General intelligence is heritable, and so are the five major ways in which personality can vary . . . openness to experience, conscientiousness, extroversion-introversion, antagonism-agreeableness, and neuroticism. And traits that are surprisingly specific turn out to be heritable, too, such as dependence on nicotine or alcohol, number of hours of television watched, and likelihood of divorcing. Thomas J. Bouchard, "Genetic Influence on Human Psychological Traits," *Current Directions in Psychological Science* 13, no. 4 (2004), doi:10.1111/j.0963–7214.2004.00295.x; Robert Plomin, *Nature and Nurture: An Introduction to Human Behavioral Genetics* (Stamford, CT: Wadsworth, 1996); Robert Plomin, "Why We're Different," Edge, June 29, 2016, https://soundcloud.com/edgefoundationinc/edge2016-robert-plomin.

220 **There's a strong genetic component:** Daniel Goleman, "Major Personality Study Finds That Traits Are Mostly Inherited," *New York Times*, December 2, 1986, http://www.nytimes.com/1986/12/02/science/major-personality-study-finds -that-traits-are-mostly-inherited.html?pagewanted=all.

220 **Robert Plomin:** Robert Plomin, phone call with the author, August 9, 2016.

221 **more likely to become introverts:** Jerome Kagan et al., "Reactivity in Infants: A Cross-National Comparison," *Developmental Psychology* 30, no. 3 (1994), doi:10.1037//0012–1649.30.3.342; Michael V. Ellis and Erica S. Robbins, "In Celebration of Nature: A Dialogue with Jerome Kagan," *Journal of Counseling and Development* 68, no. 6 (1990), doi:10.1002/j.1556–6676.1990.tb01426.x; Brian R. Little, *Me, Myself, and Us: The Science of Personality and the Art of Well-Being* (New York: Public Affairs, 2016); Susan Cain, *Quiet: The Power of Introverts in a World That Can't Stop Talking* (London: Penguin, 2013), 99–100.

221 **People who are high in agreeableness:** W. G. Graziano and R. M. Tobin, "The Cognitive and Motivational Foundations Underlying Agreeableness," in M. D. Robinson, E. Watkins, and E. Harmon-Jones, eds., *Handbook of Cognition and Emotion* (New York: Guilford, 2013), 347–364.

221 **They also tend to have higher natural oxytocin levels:** Mitsuhiro Matsuzaki et al., "Oxytocin: A Therapeutic Target for Mental Disorders," *Journal of Physiological Sciences* 62, no. 6 (2012), doi:10.1007/s12576–012–0232–9; Angeliki Theodoridou et

al., "Oxytocin and Social Perception: Oxytocin Increases Perceived Facial Trust-worthiness and Attractiveness," *Hormones and Behavior* 56, no. 1 (2009), doi:10.1016/j.yhbeh.2009.03.019; Anthony Lane et al., "Oxytocin Increases Will-ingness to Socially Share One's Emotions," *International Journal of Psychology* 48, no. 4 (2013), doi:10.1080/00207594.2012.677540; Christopher Cardoso et al., "Stress-Induced Negative Mood Moderates the Relation between Oxytocin Ad-ministration and Trust: Evidence for the Tend-and-Befriend Response to Stress?" *Psychoneuroendocrinology* 38, no. 11 (2013), doi:10.1016/j.psyneuen.2013.05.006.

221 **hypersensitivity of the amygdala:** J. Ormel, A. Bastiaansen, H. Riese, E. H. Bos, M. Servaas, M. Ellenbogen, J. G. Rosmalen, and A. Aleman, "The Biological and Psychological Basis of Neuroticism: Current Status and Future Directions," *Neuroscience and Biobehavioral Reviews* 37, no. 1 (2013), doi:10.1016/j.neu biorev.2012.09.004. PMID 23068306; R. A. Depue and Y. Fu, "Neurogenetic and Experiential Processes Underlying Major Personality Traits: Implications for Modelling Personality Disorders," *International Review of Psychiatry* 23, no. 3 (2011), doi:10.3109/09540261.2011.599315.

221 **Our deeply rooted preferences make certain behaviors easier:** "For example, all people have brain systems that respond to rewards, but in different individ-uals these systems will respond with different degrees of vigor to a particular reward, and the systems' average level of response may be associated with some personality trait." For more, see Colin G. Deyoung, "Personality Neuroscience and the Biology of Traits," *Social and Personality Psychology Compass* 4, no. 12 (2010), doi:10.1111/j.1751–9004.2010.00327.x.

222 **If your friend follows a low-carb diet:** Research conducted in major random-ized clinical trials shows no difference in low-carb versus low-fat diets for weight loss. As with many habits, there are many ways to the same destination if you stick with it. For more, see Christopher D. Gardner et al., "Effect of Low-Fat vs Low-Carbohydrate Diet on 12-Month Weight Loss in Overweight Adults and the Association with Genotype Pattern or Insulin Secretion," *Journal of the American Medical Association* 319, no. 7 (2018), doi:10.1001/jama.2018.0245.

223 *explore/exploit trade-off:* M. A. Addicott et al., "A Primer on Foraging and the Explore/Exploit Trade-Off for Psychiatry Research," *Neuropsychopharmacology* 42, no. 10 (2017), doi:10.1038/npp.2017.108.

223 **Google famously asks employees:** Bharat Mediratta and Julie Bick, "The Google Way: Give Engineers Room," *New York Times,* October 21, 2007, https://www .nytimes.com/2007/10/21/jobs/21pre.html.

224 **"Flow is the mental state":** Mihaly Csikszentmihalyi, *Finding Flow: The Psy-chology of Engagement with Everyday Life* (New York: Basic Books, 2008).

225 **"Everyone has at least a few areas":** Scott Adams, "Career Advice," Dilbert Blog, July 20, 2007, http://dilbertblog.typepad.com/the_dilbert_blog/2007/07 /career-advice.html.

CHAPTER 19

230 **most successful comedians:** Steve Martin, *Born Standing Up: A Comic's Life* (Leicester, UK: Charnwood, 2008).

230 **"4 years as wild success":** Steve Martin, *Born Standing Up: A Comic's Life* (Leicester, UK: Charnwood, 2008), 1.

231 **"just manageable difficulty":** Nicholas Hobbs, "The Psychologist as Administrator," *Journal of Clinical Psychology* 15, no. 3 (1959), doi:10.1002/1097–4679(195907)15:33.0.co; 2–4; Gilbert Brim, *Ambition: How We Manage Success and Failure Throughout Our Lives* (Lincoln, NE: IUniverse.com, 2000); Mihaly Csikszentmihalyi, *Finding Flow: The Psychology of Engagement with Everyday Life* (New York: Basic Books, 2008).

232 **In psychology research this is known as the Yerkes-Dodson law:** Robert Yerkes and John Dodson, "The Relation of Strength of Stimulus to Rapidity of Habit Formation," *Journal of Comparative Neurology and Psychology* 18 (1908): 459–482.

233 **4 percent beyond your current ability:** Steven Kotler, *The Rise of Superman: Decoding the Science of Ultimate Human Performance* (Boston: New Harvest, 2014). In his book, Kotler cites: "Chip Conley, AI, September 2013. The real ratio, according to calculations performed by [Mihaly] Csikszentmihalyi, is 1:96."

234 **"Men desire novelty to such an extent":** Niccolò Machiavelli, Peter Bondanella, and Mark Musa, *The Portable Machiavelli* (London: Penguin, 2005).

235 *variable reward:* C. B. Ferster and B. F. Skinner, "Schedules of Reinforcement," 1957, doi:10.1037/10627–000. For more, see B. F. Skinner, "A Case History in Scientific Method," *American Psychologist* 11, no. 5 (1956): 226, doi:10.1037 /h0047662.

235 **This variance leads to the greatest spike of dopamine:** Matching Law shows that the rate of the reward schedule impacts behavior: "Matching Law," Wikipedia, https://en.wikipedia.org/wiki/Matching_law.

CHAPTER 20

240 **there is usually a slight *decline* in performance:** K. Anders Ericsson and Robert Pool, *Peak: Secrets from the New Science of Expertise* (Boston: Mariner Books, 2017), 13.

242 **"The pundits were saying":** Pat Riley and Byron Laursen, "Temporary Insanity and Other Management Techniques: The Los Angeles Lakers' Coach Tells All," *Los Angeles Times Magazine,* April 19, 1987, http://articles.latimes.com/1987–04–19/magazine/tm-1669_1_lakers.

242 **a system that he called the Career Best Effort program or CBE:** MacMullan's book claims that Riley began his CBE program during the 1984–1985 NBA season. My research shows that the Lakers began tracking statistics of individual players at that time, but the CBE program as it is described here was first used in 1986–1987.

243 **If they succeeded, it would be a CBE:** Larry Bird, Earvin Johnson, and Jackie MacMullan, *When the Game Was Ours* (Boston: Houghton Mifflin Harcourt, 2010).

244 **"Sustaining an effort":** Pat Riley and Byron Laursen, "Temporary Insanity and Other Management Techniques: The Los Angeles Lakers' Coach Tells All," *Los*

Angeles Times Magazine, April 19, 1987, http://articles.latimes.com/1987–04–19/magazine/tm-1669_1_lakers.

244 **Eliud Kipchoge:** Cathal Dennehy, "The Simple Life of One of the World's Best Marathoners," *Runner's World,* April 19, 2016, https://www.runnersworld.com/elite-runners/the-simple-life-of-one-of-the-worlds-best-marathoners. "Eliud Kipchoge: Full Training Log Leading Up to Marathon World Record Attempt," Sweat Elite, 2017, http://www.sweatelite.co/eliud-kipchoge-full-training-log-leading-marathon-world-record-attempt/.

245 **her coach goes over her notes and adds his thoughts:** Yuri Suguiyama, "Training Katie Ledecky," American Swimming Coaches Association, November 30, 2016, https://swimmingcoach.org/training-katie-ledecky-by-yuri-suguiyama-curl-burke-swim-club-2012/.

245 **When comedian Chris Rock is preparing fresh material:** Peter Sims, "Innovate Like Chris Rock," *Harvard Business Review,* January 26, 2009, https://hbr.org/2009/01/innovate-like-chris-rock.

245 *Annual Review:* I'd like to thank Chris Guillebeau, who inspired me to start my own annual review process by publicly sharing his annual review each year at https://chrisguillebeau.com.

248 **"keep your identity small":** Paul Graham, "Keep Your Identity Small," February 2009, http://www.paulgraham.com/identity.html.

CONCLUSION

251 **No one can be rich unless one coin can make him or her so:** Desiderius Erasmus and Van Loon Hendrik Willem, *The Praise of Folly* (New York: Black, 1942), 31. Hat tip to Gretchen Rubin. I first read about this parable in her book, *Better Than Before,* and then tracked down the origin story. For more, see Gretchen Rubin, *Better Than Before* (New York: Hodder, 2016).

LITTLE LESSONS FROM THE FOUR LAWS

260 **"Happiness is the space between one desire":** Caed (@caedbudris), "Happiness is the space between desire being fulfilled and a new desire forming," Twitter, November 10, 2017, https://twitter.com/caedbudris/status/929042389930594304.

260 **happiness cannot be pursued, it must ensue:** Frankl's full quotation is as follows: "Don't aim at success. The more you aim at it and make it a target, the more you are going to miss it. For success, like happiness, cannot be pursued; it must ensue, and it only does so as the unintended side effect of one's personal dedication to a cause greater than oneself or as the by-product of one's surrender to a person other than oneself." For more, see Viktor E. Frankl, *Man's Search for Meaning: An Introduction to Logotherapy* (Boston: Beacon Press, 1962).

260 **"He who has a why to live for can bear almost any how":** Friedrich Nietzsche and Oscar Levy, *The Twilight of the Idols* (Edinburgh: Foulis, 1909).

261 **The feeling comes first (System 1):** Daniel Kahneman, *Thinking, Fast and Slow* (New York: Farrar, Straus and Giroux, 2015).

261 **appealing to emotion is typically more powerful than appealing to reason:** "If you wish to persuade, appeal to interest, rather than reason" (Benjamin Franklin).

263 **Satisfaction = Liking – Wanting:** This is similar to David Meister's fifth law of service businesses: Satisfaction = perception – expectation.

263 **"Being poor is not having too little, it is wanting more":** Lucius Annaeus Seneca and Anna Lydia Motto, *Moral Epistles* (Chico, CA: Scholars Press, 1985).

264 **As Aristotle noted:** It is debated whether Aristotle actually said this. The quote has been attributed to him for centuries, but I could find no primary source for the phrase.

Index